Deathtrap

Boston's Pickwick Club Disaster

John E. Keefe

DEATHTRAP
Boston's Pickwick Club Disaster

ISBN 979-8-9877300-1-0

Cover design by
Creative Publishing Book Design

Menotomy Publishing
Arlington, MA
www.menotomypublishing.com

To my mother

The people of Boston are looking, and with good reason, to the District Attorney for Suffolk County, the Mayor of Boston, and the Governor of Massachusetts for the truth about the most disgraceful disaster in the city's history.

Boston American
July 7, 1925

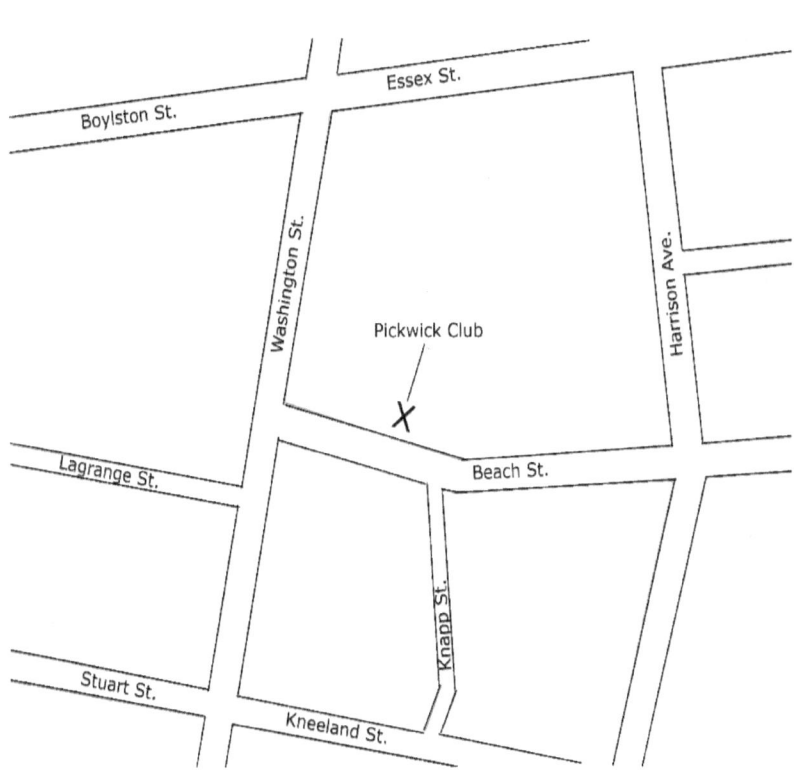

| CONTENTS |

Part One – The Collapse

Part Two – The Aftermath

Appendices

| ONE |

The small, five-piece orchestra had played just a few notes of the up-tempo and easily recognized "Twelfth Street Rag" when couples began to make their way toward the dance floor from every corner of the crowded room. The women, in their knee-length shift dresses, looked somewhat more fashionable than their partners. Most of the men had left their jackets draped over the back of their chairs, and were approaching the floor in their shirtsleeves. The tune the orchestra had begun playing was a perfect match for what was then the most popular dance craze in the country—the Charleston.

Once again, John Owen and Mae Lawson made no attempt to get up from their chairs. Owen had decided to sit this one out, just like he sat out the last one, and the one before that. The thirty-one-year-old Back Bay man didn't care much for dancing—especially the fast, modern steps—and in the summer of 1925 there wasn't much call for anything else.

"I'm kind of clumsy, so I didn't dance much," Owen told a reporter the next day.

Mae Lawson, on the other hand, loved to dance, and someone in the room noticed her disappointment. People were still converging on the dance floor when a stranger approached the table.

"Would you mind if I ask the young lady to dance?" he asked Owen.

"Not at all, go right ahead," Owen replied.

The couple were on their first date that night. Twenty-nine-year-old Mae Lawson was a newcomer to the Boston area, and lived with her younger sister in Brookline. "Mrs. Lawson had recently separated from her husband," Owen said later. "They hadn't been married very long, and she was brokenhearted. I knew she liked to dance, and I urged her to accompany me to the club. We got there shortly after midnight."

If Owen was trying to impress Mrs. Lawson, he took quite a chance when he brought her to the Pickwick Club. It was still one of Boston's more popular speakeasies, but the regulars who came every night were a far cry from the in-crowd it attracted when it first opened eighteen months earlier. The club's location, in what had formerly been the elegant Café Dreyfus on Beach Street, doubtlessly played a part in drawing some of those original visitors.

In its heyday, the Dreyfus ranked up there with the finest restaurants in the city, and was the unquestionable centerpiece of the five-story Hotel Dreyfus. The *Boston American* called it "one of the most ornate eating places in the country." The Dreyfus had begun to lose some of its allure by the time the United States entered the First World War, and it closed a few years later when the owner decided to call it quits and shut down the entire hotel. The old building then remained more or less vacant for almost four years until the Pickwick Club moved into the ground floor.

Chapter One

It didn't take long for the Pickwick to become one of the best-known nightspots in the city. It was a place where truck drivers, hairdressers, and grocery store owners could rub elbows with bankers, executives, politicians, athletes, and people in show business. The *Boston Sunday Globe* described the club's clientele as, "Men without collars, men in evening dress, heavily painted women, middle-aged couples from the country, schoolmarms, and flappers."

The good times rolled on for several months, and then things began to change. Regular customers couldn't help but notice that the well-known and the well-to-do weren't stopping by nearly as often as they once had, and a louder, rougher element had begun to fill the void. What's more, the club's open and flagrant violations of the Volstead Act—the law that enforced the ban on the manufacture and sale of alcoholic beverages—hadn't gone unnoticed. Federal Prohibition agents raided the club in January, and the Boston Police conducted another raid a few weeks later. As if those problems weren't enough, the club's owners received some unexpected and very unwelcome news when their one-year lease came up for renewal. A group of local businessmen had decided to open a new restaurant, and they began by scouting several downtown streets in search of a suitable locale. The Pickwick Club's prime, ground floor site suited them to a T. It didn't matter that someone else already leased the space. The three men were part of the inner circle at city hall, and they had no intention of taking no for an answer. That left the Pickwick Club's officers with only two choices, and neither one was very attractive. They could relocate the club upstairs to the former banquet hall on the second floor, or they could move somewhere else. Although they weren't happy about it, they agreed to move upstairs.

The change did nothing to bolster the club's reputation. If

anything, it tarnished it further. The old banquet room, with its plain, dated décor, paled in comparison with the swanky ground floor café. It wasn't long before the last few upper-class customers stopped coming. One newspaper even said the Pickwick Club was turning into something of an underworld social center. Arguments, confrontations, and even fistfights became an almost nightly occurrence. Some of them escalated into brawls so large the club's bouncers had to seek help from the police. That holiday eve was no exception. The Boston Police were there twice during the three hours that Owen and Mrs. Lawson were inside.

"It was pretty wild in there—horns, and rattles, and firecrackers too. People had been lighting and throwing them all night," Owen told a reporter.

Thanks to its state charter, the club was exempt from Boston's stringent closing laws, and could have remained open all night, but manager Jimmy Glennon always closed at four. The orchestra, conducted by his younger brother Billy, stopped playing an hour earlier. Neither of the Glennon brothers objected if a customer wanted to get up and croon a song or two with the orchestra. Quite the opposite, they encouraged it, and on any given night several singers were likely to stop by. Patrons who came that Fourth of July eve enjoyed a special treat. A seven-piece Hawaiian orchestra made up of recently discharged sailors played for a while. Like the other guest entertainers, they didn't receive any compensation for their performance. The Hawaiians, with their mandolins, guitar, violin, and banjo, played to a different beat than the regular orchestra, and while some of the dancers had trouble keeping step, everyone enjoyed the music. The ex-sailors left right after midnight because one of them had to go to work the next morning. The Pickwick Club orchestra then took over.

Several singers stopped by the club that night, and they took

4

Chapter One

turns entertaining the patrons with popular tunes like "Sweet Georgia Brown", "If You Knew Suzie", and "Yes Sir, That's My Baby". At one point four of them got up and joined in a vocal rendition of another popular song called "West of the Great Divide". It was almost ten minutes to three when they stepped down and returned to their seats. The orchestra still had time to play two more numbers. The last dance was always something mellow, but for the second-last, Billy Glennon chose a fast number. Although the crowd had gradually begun to thin, somewhere around 125 people were still inside, seated around the club's forty-plus tables, and many of them were eager for one last chance to do the Charleston. The small, fifteen-by-thirty-five-foot, linoleum-covered dance floor quickly filled.

Anna McKee was the club's coatroom attendant that night. The widowed mother of three spoke with a reporter who came to her Dorchester home the next day. "It was really crowded," she told him, "and it was really hot. None of the men on the dance floor had their jackets on. They brought in extra tables last night because the crowd was so large. They even put tables in front of the bar."

Joe Downey played trumpet with the Pickwick Club orchestra. He said he had never seen so many couples on the dance floor. "Most people knew the song and liked to dance to it, and the dance space was packed," he added.

Owen's table was on the far side of the smoke-filled room—almost up against the outside wall, and separated from the door by the jam-packed dance floor. He was still sitting there when the pulsating music finally ended. A few of the dancers started to make their way back to their seats, but most of them remained on the floor, applauding while they waited for the last dance. Owen wasn't surprised to see that Mrs. Lawson and her partner were among them.

Billy Glennon had just begun to look through his sheet music for a suitable piece when the tiny red, yellow, and green light bulbs that dotted the ceiling grew noticeably dim. Earl Davis, the club's busboy, was a few feet away and he felt something trickle onto his hand. His first thought was that one of the toilets on the third floor had overflowed, but when he looked up, the ceiling was bone dry. Some kind of dusty powder was drifting down. "Billy, there's sand coming down from the ceiling," he said. Glennon glanced up just in time to see a big piece of plaster fall. A moment later the lights began to flicker just as a loud crack like the snap of a bullwhip resounded throughout the room. Thirty-one-year-old Arthur McNeil of Jamaica Plain thought someone had fired a revolver. To Owen, it sounded like a very loud firecracker.

Cambridge cab driver Tom Garvey was just inside the door, waiting for a fare, when the lights went dim. "I looked over at the corner and I saw everyone jump up," he told a reporter from the *Boston Globe*. "I thought it was a fight at first, but all of a sudden there was a big noise and the lights went out. The next thing I knew I was lying down with things pressing into my back and sides. Someone's foot was on my shoulder. I tried to get up on my hands and knees, but something heavy was on top of me, and I was choking on the dust and dirt. A lot of things went through my head. I could hear people fighting to get out when someone grabbed hold of me." Garvey escaped with only minor injuries.

Clifford Cusick of Dorchester was standing near Garvey, just inside the door, when the floor began to sag. "I fell onto my hands and knees," he told a reporter, "and I grabbed hold of a table leg in front of me and pulled myself along. The floor seemed to be cracking, piece by piece. There was a jam of people on the stairs, under me and on top of me, all fighting to get out." Clifford suffered a broken arm while fleeing the building.

Anna McKee also thought a fight had broken out, but then the wall started to crumble, and pieces of the ceiling began to rain

6

Chapter One

down. The plaster and dust swept across the room like a wave, headed right toward the people on the dance floor. Just then, the lights went out, and the room became pitch black. McKee began to panic. Her hand brushed against a man's shirtsleeve in the darkness, and she screamed for help. She could barely hear her own voice over the deafening roar, and she was afraid he hadn't heard her, but he grabbed hold of her hand and pulled her toward the stairway. She remembered being aware that the hem of her dress caught on something as she rushed down the stairs and had started to tear, but she had no recollection of how she received the injuries that left her arms and legs covered with scrapes and bruises. Anna McKee never learned the name of the man who pulled her to safety.

John Owen spoke afterward about what happened right after the loud, explosive noise: "A second later the room was filled with shrieks, and the floor on one side started to give way, and the dancing couples were thrown into a gaping wound in the floor. I turned around just in time to see Mrs. Lawson and her partner disappear through the floor. There was screaming as a whole bunch of dancers were suddenly just swallowed up."

Owen said he jumped up just as the lights went out and started for the door, but he lost his balance and began to slide toward the hole. "It looked like a black pit and I couldn't see the bottom. I tried to crawl back, but there was nothing to grab hold of. It was too steep and I kept slipping," he recalled. Owen slid feet first into the cavernous hole, and fell almost twenty feet in total darkness before he landed on something solid. Bricks and furniture and pieces of wood continued to crash down all around him, and a large piece of flooring landed on his leg. He tried to lift it, but it was much too heavy. "It seemed like I was trapped there for hours until the police rescued me," he said.

Pickwick Club coat room attendant Anna McKee,
speaking with reporters at her Dorchester home several
hours after the collapse.

Chapter One

John Owen suffered only a few bruises and a twisted knee; Mae Lawson wasn't that lucky. Firefighters found her body buried deep in the rubble almost twenty hours after the collapse. The fate of the unidentified man who asked her to dance remains unknown.

Catherine Walker didn't even get to her feet before the floor gave way. The twenty-five-year-old Roxbury woman was sitting at a table near Owen, chatting with some friends while they watched the crowd on the dance floor. She told a *Boston Sunday Advertiser* reporter: "Suddenly, without any warning, the wall of the building fell in, bringing me down with it. I felt like I was falling down, down, down into a bottomless pit. Then something heavy, I think it was a falling timber, caught one of my feet and pinned me beneath it."

Patrons like Owen and Walker had no chance of escape. The former banquet room had only one doorway, and it was just too far away.

Mary Peterson of Charlestown told a reporter from the *Boston American*: "Everybody ran for the exit at once. The floor fell down in a slanting way and I could see girls and men slide to their death. There was one table with five people, and they just dropped into the hole—the table, the chairs, and the food." Peterson joined the panic-stricken crowd that made a mad dash for the stairs. She remembered that someone gave her a hard shove on the way down. The next thing she remembered was being outside on the sidewalk.

Trumpet player Joe Downey later recalled: "The walls shook and rattled, and then the whole ceiling crashed down upon us while the floor slipped away from beneath our feet. I thought it was an earthquake. Those in the center of the floor got it worse. I saw a couple torn apart. The man was struggling to pull his partner back to safety, but she was carried down by the debris."

Nineteen-year-old John McLaughlin had no intention of

going to the Pickwick Club that night. He and his friend Eddie Whalen were on their way home from a midnight bonfire in South Boston when someone in their group suggested they stop at the Pickwick Club. McLaughlin tried to beg off. He had to work the next morning even though it was a holiday, and he told his friends he thought he would call it a night and go home, but they insisted he come in for just one drink. McLaughlin didn't want to be a spoilsport, and he agreed. The group had only been in the club for about fifteen minutes when the loud crack thundered throughout the building just as it began to shake.

"John and I grabbed hold of each other for support," Whalen told a reporter, "but then the floor started to give way and we couldn't hold on. John slipped and fell. I watched him slide down into the hole in the floor and disappear. I couldn't do anything to save him."

Jimmy Corso had traveled to Boston from his home in West Haven, Connecticut to spend the holiday weekend with friends. A visit to the Pickwick Club was one of the top items on their to-do list. "While I was watching the dancers," Corso recalled, "the wall began to fall in one corner. It just seemed to slip down. I ran for the door, but I couldn't reach it before the floor gave way. I slid down into the cellar with five other fellows and a pile of wreckage on top of me. I could hear firemen chopping their way through the wreckage, but they sounded a long way off. It seemed like they were taking centuries to reach us." It took three hours before rescue workers were able to reach the Connecticut man. He was hospitalized with multiple contusions and abrasions.

A twenty-four-year-old chemist from Everett was trapped close by. Richard Lovejoy told a reporter he heard a cracking sound and saw the floor begin to lift right in front of him. "I started for the door, but before I got there the floor caved in and I went down with it." Lovejoy tumbled into the hole head first, and he was pinned in that position for three hours with another man's foot pressing down on his head. "Every once in a while, I would see some light which indicated rescuers were getting close, but then the light would disappear. I kept yelling continually," he recalled. Firemen reached him shortly after they extricated Corso. He was taken to Boston City Hospital with a dislocated right shoulder.

Frank Castelone was the man whose foot rested on Lovejoy's head. He credited Lovejoy with saving his life. "I would have suffocated if it weren't for him." Castelone said he saw the wall give way, and he yelled a warning to the people on the dance floor. "As I ran, the floor gave way beneath me, and I slid down on top of Lovejoy." He said Lovejoy was able to reach out and grab hold of a stick. "He poked an air hole in the wreckage for me. When the hole filled up, he made a new one." Castelone was hospitalized with a fractured skull.

Leo Romano made a dive for the wall when the floor began to sag. The thirty-three-year-old West End grocer later recalled: "Beams and other things were falling all around us, but somehow, we didn't get hit. We stood still and found ourselves in sort of a cave under the rafters. Sal Jefferson was right behind us, but a beam fell and pinned him down. We were able to lift it off and get him out. Someone on the street raised a plank to us and we used it to slide down. Jimmy Corso and Frank Castelone were with us, but they couldn't reach the wall and they went down with the dance floor."

Sadie Belan was near the edge of the dance floor when it began to collapse. "I heard a rumbling noise and then the ceiling crashed down on our heads," the thirty-year-old Dorchester woman recalled. "Some man grabbed me and pushed me toward the doorway. I was caught in the jam at the door and swept downstairs." Belan escaped with only a few bruises. A reporter who caught up with her at home the next day said she was still quite upset about the loss of her pocketbook and her fur wrap.

Rocco Scarparto had vivid memories of the thunder-like rumble that nearly drowned out Anna McKee's cries. The heavyset East Boston man was the second-floor doorman at the club that night. "It sounded like every building in the neighborhood was being pulled apart," he told a reporter.

The hysterical screams of the terrified people tumbling into the deep, black hole troubled Ethel Conlon the most. "I couldn't get them out of my mind for days," she said. "They were just awful."

Max Gartz was dead tired when he and his girlfriend arrived at the club about twenty minutes to three that morning. They had been at a party in Revere, and stopped in for a drink on their way home. Gartz found a table just inside the doorway, only a short distance from the stairs. He placed his hat on a chair, ordered a beer, and then looked at his watch. It was exactly 2:45. The orchestra was playing, and the dance floor was packed. He thought there might have been about 150 people in the club. His girlfriend wanted to dance, but Gartz said no. He told her he was just too tired. That decision almost certainly saved their lives. The waitress had just brought his beer when he heard a loud crash and saw the floor begin to quiver and shake. He too thought an earthquake had struck. Gartz and his girlfriend ran for the door, and managed to escape down the stairs in the darkness. Like several other survivors, he was sure that he was the last one to make it out to the street.

Virginia Vara was there with her husband that night. She reached out and immediately grabbed hold of his hand when the loud crack thundered throughout the room. The two West Enders ran for the door, but the lights went out before they reached it. People were pushing and shoving, and she lost her grip on her husband's hand.

"Frank," she screamed in panic.

"I'm all right. Keep going," he shouted back.

Chapter One

Virginia Vara was one of the last, if not the very last, person to escape through the doorway that night. Her husband was just a bit too far behind. She made it down the stairs to safety; twenty-five-year-old Frank Vara plummeted to his death amidst a thunderous avalanche of debris.

DEATHTRAP

| TWO |

The holiday revelers who packed the Pickwick Club that Friday night hadn't the slightest inkling that the old building was unsafe. The sight of a trapdoor almost right alongside the dance floor must have puzzled the first-time visitors. Some of them no doubt noticed that the large room had only one doorway, but that was not unusual at the time. The City of Boston didn't adopt its first building code until 1871, but the regulations only applied to new construction and major renovations. Existing structures like the one that later housed the Pickwick Club were exempt from the provisions of the new code. A subsequent amendment mandated that all buildings over a certain size must have a second means of egress, regardless of their age. The owners of the old building on Beach Street were able to comply with the new dictate by adding an external fire escape to the back wall.

Some of the newcomers that night must have been surprised when they discovered the second floor had no restrooms. The only facilities in the building were on the first and third floors, but the first-floor toilets were off limits at the time. A patron or employee who wished to use a restroom had no choice but to climb a narrow flight of stairs to the third floor. When they reached the top, they couldn't help but notice the obvious, telltale signs of a recent fire. The charred woodwork and blackened ceiling gave mute testimony to the intensity of the three-alarm blaze that tore through the building's upper floors a few months earlier.

About twenty people were inside the building when the fire broke out around ten o'clock on a weekday night. All of them were on the first floor, and they escaped without injury. The Pickwick Club hadn't opened for the evening, and the only business on the third floor, where the fire began, was a small tailor shop that had closed hours earlier. No one had used the fourth or fifth floors for several years. The fire heavily damaged the upper floors of the building before it burned a hole in the roof. Firefighters had to pump about 3,000 gallons of water onto the blaze before they brought it under control, and much of the water splashed down into the interior. Before they returned to their stations, the firefighters chopped holes in each floor so the water could drain into the basement.

The Pickwick Club had to remain closed for more than a week until a construction crew finished covering the hole in the roof with a temporary patch. During that time, one of the club's officers hired a carpenter to repair the gaping hole in the floor that firefighters left behind. The easiest way to do that was to build a trapdoor. In the months to come, staff members had to open it more than once to drain water that came in after a heavy rainfall. The first-floor restaurant that had forced the club's relocation never reopened after the fire, nor did the tailor shop on the third floor. No one had any reason to go up there afterward except to use the restrooms.

Several of the patrons undoubtedly remembered that the old

building was once home to the Hotel Dreyfus, but none of them would have ever suspected that it was also the site of a sex scandal that some of the area's most influential citizens managed to keep under wraps for over eighty years. More about that later.

Arthur Dreyfus had just turned eighteen when his family left their native France and moved to Boston. A few months later, he learned that a fellow French immigrant named Henri Marliave was about to open a new restaurant. Dreyfus stopped by, filled out an application, and landed a job as a busboy. That restaurant went on to become a Boston landmark. Marliave has been serving meals at the same Boswell Street address since the day it first opened in 1885. It is the third-oldest restaurant in the city.

Dreyfus was ambitious and clever, and he quickly rose through the ranks—first to waiter, and then maître de. The young Frenchman gained invaluable experience during his seven years at Marliave, and his position as maître de put him in daily contact with a number of influential and well-to-do Bostonians. By 1892, he was confident that he had learned enough about food service and hospitality to open his own restaurant. He left his job at Marliave and, with a great deal of borrowed money, bought a small hotel and restaurant on Hayward Place in downtown Boston. He renamed it the Hotel Dreyfus. It was a risky move, and it almost ended on a disastrous note when creditors forced him into involuntary bankruptcy three years later. A judge allowed the business to remain open, but under court supervision. It only took a few months for Dreyfus to begin to turn things around, and the operation once again became profitable.

Buoyed by his success, he decided to open a second Hotel Dreyfus in Providence, Rhode Island, this time in partnership with another man. Things didn't work out nearly as well in Providence as they did in Boston. Dreyfus and his partner failed to see eye to eye on several matters, and the two men ended up in court, battling for control of the hotel. In October 1901, a judge ruled in Dreyfus's favor. Under his sole leadership, the hotel went on to become a landmark in the city's theatre district for the next seventy-five years. Much of that success was attributable to the popularity of its signature, oak-paneled dining room, the Dreyfus Restaurant.

Two years after his victory in Providence, Dreyfus was back in court—this time seeking to block his eviction from the Boston property. The building's owner wanted to demolish it and erect a large department store in its place. Dreyfus lost a lower court bid to overturn the eviction order, but he filed an appeal with the Massachusetts Supreme Judicial Court. This time Dreyfus prevailed. The SJC overturned the lower court decision, and allowed Dreyfus to remain in the building, but only until his lease expired.

The young entrepreneur wasted no time taking action. His first move was to change the name of his hotel, and a month after the court's ruling, the old Hotel Dreyfus became the new Hotel Lafayette. Dreyfus then set out to secure another location. He found what he was looking for in an old, five-story, red brick warehouse at number 6 to 10 Beach Street. It wasn't a large building by any means, but Dreyfus found it appealing for two reasons—it was close to Hayward Place, and it was vacant. He wasted no time negotiating a long-term lease for the property. The old warehouse needed extensive renovations before Dreyfus could use it as a restaurant. The work took several months to complete. When a city building inspector came to check the improvements, he discovered that Dreyfus had failed to enclose the dumb waiter that connected the basement kitchen with the first and second floors as the plans specified. The additional work delayed the hotel's opening until May 1905, almost a year after Dreyfus took over the property.

The elegant, street-level Cafe Dreyfus was the unquestioned centerpiece, and it quickly gained acclaim for its classic French

Chapter Two

cuisine. James O'Connell, in *Dining Out in Boston: A Culinary History,* noted that a customer who desired a sirloin steak could choose from nine different preparations. The hotel had a banquet room on the second floor, and several private dining rooms on the two floors above. Dreyfus used the fifth floor only for storage. Even though the city's newspapers routinely referred to the new venture as the Hotel Dreyfus, it was in fact a dining establishment. None of its advertisements ever mentioned guest rooms.

The owners of the building on Hayward Place never followed through with their plans to demolish it, but they did raze the building next door the following year and replaced it with an eight-story department store. The June 1905 *Boston Directory* listed Arthur Dreyfus as the owner of two properties in Boston— the Hotel Lafayette on Hayward Place, and an unnamed restaurant at 10 Beach Street. By the end of 1906, Dreyfus had severed all ties with his original hotel, and it had reopened as the Hotel Epicure under new ownership. A spectacular fire gutted the entire building four years later, only a few weeks after the completion of a major top-to-bottom refurbishment.

The Café Dreyfus had been open for less than two months when a local business executive read the favorable reviews, and decided it would be the ideal place for an upcoming luncheon meeting. Robert Bourne's guest was a man named Timothy Swift, the chief custodian of the Federal Post Office Building in Boston. During the course of their meal, Bourne offered him a substantial bribe to help land a lucrative furniture supply contract. The temptation proved too strong, and Swift took the money. That mistake cost him his job, and earned him a fifteen-month prison sentence.

Dreyfus brought his eighteen-year-old son Henry aboard in 1909, right after the young man graduated from high school. Harry, as his friends called him, moved up rapidly, and his father eventually placed him in charge of the entire Boston operation. Harry was a well-known figure in Boston's gay community, and it wasn't long after he took over that the Café Dreyfus began to gain a reputation as a gathering spot for homosexuals. A few years later, it was embroiled in a scandal that tarnished the reputations and altered the career plans of several prominent young men. Harry Dreyfus was twenty-nine years old at the time.

It began with the May 1920 suicide of a twenty-year-old Harvard student. The night before Cyril Wilcox took his life at his parent's home in Fall River, Massachusetts, he confided in his older brother George that he was gay, and confessed to having had an intimate relationship with an older man who managed a Boston restaurant. He said the two often spent the night together in the manager's Beacon Street apartment. George Wilcox decided to look through his late brother's correspondence a few days after the funeral, and he discovered that his brother was one of several Harvard students who had taken part in frequent, clandestine homosexual activities. The letters spoke of sordid parties in dormitory rooms where students—one of them the son of a well-known and still influential former US Congressman from Massachusetts—had sex with young sailors they picked up on the streets of Boston. The activities extended beyond the campus walls, and several letters mentioned uninhibited get-togethers at the Cafe Dreyfus where the manager and several members of the waitstaff routinely took part.

Wilcox took the train to Boston where he confronted Dreyfus and demanded to know who else had seduced his brother. When Dreyfus refused to tell, Wilcox proceeded to give him a sound beating that ended only when the badly bruised manager gave in and furnished the names. He never reported that incident to the police. Wilcox then brought the incriminating letters and the names he had pried from Dreyfus to Harvard Dean Chester Noyes Greenough. The next day Greenough met with Harvard

Chapter Two

President Abbott Lowell. The two men decided to select a five-member panel to look into the allegations. Academic historians call that panel "The Secret Court of 1920". By the time the probe ended, the university had fired an assistant professor, expelled eight students, and barred a recent graduate from setting foot on school property. The panel concluded there was no legal recourse they could take against Dreyfus and the waiters.

Arthur Dreyfus closed his hotel a short time later. The overseers and trustees of Harvard may have exerted some pressure, but the most likely reason was the recently enacted Prohibition amendment. Greenough's investigation, and the subsequent dismissals, remained cloaked in secrecy until 2002 when a reporter for the student newspaper *The Crimson* stumbled across a box of old files while researching a story.

The news that Arthur Dreyfus was leaving had to be the last thing John Flavin wanted to hear. Flavin owned the Beach Street property, and Dreyfus had been the sole tenant for more than fifteen years. His departure meant the steady, dependable rental income was about to grind to an abrupt halt. The odds of finding another tenant like Dreyfus—someone who wanted all five floors—were practically nil. Flavin mulled things over for a while, and then decided to let someone else search for renters. He agreed to lease the entire building to the David A. Schulte Company of New York City, the owner of a nationwide chain of tobacco stores. Schulte had recently branched out into real estate speculation, especially in the area around Times Square. Leasing the building to Schulte was the first step in what morphed into a rather convoluted arrangement, not just for leasing and subleasing, but for property management as well. A short time after they signed the lease, Schulte turned around and did the same thing Flavin had done. They sublet the entire building to the Hayward Realty Company of Boston.

DEATHTRAP

A Roxbury man named Hyman Bloomberg owned Hayward Realty, but for some reason, the forty-six-year-old Russian immigrant didn't want his name to appear on the lease. He asked Schulte to use his son's name instead. It was just for bookkeeping reasons, he said, and he assured the New Yorkers he was the only person who had the authority to make decisions. A short time later Schulte hired the Boston real estate firm Whitcomb & Company to look after their interests in a loosely defined role that entailed little more than collecting the rent from Bloomberg. John Flavin kept the building for another year, and then sold it to a man named Albert Rosenthal with the stipulation that the Schulte Company lease remain in force. Rosenthal died soon afterward without leaving a will. The building then came under the control of his brother-in-law, Nathan Ginsberg, in his capacity as executor of the estate.

Finding suitable tenants proved to be a lot more difficult than Bloomberg anticipated. Occasionally someone rented one of the former private dining rooms on the third floor, but most didn't stay very long. Bloomberg's lease agreement with the Schulte Company made him responsible for paying the building's property taxes and insurance premiums, in addition to his $266 monthly rent. Those costs totaled $473 a month, or about $7,000 at today's prices. By the dawn of 1924, the situation looked bleak. There was only one tenant in the entire five-story building—a small tailor shop on the third floor. Bloomberg was losing a lot more money than he could afford. Unbeknownst to him, things were about to change.

A stranger called unexpectedly a few weeks later and said he might be interested in renting the site of the old Café Dreyfus on the first floor if the terms were agreeable. The man's name was Timothy Barry, and he went on to explain that he was one of several investors who wanted to open a new social club, but they needed to find a suitable location before they submitted their application for a state charter. The two men came to a satisfactory arrangement, and Barry signed a one-year lease that placed no restrictions on what he could do with the space. The *Boston Sunday Globe* later described Barry as a man who had many friends in Boston political, legal, and newspaper circles.

The club's application breezed through the approval process, and on March 20, 1924, the Massachusetts Department of Corporations and Taxation granted a charter to the Commercial Men's Club. Barry then turned around and sublet the space to his new organization. The newly chartered club opened its doors a few days later, but it bore little resemblance to a private social club. It was a public speakeasy in every sense of the word. There was one other change. Barry called his new venture *The Pickwick Club*. From that day forward, no one ever referred to it as the Commercial Men's Club.

As a private club, Barry's organization was supposed to impose some meaningful or fraternal condition for membership. It was also supposed to restrict admittance to current members and their guests, but no one ever paid much attention to the members-only rule. A heavyset man stood by the front door during opening hours, but he was there to sound the alarm at the first sign of a police raid, not to check the freely distributed membership cards. Regular patrons had no problem gaining admission. If a questionable looking person tried to get in, the doorman pressed a button that summoned the manager who came to the door and made the decision.

The club served light meals and mixers while an orchestra played dance music. Like most speakeasies, it technically did not sell alcoholic beverages. Instead, customers could be sure of finding a resident bootlegger who sold alcohol by the bottle at greatly inflated prices. He, in turn, kicked back a large part of his profits to the club's owners. Waiters often made the purchase on the customer's behalf.

DEATHTRAP

The operation had been up and running for almost a year and was returning a tidy profit when Hyman Bloomberg gave Barry the bad news that he had to make way for the three men with city hall ties. Nat Clark was a clerk in the city's licensing bureau, John Glynn's brother Theodore was the Boston Fire Commissioner, and Michael Ward worked at the mayor's secretarial bureau. Whether they applied some pressure, or perhaps just slipped Barry and his associates some money, remains a mystery, but Barry agreed to move the Pickwick Club upstairs to the old banquet hall on the second floor. On February 19, 1925, he signed a one-year lease for the entire second floor at $250 a month. As he had done a year earlier, he then sublet the space to his club. Boston Mayor James Michael Curley happened to be vacationing with his family at Ormond Beach, Florida when the Greenwich Village Cafe opened for business in the old Pickwick Club site. He flew into a rage when he returned and discovered the three men had mailed invitations to the grand opening with the words, "The favor of a reply will be appreciated by Nat Clark, Mayor's Office, Boston." He fired Clark on the spot.

The Pickwick Club's seemingly charmed existence came to an abrupt end when Federal Prohibition agents made a surprise raid in January 1925. After uncovering dozens of cases of whiskey, rum, and gin stashed in the basement, they took thirty-three-year-old Max Mulmat of Roxbury into custody and charged him with illegal possession of alcohol. There is little doubt that Mulmat was the club's bootlegger. He posted bail, and appeared at the US district courthouse in Boston on Monday morning, February 8, to answer the charge. The court had a number of similar cases on the docket that day, and while Mulmat waited for his trial to begin, a curious event was unfolding just a few blocks away. An attorney for the Pickwick Club came to the office of the Massachusetts Department of Corporations and Taxation that morning and filed a revised list of officers. Charles

Chapter Two

Gluck of the Hotel Avery in Boston had resigned from his position as clerk; his replacement was a Mr. Frank Ross of 24 Homestead Street in Roxbury. It was a deliberate deception. There was no "Frank Ross". The new clerk did reside at 24 Homestead Street, but his name wasn't Ross—it was Max Mulmat. The irony of filing a revised list of officers at the very same time that the newest one was in a federal courthouse awaiting trial for illegal alcohol possession must have caused a few chuckles at the Pickwick Club. The Commonwealth of Massachusetts placed only one hurdle in the path of a social club official. A person had to be squeaky-clean. No one who was involved in the sale of intoxicating liquor, or engaged in illegal gaming, or any other business or vocation prohibited by law, could serve as an officer or director. There was no question about Mulmat's guilt. He entered a guilty plea that day, and paid a $100 fine. That's the equivalent of about $1,500 today. If anyone other than the elected officers suspected that Mulmat had an official connection to the club, they kept it to themselves. None of the Boston newspapers ever mentioned it.

The Boston Police had staged their own raid at the club in the early hours that same morning, and taken nine men into custody. They booked eight of the men on charges of public drunkenness, but they charged a twenty-nine-year-old Dedham man named William Fitzhenry with assault and battery on a police officer. Fitzhenry allegedly hit Patrolman John Laidlaw with a sucker punch that sent him reeling to the floor in a daze.

James Phillips was unquestionably drunk when he staggered out of the Pickwick Club with three friends at four o'clock in the morning a few weeks later. *Plastered* is perhaps a better word. The four men climbed into Phillips' car, and the Roxbury man drove away. He didn't get far before a police officer noticed his erratic driving, and signaled him to stop. Phillips sped off, and led the police on a two-and-a-half-mile, high-speed chase through the streets and onto the sidewalks of Boston's Back Bay neighborhood. At one point, he nearly hit an officer who was trying to stop him. The wild ride finally ended when the police forced his car to the curb on Bay State Road, and took the occupants into custody. They charged all four men with public drunkenness. They also charged Phillips with operating an automobile while under the influence of alcohol. A Municipal Court judge found him guilty on both counts, and sentenced him to six months in the Suffolk County House of Correction.

Another fight broke out inside the club about two weeks after the Phillips incident, and it escalated into a full-fledged brawl. When the melee was over, a South End man named Michael Galvin was lying under a table with a stab wound in his left thigh. One of his friends helped him to his feet and brought him to the Haymarket Relief Station for treatment. When a nurse spotted the stab wound, she followed the clinic's established procedure and notified the police. An officer came to the Relief Station and questioned Galvin. A dispatcher then sent Patrolman Paul Halleran to the Pickwick Club to investigate. Halleran encountered a situation inside the club that no police officer wants to face alone. Several of the patrons were drunk, and an atmosphere of belligerence and hostility hung heavy throughout the room. It was like an explosive mixture just waiting for a spark. According to Halleran's report, he found "six or seven men creating a considerable disturbance." He told one group of men to "beat it," but no one made any attempt to move. He then tried to take a thirty-two-year-old Jamaica Plain man into custody. He no sooner grabbed hold of James Montrose when another man in the group came over and pulled Montrose away. Halleran backed off and went down to the street where he found Officer Frank Callahan. The two police officers returned to the club and, after a brief struggle, they managed to get both men into handcuffs. The police charged Montrose with public drunkenness, and James Ross of Charlestown with attempting to rescue a prisoner. The story made the front page of the next morning's *Boston Globe*, under a banner headline:

STABBING AND SMALL RIOT
IN PICKWICK CLUB

Investigators later determined there was no connection between the earlier stabbing and the disturbance that led to the two arrests.

On May 14, five men held up a bank messenger at gunpoint as he was about to deliver the weekly payroll to the Lever Brothers Soap Company in Cambridge. Four days later, an informant told the police he heard some of those men planned to stop by the Pickwick Club that night. Inspectors from Boston and Cambridge went to the club, accompanied by Harold Coneeny, the bank messenger. They weren't inside very long when Coneeny spotted thirty-six-year-old Lester Fogg of Allston and shouted, "That's him. He's the man who stuck a gun in my face." The police took Fogg into custody, and he spent the next five weeks in jail, unable to raise the needed $50,000 bail. On June 24, prosecutors told the judge they weren't ready to move forward, but they didn't let on that they had begun to question the messenger's identification. The judge then reduced Fogg's bail to $300. His mother came up with the money, and a few hours later Fogg was back at his favorite speakeasy celebrating his release.

It's no wonder that one Boston newspaper said the club was fast becoming a gathering spot for gangsters and their girlfriends. That claim was a bit of an exaggeration. The so-called "gangsters" were little more than petty criminals. Boston's top racketeers never came to the Pickwick Club. Men like Charles "King" Solomon, Hyman Abrams, Joseph Linsey, and the Fox brothers were more likely to patronize mixed-race clubs in Roxbury like the Phalanx (popularly known as the *Black and White Club*) and the Cotton Club, where Solomon was later shot to death in the men's room.

Two separate disturbances broke out at the club during the early morning hours of July 4. The downtown streets had teemed with holiday revelers for much of the evening, but by one thirty, the almost-relentless din of exploding firecrackers and cherry bombs had tapered off to an occasional crack, pop or boom, and the section of Washington Street that stretched between Boston's theatre district and Chinatown had grown quiet. Vaudeville star Harry Steppe, and what the marquee boasted "his large chorus of pretty girls," had wrapped up their last show of the night at the Gayety almost two hours earlier, and the theater was dark. So was Gordon's Olympia Theater across the street. Thompson's Restaurant had closed, but the Grand Garden Chinese restaurant upstairs on the second floor was still open, and would remain so until dawn. Six-year veteran police officer Frank Callahan—the same man who helped Patrolman Paul Halleran subdue an angry crowd at the Pickwick Club a few months earlier—was walking his beat along that stretch of Washington Street when he heard the sound of men shouting somewhere up ahead, their heated words laced with profanity. There was no sign of any trouble on Washington Street. The noise had to be coming from around the corner on Beach Street, and at that hour of the morning, it was all but certain to be at the Pickwick Club. Callahan turned the corner and spotted the men right away. They were blocking the sidewalk in front of the Pickwick Club as they yelled and screamed insults at one another. Six years spent walking a beat in downtown Boston had given Callahan a keen sense of street smarts, and he knew the argument could easily escalate into a shoving match. From there, it was just one step away from a full-fledged brawl.

"Hey. Break it up." Callahan's deep voice was loud enough to drown out the noise of the melee.

"Go to hell," someone in the group shouted back, and then tacked an especially vulgar obscenity.

The speaker was a man about forty. His work clothes and scuffed boots suggested he was a laborer of some sort, while his slurred speech, bloodshot eyes, and glassy stare confirmed what was already apparent. To use the vernacular of the day, he was *stinko*. Callahan later learned that the man's name was Murphy. The club's bouncers had just ejected the men after they were involved in some sort of altercation. At the moment, it didn't matter that Murphy was drunk, and in the morning would probably have only a fuzzy recollection of what had happened. Nobody spoke to Frank Callahan like that, especially when he was in uniform.

He stepped over and grabbed the man's wrist while he reached in back for his handcuffs. It happened all the time. Taking a drunk into protective custody was an everyday occurrence. What happened next was anything but an everyday occurrence. Another man in the crowd suddenly lunged at Callahan hard enough to knock him off balance, and tried to wrestle him to the ground. Murphy was able to break free and get away. Callahan then went after the man who attacked him. Tommy Conroy was a thirty-six-year-old former welterweight, and a well-known West End troublemaker. His brief career in the ring came to an abrupt end fifteen years earlier when he lost his one and only professional fight. He and Callahan got into a no-holds-barred struggle, and it was only after Conroy dislocated his thumb that Callahan was able to get him into handcuffs.

Two police officers brought Conroy to Boston City Hospital where doctors treated his injured thumb and applied a splint.

The officers then took him to the station house on Lagrange Street where he was booked on a charge of interfering with an officer making an arrest. Frank Callahan resumed patrolling his beat on Washington Street.

The police were back at the club an hour later. Several men tried to get in, but the downstairs doorman barred their way when he saw they were drunk. He called the police when one of them retaliated by smashing a bottle against the front door. The dispatcher sent officers Frank Mullen and Neal McDevitt to investigate, but when they arrived, the doorman was all apologies. "Everything is all right, guys," he told them. "The manager came down and talked to them, and they left. Sorry about that."

McDevitt had trouble hearing the doorman because of the noise coming from the second floor—a motley blend of people talking and laughing, of shuffling feet on the dance floor, and a few male voices crooning a popular tune while the orchestra played a bit too loud. He did notice that no one had bothered to sweep up the broken glass on the sidewalk. Before he left, McDevitt walked upstairs to take a quick glance. He thought that perhaps 125 people were up there.

Mullen took the patrol car back to the station, and McDevitt went back to walking his beat. In their wildest dreams, neither man could have imagined that the old five-story building had all but come to the end of its existence, and within a matter of minutes would be nothing more than an ugly pile of rubble.

| THREE |

Boston-based Jordan Marsh & Company was by far and away the largest retail chain in New England during the first half of the twentieth century. Eben Dyer Jordan was only fourteen when he left his family's farm in Danville, Maine in 1836 and moved to Boston to take a job in a dry goods store. He worked there for five years, and then teamed up with a partner named Benjamin Marsh, and opened a wholesale import business. In 1861, the two men purchased a large, five-story brownstone building in the heart of the city's downtown shopping district and began to sell their merchandise directly to the general public. The store went on to enjoy a period of phenomenal growth in the aftermath of the Civil War. Much of that success was the direct result of its innovative merchandising policies. Jordan Marsh was the first retailer in Boston to install glass showcases, and it was one of the first department stores in the country to provide elevators and electric lights. It also offered something else that proved immensely popular—charge accounts.

The store catered primarily to local city residents for much of the nineteenth century, but it began to attract more and more shoppers from the streetcar suburbs as that era drew to a close. By the early 1920s, the country was seeing a significant growth in automobile ownership—and in the number of women drivers. The company's directors decided it was time to accommodate shoppers who preferred to drive to the store. They decided to purchase two adjoining buildings on Beach Street—one of them next door to the Pickwick Club, demolish both buildings, and erect a multistory parking garage on the site. It was only a few hundred yards from their flagship downtown store. The *Boston Globe* touted the planned garage as "one of the most modern of its kind in this section of the country". No one could have foreseen that the directors' well-intentioned plans would one day lead to the deadliest building collapse in the city's history.

It took some time to evict the tenants and remove all of the furniture and fixtures, and it wasn't until the closing days of 1924 that Jordan Marsh could award the Thomas Elston Wrecking Company with a contract to level the vacant structures. Elston's workers began to dismantle the six-story building next door to the Pickwick Club in February 1925, and they had taken down the top three floors by the time of the April fire. It was a slow process because the crew didn't merely raze the old structures; they also salvaged every item that had any resale value.

One of the many problems that challenged eighteenth and nineteenth century architects was the tendency of exterior brick walls to bulge outward. The tried-and-true remedy was simple, but costly. To keep parallel walls from spreading apart, they ran a series of tie rods under the floor boards, and connected the tie rod ends to anchor plates positioned on the outside of both walls. Those cast-iron plates tended to be quite decorative, and often had the shape of a five-pointed star. Architects generally had no

32

choice but to incorporate tie rods and anchor plates into the front and back walls, but they could sometimes support the sidewalls with a less-expensive alternative. They designed a structure so its sidewall rested flush against the building next door. It was an effective and economical way to provide strength and support, as long as both buildings remained in place. Taking one of them down, however, could significantly weaken the sidewall of the building left standing.

That was the predicament that confronted engineers after Elston's crew razed the building next door to the Pickwick Club. For nearly sixty years, the sides of the two structures had rested against one another, and the sidewall next door provided more than enough support. Elston later said it was twenty inches thick, from the basement right up to the roof. He added that in his twenty-eight years' experience as a building wrecker, he had never found a structure built more on honor. The term "honor built" implied high quality—the type of work on which a builder took pride.

The architectural firm that Jordan Marsh chose to design the new garage came up with a solution. The best way to stabilize the weakened wall, they decided, was to shore it up with concrete support piers. It wasn't a new idea by any means. Engineers had used concrete piers to support heavy loads for some time. To construct a support pier, one or more workers had to dig a hole alongside the foundation to the very bottom, and then continue down another ten feet or more while they also extended the hole inward under the foundation for at least three feet. They then built a series of eighteen-inch-high wooden forms that extended from the bottom of the excavation up to the base of the foundation wall, and poured concrete into the forms. When the concrete was dry, they shoveled dirt back into the hole and tamped it down.

There was no question that the scheme involved a certain

amount of risk. Some people weren't sure it was a risk worth taking. Thomas Elston, the demolition contractor, was one of them. Along with several others, he thought the sidewall was too unstable to gain much benefit from support piers, but the proponents were able to convince Nathan Ginsberg, the executor of the late building owner's estate, that the plan was feasible, and he bought into it. The contractor for the new garage then awarded a subcontract to the Charles Gow Company to construct the support piers.

Gow was twenty-seven years old when he started his construction company in 1899, and had already begun to make a name for himself in civil engineering circles. His particular area of expertise was in the rapidly evolving field of heavy-structure foundations, and the company he established went on to gain international acclaim for their innovative developments in structure support. Their signature product, the Gow Caisson, became the de facto standard for anchoring foundations. As the years went by, Gow began to spend more and more time on outside consulting—an endeavor he really enjoyed—and less and less time in the office. In 1922, he sold his business to the Raymond Concrete Pile Company of New York City with the agreement that he would stay on, but only on a part-time basis. Gow was deeply involved with consulting projects for transit systems in Boston, New York, and Philadelphia when work began on the Pickwick Club building, and his visits to the office had all but ceased.

On Monday, June 29, those support piers had been in place for more than a month, and they had hardened and cured enough to allow a crew from the Fritz Construction Company to begin repairing the damage caused by the April fire. The first order of business was to rebuild the burned-out roof. Around one o'clock that afternoon, some employees of the Parke-Davis Drug Co. happened to be walking down Beach Street on their way back from lunch just as a crane hoisted an eight-by-fourteen-inch timber onto the roof of the Pickwick Club building. Several of them were sure they saw the building sway when the crane lowered the heavy timber into place.

John Goff was one of several carpenters who worked on the new roof, and he spotted a few things that made him nervous. Some of the beams noticeably sagged, and one interior wall had a large, wide crack that ran from top to bottom. He pointed them out to his supervisor, but the man wasn't very concerned. He told Goff to forget about it and get back to work. Goff went back to work, but he didn't forget about it. Two days later, he told company owner Nathan Fritz he was afraid the building might collapse, and he didn't want to work on it any longer. Fritz gave him his pay envelope, and he left.

It was hot and sultry the day Goff walked off the job, but weather forecasters had their eyes on an approaching cold front. They were all but certain that a line of severe thunderstorms would reach eastern Massachusetts by sunset. The new roof was still unfinished that afternoon, and the crew from Fritz Construction Co. covered an open area with a tarpaulin before they left. The promised thunderstorms came as expected a few hours later, and the gusty winds from the squall line that preceded them tore the tarpaulin loose. Almost an inch of rain fell on the city that night. The first Pickwick Club employees showed up for work an hour later, and they found the dance floor covered with water. Timothy Barry arrived soon afterward, took one look, and said, "It's a no go tonight." He told the janitor to open the trap door and sweep the water into the hole where it splashed down onto the vacant ground floor.

If the Fates had already decided to destroy the old building, they had one more card to play. The new garage would provide multiple floors of above-ground parking, along with two levels that were below ground. To accommodate the underground levels, the excavation contractor had to dig down at least sixteen feet below the sidewalk. That was almost eleven feet below the bottom of the nearby foundations. By the time his men finished work on Friday afternoon, July 3, they had brought the edge of the crater-like excavation so close to the Pickwick Club building that they exposed the newly poured concrete support piers. When the club opened its doors to the holiday eve revelers that night, the stage was already set for a catastrophic collapse.

Mae Lawson and her companion were blissfully unaware of any danger as they joined the dozens of other couples who had already started doing the Charleston. That energetic dance made its first appearance on the New York stage three years earlier as part of an all-black review called *Liza*. Cast members Maude Russell and R. Eddie Greenlee led off the second act with a specialty dance number while the ensemble belted out a song called "The Charleston Dancy". Russell later said she used to kick so high that her legs nearly hit her nose. "I was a dancing fool," she added. New York reviewers generally gave the show good marks, but none of them singled out the Russell-Greenlee number for special mention.

Liza closed after 172 performances, but a sequel called *Runnin' Wild* was already in the works. The producers decided to retain the same spirited dance steps, but incorporate them into a featured production number that would bring down the curtain at the end of Act One. They scrapped "The Charleston Dancy" and hired veteran songwriters James Johnson and Cecil Mack to create a new number for the show. The two men came up with several possible titles before they settled on the shortest one. Johnson and Mack called their new song "The Charleston".

The director then chose an unknown, nineteen-year-old cast member named Elisabeth Welch to sing the driving, rhythmic lyrics. *Runnin' Wild* opened at New York's New Colonial Theatre on October 29, 1923. Some claim the opening night per-

Chapter Three

formance made American musical theatre history. The Charleston blossomed into an overnight sensation; its popularity exploded across the country like no dance craze had ever done before, and Elisabeth Welch's rousing rendition of the up-tempo melody propelled her into a successful career in show business that spanned almost seven decades and two continents.

The Charleston was still the most popular dance in the country that summer of 1925. The basic steps were easy to learn. They resembled walking, or stomping, while the arms swung backward and forward. A person could do the steps alone, or with a partner, or as part of a group. Dancers more or less remained in one place, and quite a few could squeeze together into a small area. People today often associate the Charleston with the song of the same name, but the steps go well with any snappy tune played in 4/4 time. The song Glennon chose was an ideal match.

The small dance floor quickly filled. At least thirty couples were out there, clapping their hands, slapping their sides, sliding their feet, jumping, kicking, and stomping. Every two thirds of a second, sixty or more shoes slammed down onto the floor in unison. Left feet, right feet—stomp, stomp, stomp! One hundred times every minute! The old wooden floorboards under the linoleum rested on three-inch-by-twelve-inch wooden joists, spaced fourteen inches apart. As the steady pounding of feet continued, those joists began to vibrate. Structural engineers use the term *mechanical resonance* to describe what took place. Under certain conditions, a suspended beam or cross member will vibrate violently when subjected to steady, rhythmic oscillations. Those vibrations have caused catastrophic failures in bridges, buildings, and even airplanes.

Many people cite the 1940 collapse of the mile-long Tacoma Narrows Bridge in Washington as a classic example of destruction caused by mechanical resonance. In that instance, forty-mile-per-hour crosswinds blowing through the suspension cables set up the vibration. Soldiers marching four abreast caused the vibration that led to the collapse of the Broughton Suspension Bridge near Manchester, England in 1831. The water in the river below was unusually shallow, and although several soldiers sustained serious injuries, no lives were lost. A similar accident twenty years later claimed more than 200 lives when a suspension bridge that spanned the Maine River in France collapsed after a battalion of soldiers began to march across it. On a more recent note, mechanical resonance problems forced a two-year closure of London's Millennium Pedestrian Footbridge over the Thames after it began to sway as thousands of pedestrians walked across it on opening day. Authorities had to evacuate a thirty-nine-story building in Seoul, Korea in 2011 when it began to shake violently. Investigators determined that the steady, rhythmic stomping of a Tae Bo exercise class dancing to the tune "The Power" had triggered the resonance.

The Pickwick Club dancers knew nothing about resonance; they had no idea what was going on under their feet. Those vibrating joists ended at the outside walls, and they too began to vibrate—especially the weakened wall, and the newly poured concrete piers that supported it. Anyone passing by might have seen dust trickling down from the brick wall where some of the mortar had started to crumble. They would have heard what sounded like pops or snaps as some of the bricks began to crack. John Owen heard those cracks and pops, but like several other people in the club, he mistook them for the sound of firecrackers. Patrons had been lighting them and throwing them onto the floor all night.

The steady, measured pounding of feet on the dance floor went on and on without letup—a vibrating, pulsating, throbbing clamor. Billy Glennon had the orchestra run through the tune twice to give the dancers some extra time. People loved it when orchestra leaders did that, and the relentless stamping and stomping continued for several minutes. Toward the end, Glennon picked up the tempo, and the dancers quickened their pace. The joists under the old floorboards began to vibrate with even more intensity. Finally, the music stopped. Most of the dancers were still on the floor, waiting for the last dance, when the lights suddenly grew dim and began to flicker.

That was the only indication that something had gone terribly wrong. The relentless vibrations had taken their toll on the weakened sidewall, and a few sections started to crumble. When they did, some of the bricks above slid downward. At some point, the shifting weight and the resultant stress proved too much for the old bricks and mortar, and the entire wall began to break apart and fall. High above, the eight-ton tar and gravel roof crashed down onto the fire-weakened fifth floor, setting off a domino-like chain reaction as one floor after another gave way and collapsed onto the one below. It took only a few seconds for the tumbling mass to reach the second floor, but by then the lights had failed, plunging the room into darkness. Anguished shouts and screams mingled with an ear-splitting screech as boards and timbers tore apart, then the shrieking noise gave way to a thunderous roar as countless tons of bricks and debris hurtled down from the upper floors. Terrified patrons rushed for the door. Many of them didn't make it. The floor collapsed from under their feet sending everyone and everything—tables, chairs, bricks, beams, plaster, and glass—crashing downward like an avalanche into a pitch-black abyss.

Although the lucky ones who survived invariably recalled vivid details of their brush with death as if the collapse had played out in slow motion, the whole chain of events took less than ten seconds. For a few moments, nothing emanated from the rubble but an eerie silence.

DEATHTRAP

| FOUR |

Fire Chief Daniel Sennott was sound asleep at his headquarters in the Mason Street Fire Station when a sudden
clang of the Gamewell fire alarm bell reverberated
throughout every nook and cranny of the old, two-story building,
shattering the death-like silence and rousing even the soundest
sleeper. After a slight pause, the bell went on to sound out the
array: one-four-seven-one. There was a brief lull, and then the
sequence began again. By that time, every fireman in the station
was on his feet and counting the number of chimes. No one had
to search the list and find the location of box 1471. They had all
been there before—many times. The call box was, and still is,
mounted on a pedestal at the corner of Washington and Essex
Streets. It is one of the busiest intersections in downtown Boston.
Sennott glanced at the clock on the wall and noted the time. It
was one minute past three.

A Boston police officer had pulled the alarm that roused the
men on Mason Street. Sylvester Murphy was on Washington
Street a few minutes earlier when he met Sergeant John

DEATHTRAP

Montague and Patrolman Frank Callahan. The three men had worked a special 7:00 p.m. to 3:00 a.m. shift that holiday eve, and were on their way to the station house to sign out. They had just turned the corner and gone but a short way up Lagrange Street when a resounding, rumbling noise echoed through the pre-dawn tranquility like a clap of thunder. In some ways, it sounded like a huge load of coal sliding down a chute. All three turned and ran in the direction from which the sound seemed to have come. It only took them a few moments to reach Washington Street. A quick glance to the left showed that something had happened down by the corner of Beach Street. People were running from the Grand Garden restaurant, and some of them didn't stop until they reached the middle of the street. There was no sign of fire or smoke, and the lights on the second floor still shone brightly. Whatever had fallen was close by, but it wasn't the Grand Garden. The three men ran to the intersection and looked down Beach Street. Everything was clear for about a hundred feet. Beyond that, a massive cloud of grayish-white dust stretched from one side of the street to the other, and rose upward for fifty or sixty feet. Murphy and his two companions stared in disbelief. It was like peering into a fog bank. Behind that hazy veil, there should have been a five-story, red brick building. A crowd of holiday eve revelers should have been drinking and dancing on the second floor. It took a moment or two to grasp the extent of the horror. The building wasn't there. The Pickwick Club had collapsed.

Murphy turned around and ran toward the fire alarm box at the corner of Essex Street, about 300 feet away. Montague and Callahan dashed down Beach Street toward the collapsed building. Patrolman Neal McDevitt was already there when they arrived. McDevitt had responded to the call about the disturbance at the front door ten minutes earlier, but he returned to his beat on nearby Kneeland Street when he learned the troublemakers had left. He was almost at the corner of Knapp Street, about 300 feet from the Pickwick Club, when he heard the loud, crashing sound. McDevitt ran the length of Knapp Street, and almost bumped into George Callahan when he turned onto Beach Street. Callahan was the Pickwick Club doorman he had spoken with minutes earlier. Callahan was screaming, "Get a ladder. Get a ladder." He later insisted he had shouted for McDevitt to call the fire department.

Patrolman George Gardner heard the crash while walking his beat on Harrison Avenue, and he arrived only moments after McDevitt. He saw a girl struggling to climb through a ground floor window, and he ran over to assist her. Someone was screaming from just inside the window, and Gardner realized one or more people were trapped under a section of flooring that had come down from an upper story. He was able to lift it with his shoulder, and two men crawled free.

The devastation that McDevitt and Gardner encountered was so extensive that many first responders thought a bomb had exploded. The entire east wall that faced the excavation was gone, as was most of the back wall. Half of the front wall had fallen too; the section that remained standing leaned way out over the sidewalk, and looked like it could fall at any moment. Only the west wall, the one nearest Washington Street, was intact. The roof had collapsed, along with almost the entire interior. A few large sections of floorboard still clung to the west wall, but they dangled almost straight down, ready to tumble at any moment. In some places, the debris towered almost fifteen feet high, but much of it had slid into the deep excavation next door. Bricks and shards of glass from the collapsed section of the front wall blocked the sidewalk and spilled out onto the street.

A tiny section of the fourth floor in the back left corner had somehow withstood the tons of debris that crashed down upon it. It wasn't any more than ten feet across, but it acted like a canopy and deflected enough of the falling rubble so that the corner sections directly below also remained intact. It was by sheer good luck that six people happened to be standing in that back corner of the second floor when the rest of the floor collapsed. All six were Pickwick Club employees—the five members of the orchestra, and Earl Davis, the busboy. They were still there when the first people came running, but only for a moment. One of them crawled over to the back wall, opened a window, and climbed through. The others quickly followed. People on the street couldn't see that the window opened onto a fire escape that led to the roof of the Grand Garden. The six crossed the roof and then made their way down the Grand Garden's fire escape to an alley alongside the restaurant. Four of the men escaped without a scratch. Pat Curran, the piano player, and Johnnie Donovan, the drummer, suffered minor injuries when they were struck by chunks of plaster from the ceiling. Curran had a cut on his head; Donovan had one on his arm. Neither McDevitt nor Gardner saw the six men, but doorman George Callahan apparently did, and that no doubt was the reason for his frantic shouts to get a ladder.

Billy Glennon told a *Boston Globe* reporter the next day he had no recollection of his escape, but he had vivid memories of seeing people frantically try to grab hold of anything to keep from sliding into the deep hole. Another musician spoke with a reporter from the *Boston Herald.* "It was all so terrible that I can hardly believe it happened, and I can't remember any details. At first, as I crawled toward a window that led to the fire escape, I thought that only part of the ceiling had fallen. The lights had gone out, and I bumped against two or three other fellows as I made my way to the fire escape and down to an alley. It wasn't until we reached safety that we knew the whole building was gone."

McDevitt heard screams coming from somewhere inside, and

he tried to push his way up the tottering front stairs only to find them blocked by fallen timbers. It wasn't until he was back outside that he glanced up and noticed that the top of the five-story brick wall tilted way out over the sidewalk. By that time, several spectators had rushed to the scene—many of them patrons and employees of the Grand Garden who fled down the stairs in near panic when they heard the thunderous noise just as the building began to shake. Like many other people, most of them thought an earthquake had struck. McDevitt told a *Boston Herald* reporter the next day that the first police officers at the scene were able to free as many as a dozen people from the tangled wreckage before the firefighters arrived. Frank Callahan continued his frantic efforts until he broke his finger while helping several men lift a heavy beam to reach a woman pinned underneath.

South Boston pals Thomas Horan and Patrick Greene were on Washington Street, a few blocks away, when the thunderous crash echoed through the neighborhood. The two men raced toward the sound. They had no sooner arrived when they saw three men crouched down at the edge of the tangled wreckage, about eight feet above the sidewalk. A massive beam rested only a few inches above their heads. The newcomers found a wooden plank and raised it against the debris so Leo Romano and his friends could slide down.

Chief Sennott and his crew made the three-quarters-of-a-mile run from the Mason Street station in less than three minutes. Sennott was sixty-two years old at the time, and a forty-three-year veteran of the Boston Fire Department. He had spent the last twenty of those years in the downtown district. It was the most congested commercial section of the city, and was the home of numerous department stores, hotels, and theatres. Even after his appointment to the department's top slot in 1924, he continued to use the Mason Street Station as his headquarters.

DEATHTRAP

Years of experience had taught him that it was vitally important to get a clear overview of the entire situation before he took any action. While some of the first responders, particularly the police officers who arrived right after the crash, rushed into the wreckage to free the trapped victims, Sennott made a quick but thorough scan of the entire crash site. Nothing escaped his careful scrutiny. There was no smoke, no sign of fire. That in itself was a blessing, but the twisted wreckage posed a grave risk to his men when they crawled onto it in search of victims. The five-story brick wall that leaned way out over the sidewalk was the immediate threat. Sennott realized he had to try to stabilize it with the limited equipment he had at his disposal. He told the crew of a ladder truck to extend the ladder full height and rest it against the top floor of the wall. Newspaper photos of the flimsy aerial ladder leaning against the massive, five-story brick wall that weighed hundreds of tons make it obvious the ladder provided little if any help. Had the wall begun to topple, it would have reduced the ladder to splinters and buried the fire engine under tons of rubble.

Sennott also noticed that several bystanders had begun to climb out onto the wreckage to try to free some of the trapped victims. He told the police he wanted every civilian moved back to the other side of the street—it didn't matter whether they were trying to help or not. A few of the would-be rescuers ignored those orders, and police officers had to go in and pull them from the rubble. Pickwick Club doorman George Callahan was one of the worst offenders. He broke away from the police repeatedly and tried to climb back onto the wreckage. Sergeant Montague finally had to have him removed from the scene.

It was pitch dark when the crew arrived from Mason Street, and sunrise was still two hours away. Streetlights in the 1920s didn't provide anywhere near the illumination of today's modern

46

Chapter Four

lamps, so the first police and firefighters on the scene had to rely on flashlights. Sennott told an aide to ask the Boston Edison Company to send over some floodlights right away.

The first responders could hear frantic pleas for help arising from all over the wreckage, but they often couldn't see the person who was crying out. Some of the victims who fell into the deep excavation next door were buried under as much as fifteen feet of debris. Rescue workers tried not to think about it, but they realized some of those people who were begging for help down there in the darkness would probably never make it out alive. In time, the pathetic screams began to grow faint as injuries and loss of blood sapped the victim's strength. By the time daylight arrived, the cries coming from the lowest depths of the rubble had all but ceased. The Suffolk County Medical Examiner later said that some victims could have lingered for several hours before they finally suffocated on the dust and dirt that continued to trickle down into the lowest depths of the debris.

Firefighters made one valiant rescue effort after another as they crawled deeper and deeper into the tangled and twisted debris. Eddie Doyle of Ladder Eight was able to free three victims. The hardest one to extricate was a twenty-two-year-old South End hotel employee named Oreste Cheba. He was wedged between two timbers, and there wasn't nearly enough room for Doyle to lift him. The only option was to crawl as close to the injured man as he could, tie a rope around his waist, and then try to drag him out. Cheba continued to scream at the top of his lungs, "Stop. You're tearing me apart. You're going to kill me," but Doyle kept on tugging until he pulled the South End man free. A few other firefighters then helped carry Cheba to the street and place him into an ambulance. Doctors at Boston City Hospital found that he had dislocated his left shoulder.

Doyle turned around and crawled back down into the wreckage once again, and soon spotted a woman's legs dangling down between two heavy beams. He pulled and tore at the rubble until the gap was wide enough to reach her. That's when he discovered she was dead, and had probably died instantly. Her spine was snapped backward at a ninety-degree angle. It took firefighters another half hour before they could carry thirty-six-year-old Loretta Keegan's body to the street. By that time, Doyle had spent over an hour in the stagnant, dusty air deep in the wreckage, and he collapsed a few minutes later. He was unconscious and covered with grime when his fellow firefighters brought him to the street, but he recovered a few minutes later. Doyle tried to go back into the rubble, and it took four firefighters to get him into an ambulance that brought him to the hospital where doctors treated him for exhaustion.

Soon afterward, rescue workers freed a man who had suffered critical injuries but was still alive, and a woman who was so drunk she didn't realize she was hurt. The injured man was thirty-three-year-old Max Mulmat of Roxbury. Reporters didn't identify the woman. Although every newspaper in Boston reported Mulmat's name, none of them mentioned that he was an officer of the club. It's quite possible that there wasn't any reporter in Boston who had even the slightest suspicion.

Dr. Michael McGarty was one of several physicians who rushed over to Beach Street when news of the collapse reached Boston City Hospital. He wasn't there very long when a police officer told him a man was lying deep in the rubble, his finger crushed by a heavy beam. There was no way they could lift that beam. McGarty had to crawl along a large beam on his hands and knees to reach the victim. When the man saw him, he asked if he could have a cigarette. All the doctor could do was light one and blow smoke into the man's mouth. McGarty realized that he had only one option—he had to amputate the crushed finger, and do so with just a local anesthetic while lying on his stomach on a fallen timber. McGarty's actions saved the man's life.

Another man also hurried to the Pickwick Club to offer assistance that night. Rev. Lawrence Morrisroe came from nearby Saint James Catholic Church. Time and time again he made his way down into the wreckage, sometimes crawling along a beam or heavy plank, to give the Church's sacramental last rites to a lifeless victim as police and firefighters stood by with their hats or helmets in hand in a moment of silent prayer.

Boston Fire Commissioner Theodore Glynn arrived shortly after dawn. Chief Sennott gave him a detailed update, after which Glynn told reporters, "This is the worst catastrophe I have ever seen. I'm surprised to see that such a dilapidated building was allowed to stay open for public use." Glynn neglected to mention that his brother had co-owned a restaurant in the building until quite recently.

The *Boston Advertiser* was the first of the morning dailies to hit the streets with news of the disaster. The popular tabloid rushed a special edition into print with the banner headline:

75 DEAD, SCORES HURT
IN HUB CLUB COLLAPSE

It was just a wild guess, but it served as a precursor for the deluge of false reports that surfaced in the days to come. There were only six known dead when the staff writers of the *Advertiser* composed their story.

The headlines of the early editions of the *Boston Globe* and the *Boston Post* were no less sensational. The *Globe's* headline was especially dramatic:

HUNDREDS MAY BE DEAD
IN PICKWICK CLUB CRASH

Headline in an early edition of Saturday morning's *Boston Globe.*

The *Post* followed a short time later with a slightly more sub-dued headline:

PICKWICK CLUB CAVES IN
125 DANCERS TRAPPED

It went on to say that police officials estimated there were be-tween 175 and 200 patrons in the club when it collapsed. As of five thirty Saturday morning, they could account for only seventy-five of them. They feared that at least twenty were dead.

Chief Sennott kept his eye on the narrow section of the front wall that remained upright. He wasn't the only one. Every person at the scene, rescue workers and spectators alike, realized it could crash down at any moment. After a while, the apprehension be-came almost unbearable, and Sennott told one of his aides to call

Chapter Four

Thomas Elston, the veteran demolition contractor who had taken down the building next door. Elston arrived soon afterward, accompanied by his foreman, John Hudson. The two men had worked together for almost twenty-five years. They both agreed that the situation was every bit as delicate as Sennott feared. The fifty-foot-high brick wall weighed several tons, and the ladder leaning against it provided very little, if any, support. There was only one solution—push the wall back and let it fall into the rubble. No one could be sure, however, that there weren't more people buried under the debris directly below the area where the bricks would fall. Sennott, Elston, and Hudson knew they had no choice—they had to leave the precarious wall standing, and hope and pray it wouldn't fall.

It proved to be the right decision. Boston firefighters Malcolm McIntosh and John Rowan were crawling over the wreckage a few minutes later, trying to find an opening, when McIntosh heard a woman moan. The sound came from deep down in the pile of rubble. The two men shouted for someone to get help, and Fire Chief Sennott and Assistant Chief Edward Shallow came running. Boston's Fire Commissioner Theodore Glynn arrived a few minutes later. Glynn crawled onto the debris to encourage the trapped woman.

"Keep your courage up. We'll get you out," he told her.

"I'm all right. I'll stick it out," she said.

The men couldn't see the woman, but her voice came from about ten feet in from the sidewalk. Several more firefighters rushed over, and they began to tear at the debris.

"Stop it," Glynn shouted. "Don't touch that stuff. You might bring the whole wall down on her."

Thomas Elston and John Hudson had already called some of their employees and told them to hurry to Beach Street. Any attempt to free the trapped woman had to wait until they arrived with their equipment. Elston's crew first positioned three heavy-

DEATHTRAP

Beach Street, seven hours after the collapse. The fire department's aerial ladder rests against the building on the left side of the photo.

Boston Sunday Post
July 5, 1925

duty jacks under a section of the collapsed flooring, and then raised it high enough that someone could crawl underneath. Two men crept under the floorboards only to discover that two heavy beams slanted downward at an almost forty-five-degree angle. Bricks, and small pieces of wood, and other debris filled the space between them. The trapped woman was somewhere underneath. The two men tore into the pile of bricks and began to toss them out one by one, at one point in a bucket brigade-like fashion. They managed to dig out several feet of rubble before they found their path blocked by a solid timber. Two other men then crawled down into the hole with a saw. They planned to cut through the beam in two places, and then remove the center section. No one knew what might happen when the beam separated, especially with a weakened five-story brick wall towering ominously overhead. When Elton's men finally cut through the beam and cleared away the center section, their hearts sank. Behind it was a mass of torn, twisted sheet metal with razor-sharp edges. About three hours had passed since McIntosh first heard the woman cry out, and now the task looked almost hopeless. Once again, the rescue attempts had to wait—this time until someone located a pair of giant shears. It took a while to find them. Two men then crawled down into the tunnel and cut through the tangled, twisted metal. The work was difficult, and it was dangerous. Any contact with a sharp edge, no matter how slight, would have caused a deep cut. To the rescue workers standing by, it seemed like the task was taking forever, but when the two men finally cut through several feet of sheet metal, they could see the woman's head.

"Mister, here I am, over here," she cried out when she saw the first fireman. She told him her name was Edith Jordan, she was twenty-eight, and she lived in Somerville. She also said she had been married for only a few months. She and her husband had gone to the Pickwick Club with three of his friends. "I think he's trapped down here too," she said.

"No, he isn't," Glynn shouted. "He's out here waiting for you."

It wasn't quite true. Rescuers had freed John Jordan from the wreckage a few hours earlier. He had numerous lacerations and bruises, and firemen sent him to Boston City Hospital in an ambulance.

"I'd like some water," she said. Someone ran to a nearby drugstore and brought back a funnel and a length of rubber tubing. The two men in the tunnel were able to work the tubing down to her and give her a sip of water.

"Can I have something to eat?" she asked. The best the men could do was to give her some chicken broth.

She was lying face up with a heavy beam on her chest. "There are two people on top of my legs," she said. "They haven't moved. I think they are dead." She assured firefighters several times that she was all right, but as time went by, she began to implore them, "Please hurry."

Around ten o'clock, Malcolm McIntosh crawled into the hole and told her that firemen had brought her husband to the hospital as a precaution, but that he was fine. "I'm so glad to hear that," she said. "I wish I could get out and see him. It's getting very cold down here." When McIntosh came out, Fr. Morrisroe crawled down into the rubble and gave Mrs. Jordan the last rites.

The work continued to progress at a snail's pace. Only two men could work in the tunnel at the same time—sometimes only one. Eventually they came close enough to Mrs. Jordan to see there was more than just a beam pressing down on her—there was also some heavy metal lath strips. They managed to saw through the beam and then used the shears to cut away the metal lath. When they had cleared the last of the metal, they scooped enough dirt from under her waist that they were able to slip a lifebelt around her. Slowly, inch by inch, they eased her out from under the rubble. It was ten minutes to twelve, almost nine hours after the collapse, when Commissioner Glynn shouted to the ambulance driver, "Get your motor running."

A few moments later the rescue team, their faces and clothes covered with dirt, placed Mrs. Jordan on a stretcher and covered her with a bright red blanket. Five hours had passed since McIntosh first heard her cries for help. As attendants slid the stretcher into the ambulance, she asked, "Am I all right?"

Chapter Four

"You bet you are," the driver said.

He made the two-mile run to Boston City Hospital in less than five minutes. Mrs. Jordan was still conscious when attendants wheeled her into the X-ray room, but she was slipping fast. Her face had lost all color, her skin was cold and clammy, and she had begun to breathe rapidly—the telltale signs of a person going into hypovolemic shock from loss of blood. Someone sent for her husband, but by the time he arrived, she was gone. Edith Jordan died fifteen minutes after she arrived at the hospital. She was the last victim that rescue workers were able to free from the wreckage alive.

Back at the Pickwick Club, firefighters crawled down into the hole once more and retrieved the body of the man who was sprawled across Mrs. Jordan's legs. She was mistaken when she said there were two people. What she thought was a body pushing against her left side turned out to be just a beam. A man's hand was sticking out from the dirt at the bottom of the hole. It was obvious that he was dead, as was another man father back in the debris. A heavily charred beam that bore witness to the ferocity of the April fire had crushed part of his head. Firefighters could only get as far as the man's legs, but one of them was able to reach into the victim's pocket and retrieve his wallet. The dead man was Patrolman Paul Halleran of Division Nine, the same police officer who had to seek help when an unruly crowd prevented him from making an arrest at the club a few months earlier. Halleran had gone off duty at two o'clock that morning, and stopped by the Pickwick Club for a drink on his way home.

The time had come for Sennott and Glynn to make a decision— one that neither man wanted to make, yet they knew they couldn't forestall it any longer. They sent word to the rescue crews to suspend the search operation and make sure everyone moved away from the wreckage site. Commissioner Glynn then gave Thomas Elston the go-ahead order to take down the precarious section of the front wall. The two bodies buried under the rubble would have to stay there a while longer. So would any other victims, either alive or dead, although the likelihood of finding any more trapped victims who were still alive was growing more and more remote. It was far more important to safeguard the living than to recover the bodies of the dead.

| FIVE |

Fire officials would have been hard pressed to find a more experienced team of demolition experts than Thomas Elston and his foreman, John Hudson. The seasoned veterans had been razing buildings in the Boston area for more than twenty-five years. The fire engine, with its ladder leaning against the wall, had to move before any work could begin. No one could be sure how much help, if any, that ladder offered, or what would happen when the firemen eased it away. The entire brick wall might remain standing, or it might collapse straight down. If it stayed together and fell forward in one piece, however, countless tons of brick and mortar would rain down on top of the ladder truck and its crew. Ever so slowly, inch-by-inch, the crew backed the ladder away from the wall. One bystander said it was so quiet a person could hear a pin drop. Nothing happened. The wall didn't even tremble. The driver then gently moved his truck farther down Beach Street, out of harm's way. It was time for John Hudson and his crew to go to work.

The easiest and safest way to take the wall down was to loop a heavy chain around its base, or at least around most of it, and then pull the chain. Hudson's crew brought whatever equipment they thought they might need when they rushed to the scene, and one man arrived in a truck with a small crane mounted on the back. The vehicle somewhat resembled a tow truck. The driver backed close to the base of the wall and waited while other men worked a length of chain through some broken ground floor windows, and then attached both ends to a hook that dangled from the crane. Hudson then shouted out to the driver, "Take her up easy now. Keep a steady strain."

The man inched the truck forward until the chain was taut, and then he gunned the engine. The truck didn't move, but the rear wheels began to spin. One of the Elston Company's steam shovels was nearby, and Hudson told the operator to pick up a large granite block and lower it onto the bed of the truck. The truck driver then went through the same routine and took up the slack in the chain, but it snapped as soon as he pressed his foot down on the gas pedal. Everyone had to stand by until Hudson's men found another chain and strung it through the broken windows. The driver then made a third attempt. Nothing happened for a moment or two, and then the lowest bricks and mortar began to crumble. The truck lurched forward, and the wall crashed straight down behind it.

With that threat now removed, Hudson and his crew turned their attention to three sections of floorboard that still clung to the one wall left standing. All three dangled almost straight down, as if they too could fall at any minute. One had partially broken apart, but the other two were intact, with the floorboards still nailed to the underlying joists. The section of the fourth floor was the largest—about fifteen feet wide and twenty feet long. Work had no sooner started than a newspaper photographer thought he heard a woman cry for help. Everything stopped while firemen swarmed over the pile of rubble with crowbars and shovels.

Chapter Five

It turned out to be a false alarm, and Hudson's men went back to work.

Taking down those sections of floorboard proved to be even more risky than bringing down the front wall. Hudson's crew had to first climb up behind a section of flooring and loop a heavy steel cable behind it. The steam shovel and the tow truck then pulled and tugged until joists and floorboards gave way with a high-pitched screech and crashed down onto the debris, kicking up a huge cloud of dust. The crew then crawled onto the wreckage, retrieved the cable, and went to work on the next section. They repeated that process until the last of the floorboards were down.

A number of public officials flocked to the crash site that day. The first to arrive was Suffolk County District Attorney Thomas O'Brien. He showed up around midmorning, while fire fighters still struggled to free Edith Jordan. O'Brien spoke with several people at the scene, including Fire Commissioner Glynn, and then told reporters he planned to have a grand jury look into the collapse, maybe as early as Monday morning. He intended to find out who owned the Pickwick Club, who allowed it to operate, when the city had last inspected the building, and whether or not anyone had ever reported it as unsafe.

"This is a terrible catastrophe," he said, "and if there are guilty persons responsible, rest assured they will not escape punishment. I'll leave no stone unturned to uncover the facts. No one will be spared in this investigation."

Boston mayor James Michael Curley arrived soon afterward. He was at his summer home in North Scituate when an early morning phone call from one of his aides changed whatever plans he had for the holiday weekend. Curley spoke with Fire Commissioner Glynn for several minutes, and then left without speaking with reporters.

City officials confer at the collapse site on Saturday morning.
Sections of floorboard can be seen dangling almost straight
down from the back wall.

Chapter Five

Boston Building Commissioner John Mahoney was another visitor that morning. Unlike Curley, he didn't avoid the reporters, but he managed to dodge most of their questions. Mahoney said he wasn't in any position to discuss the building, and he told them he wasn't sure if his department had any reports on the structure. The Commissioner soon found out to his chagrin that his department did have a report on file—a very recent one. One of his employees had inspected the property for structural integrity just two days earlier, and failed to find any problems.

Officials had to put the rescue efforts on hold for almost three hours while the demolition crew took down the dangerous sections of flooring. It was almost four o'clock before the search resumed. This time workers were able to move a lot faster than they had in the morning. Instead of having to contend with heavy beams and sections of flooring, they pulled out planks, boards, and bricks. They did encounter one unexpected problem. A Dixieland jazz band had begun to play next door inside the Grand Garden restaurant in midafternoon, while Hudson's crew took down the last sections of flooring. The blaring music that drifted through the open windows made it difficult to hear someone who might yet cry out from the rubble. Firefighters put up with the noise for a while until a rescue worker thought he heard someone groan, but he couldn't be sure. He stomped over to a department official and told him the music was far too loud. Like many others at the scene, the fire captain was growing increasingly angry at what he considered callous and blatant disrespect. To play lively, feel-good music while firefighters searched for bodies right next door, and while anxious friends and relatives looked on in silent prayer, was completely inappropriate. "Stop that damned music," he shouted to a nearby policemen. Sergeant Thomas Harvey went over to the Grand Garden and told the manager the jazz band had to stop playing right away. The police would allow no music of any kind until all rescue operations were complete.

While the demolition team was struggling to remove the last sections of flooring, the Suffolk County Medical Examiner's office released the names of the first six victims:

Loretta Keegan, 36, Cambridge
John Scales, 22, Roxbury
Pauline DeLucca, 35, South End
Edith Jordan, 28, Somerville
Wayne Marr, 30, US Coast Guard Cutter *Mojave*
Paul Halleran, 33, Dorchester

A few hours later, William Randolph Hearst's International News Service broadcast its own tally of what it claimed were the known dead. It was riddled with errors. The names of four current or former local professional boxers were on the list: South Boston heavyweight Joe "Hambone" Kelly, Boston featherweight Morris Kaplan, who fought under the name "Red" Chapman, Frank Tillo, and Frank Russo of Somerville, whose career failed to get off the ground after he lost his first and only professional fight. Frank Tillo was the only one who had lost his life; the other three were very much alive. None of them had set foot inside the Pickwick Club that night. The collapse did claim the life of a man named Chapman, but he was an automobile salesman from Dorchester, not a professional fighter. Even after the erroneous report of Red Chapman's death was discredited, some news stories continued to describe the automobile salesman as a *pugilist.*

The I.N.S. list also included George Lowre, Frank Martello, Fred Rions, and Dave Melmont of Boston's South End, along

Chapter Five

with Hannah Nalseapple of York, Pennsylvania. Her body was "terribly crushed", according to the I.N.S. If any of those people were in the club that night, they escaped without injury. Their names never appeared in news reports again. The last victim on the I.N.S. list was an unidentified sixteen-year-old girl "with bobbed blonde hair". Like Nalseapple, her body was also badly crushed. The sixteen-year-old girl later turned out to be a thirty-three-year-old employee.

The report of Frank Tillo's death sent shock waves through Boston's predominately Italian North End neighborhood where the popular lightweight boxer still enjoyed celebrity status—especially among adolescent boys—even though he hadn't fought for more than four years. The next day, grief gave way to confusion when the *Boston Sunday Advertiser* mistakenly reported that he had survived the collapse, and was in a Boston hospital with two broken legs.

Tillo was at the peak of his career when he stepped into the ring at Boston's Mechanics Hall on June 14, 1921 before some 3,000 fight fans. They had gathered to watch a classic 1920s matchup—a North End Italian doing battle with a South Boston Irishman. Tillo had a good reason for wanting to win that night. His opponent was Eddie "Shaver" O'Brien, and O'Brien was responsible for one of only four losses on his record. Five rounds later, the fight was over—and so was Tillo's boxing career. The referee stepped in when Tillo hurt his right hand and couldn't continue. The injury never healed properly, and the popular North End man who gained local fame for his powerhouse right hand punch never fought again. That night also marked a turning point in his personal life. It was all downhill from there.

He was watching a boxing match in a local arena fifteen months later when he got into a fight with a man named Guy

Morgan. By the time the police arrived and broke it up, Morgan had stabbed him six times. An ambulance brought Tillo to Boston City Hospital where doctors had to make thirty-five stitches to close his wounds. Prosecutors summoned Tillo to Boston Municipal Court two weeks later to testify at Morgan's arraignment, but the North End man swore that Morgan hadn't stabbed him. Tillo stood by his story even after a Boston police officer testified that he saw the two men scuffling. Tillo's attempts to explain his stab wounds were so implausible the judge stepped in and asked him if he knew what the word *perjury* meant.

Six months later, Tillo found himself back in court—this time in Brookline where he pled not guilty to three counts of armed robbery after he allegedly forced his way into a garage on Dummer Street and robbed several men who were in the midst of a high-stakes crap game. One of the victims positively identified him as the man who took $300 from him at gunpoint.

The Boston Police arrested Tillo on July 13, 1923 and charged him with assault and battery on a shoe dealer from St. Louis. George Brockman was in town to attend the annual Boston Shoe Show at the Copley Plaza Hotel. The thirty-four-year-old visitor went out for an evening stroll after spending the entire day inside the hotel. A woman approached him as he neared the intersection of Worcester and Newland Streets, a residential area in the South End about a mile from the hotel. Brockman never explained why he happened to be in that neighborhood, nor did he say what transpired, but a few moments after the encounter a car pulled up alongside him and a man got out and punched him in the face. Brockman reeled backwards and fractured his skull when he hit the sidewalk. One newspaper said the woman was "well known to the local sporting community."

Tillo had another run in with the law only twenty-four hours before he met his death. The bizarre chain of events that led to

Chapter Five

his arrest began at the Armenian Club on Kneeland Street in downtown Boston where Tillo was having a few drinks with three companions. A cabaret singer named Willie Mae Burnham, or "Billie" Burnham as she was better known, came in while they were there. One of Tillo's friends liked to think of Burnham as his girlfriend, and they often spent the night together in her room at the United Hotel on Beach Street. George Assook had no reason to suspect that night would be any different, and he flew into a rage when he saw her get up and leave with two other men. He ran outside just in time to see the three get into a car and drive away. Assook shouted for a taxi. His three companions had joined him on the sidewalk by the time the cab pulled up, and the four men climbed inside. Assook told the driver to follow Burnham. The first car turned onto Commonwealth Avenue, a wide boulevard with a tree-lined mall that separates the east and westbound lanes. The taxi followed close behind. By the time the two vehicles reached Newton Center, Assook had had enough. He ordered the driver to force the other car to the curb, and then jumped out with a straight razor in his hand while he screamed at the top of his voice and threatened to cut both men's throats if Burnham didn't get into the cab. A neighbor heard the commotion and called the police. Patrolman Allan Foley was nearby, and he drove up just as the taxi with Burnham and the four men began to pull away. Assook threatened to cut his throat as well, but he backed off when Foley drew his service revolver. Three more Newton policemen arrived moments later, and they took the four men into custody. A Middlesex County District Court judge later sentenced Assook to one year in the House of Correction for assault and battery with a dangerous weapon. Tillo got off lightly—the police only charged him with creating a disturbance, and they released him on personal recognizance.

The Pickwick Club death toll might have climbed even higher if Walter Casey had met up with Tillo at the club on Friday night as the two had planned. Casey would have kept that appointment if the Brookline Police hadn't spoiled his plans when they arrested him that afternoon inside the home of Walter Evarts on Buckminster Road, and charged him with breaking and entry. Evarts and his family were at their summer cottage in Marblehead at the time, but a caretaker at a neighboring home across the street saw three men sneaking down Evarts' driveway. He knew the house was vacant, and he called the police. Within a matter of minutes, they had the house surrounded. The police quickly apprehended two of the burglars, but there was no sign of the third man. Officers fanned out and began a thorough search of the stately, mansion-like home. They looked under every bed and checked every closet and cubbyhole. An hour later, they found Casey, covered with soot from head to toe, in a firebox under the furnace.

The *Boston Advertiser* later ran a fictitious story that claimed three armed gunmen entered the club only a few moments before the crash, intent on killing Tillo, but the collapse foiled their planned, gangland-style execution. The *Advertiser* said the three unidentified men managed to escape uninjured.

When Mayor Curley stopped by the collapse site that morning, he knew quite well that his first priority would be to ensure that no one could point an accusing finger in his direction. Several hours later, his office released a prepared statement drafted by Building Commissioner John Mahoney and Licensing Board Chairman John Casey. To no one's surprise, it exonerated Curley and pinned the blame on someone else—in this case officials at the Republican-controlled state house. Boston's Democratic mayor had effectively used the "us-versus-them" style of class warfare from the time he first entered the political arena twenty-five years earlier. It was a tried-and-true political strategy that won him the hearts—and votes—of his predominantly

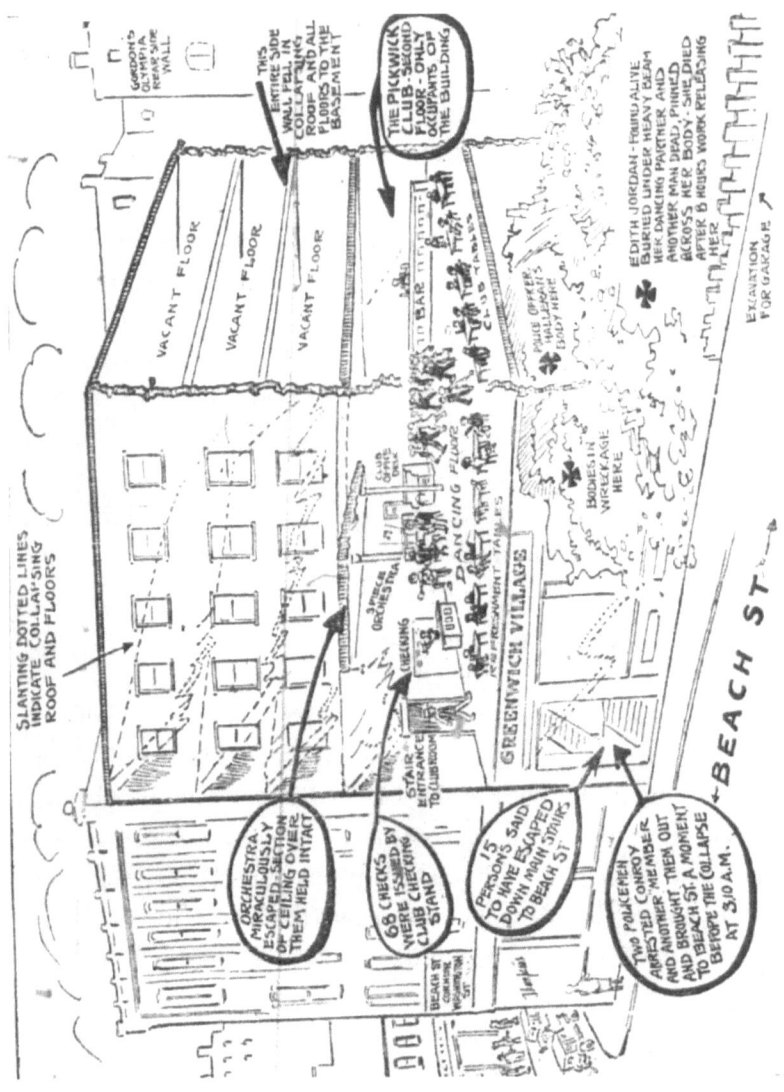

Sketch of the fallen building. The report of Conroy's arrest (lower-left balloon) is completely incorrect.

Boston Sunday Post
July 5, 1925

Irish Catholic and overwhelmingly Democratic working-class constituency.

The message was simple. Republicans, either at the state house or in Washington, were the cause of every problem the city faced. He directed his most vehement wrath and ridicule toward his favorite target—the upper-class, Harvard-educated, old-line Boston Brahmins that he invariably portrayed as the arch enemy of the working class.

Curley's statement read: "The building at 6 Beach Street which collapsed this morning was occupied by the 'Pickwick Club,' an organization which is, from information received, operating under a charter granted by the Secretary of the Commonwealth of Massachusetts, undoubtedly for social purposes, and catering to men and women seeking entertainment without interference or restraint from the city licensing authorities who have the authority to license all other places of amusement in the city.

"The recommendations of the mayor to the Massachusetts legislature for the past three years, and the endeavors of his predecessor, indicate that the mayors of Boston have sought jurisdiction over resorts of the type of the 'Pickwick Club' in order that adequate supervision might apply as in other places licensed by the mayor. In every attempt to gain this authority, the legislature has declined to take action.

"Since no official with authority to prevent overcrowding was present, it is most probable that the club management, taking advantage of the 'night before' crowds seeking unrestrained freedom in their pursuit of pleasure, readily accepted all who came to the club after the closing of the properly licensed amusement places in Boston.

"The building was undergoing alterations; the work was not completed. The Pickwick Club, occupants of the premises, apparently overcrowded the premises beyond the strength of the floors."

City hall insiders realized the press release was nothing more than a carefully crafted smokescreen. They also knew there wasn't a shred of truth to the mayor's claim that the state legislature had thwarted the city's attempt to gain jurisdiction over private clubs like the Pickwick Club. The Massachusetts House Committee on Social Welfare had held a public hearing only five months earlier on a proposed bill that would have placed regulation of private clubs and dance halls in the hands of local communities, and given Curley the very controls he claimed to have sought. A number of people attended the hearing and spoke in favor of the legislation. The *Boston Evening Transcript* described some of their heated remarks as "the most sensational attacks on Massachusetts midnight clubs and roadhouses ever heard in public."

To many people's surprise, the Curley administration opposed the measure. The mayor was on vacation in Florida at the time, but he sent the city's assistant corporation counsel, H. Murray Pakulski, to the hearing in his place. Pakulski told the committee members there was no need for the proposed legislation. He said there were already enough laws on the statute books to control private clubs and to regulate dance halls. Representative Francis X. Coyne of Boston's Dorchester section also spoke in opposition to the proposed legislation. Based undoubtedly on what they perceived as lack of support, the committee issued an adverse report, and House Bill 91 never came up for a vote before the Massachusetts House of Representatives.

The crowd of spectators at the Pickwick Club began to thin as darkness fell, but hundreds of people still lined the barricades and watched the grim search for bodies in silence. On nearby Boston Common, only a few blocks away, thousands of celebrants gathered to watch the scheduled fireworks display. The brilliant flashes of light and the loud booms from the aerial pieces struck many of the people on Beach Street—firemen and spectators alike—as surprisingly callous. Some of those fireworks were so loud that workmen had difficulty hearing. Fortunately, the display lasted less than fifteen minutes.

It was almost midnight when a rescue worker spotted a man's shoulder protruding from under the edge of a large section of flooring that slanted downward toward the debris-filled excavation next door. Several men rushed over to help, and when they had torn it apart, they found two bodies underneath—a man and woman whose arms were so tightly gripped around one another that firemen had trouble prying them apart. When the authorities began their search for identification, they found a loaded, .44-caliber revolver in the man's pants pocket. The two victims turned out to be thirty-four-year-old Mabel Dixon of 461 Audubon Road in the Back Bay, and Joseph Phaneuf, a chauffeur who lived at the same address. Why he was carrying one of the most powerful handguns ever made remains a mystery.

Contemporary newspapers had little to say about either victim. He was thirty-eight and divorced; she had formerly lived in Amherst, Nova Scotia. They were mistaken in saying Phaneuf was thirty-eight. He was actually forty-six, which made him the oldest of the forty-four victims. Those few sparse details, along with the fact that they lived at the same address, could easily lead a person to believe the two were romantically involved. They weren't! Dixon and Phaneuf had only met a few days earlier, and were most likely on their first date. The fact that they both lived at 461 Audubon Road was sheer coincidence. Mrs. Dixon had come to Boston from her native Canada two weeks earlier, and was staying with a friend who just happened to live in the same apartment building as Phaneuf.

Chapter Five

She was born Mabel Gertrude Higgins on February 8, 1891 in the small village of Bear River, Nova Scotia. Her US Immigration application stated that she was a widow, worked as a bookkeeper, planned to live with her friend May Bitte at 461 Audubon Road in Boston, and intended to become a permanent US resident. Mabel Dixon arrived in Boston on June 20, 1925, filled with excitement as she looked forward to a new life in a new country. Fourteen days later she was dead, buried under a pile of rubble in the Pickwick Club ruins.

While newspapers had little to say about Phaneuf, US Census records show that he was born in Canada on May 2, 1879, and came to the US when he was thirteen years old. In 1910, he was living in Quincy, Massachusetts and working as a coppersmith at the nearby Fore River Shipyard. Like many other shipyard workers, Phaneuf lost his job shortly after the November 1918 Armistice ended World War I. He left Quincy and moved into a rooming house on Lawrence Street in Boston's South End, right around the corner from his sister's apartment.

He and Dixon had gone out on a double date that night with a friend of his named Al Shepard, and Shepard's unidentified girlfriend. When Shepard spoke with reporters the next day, he told them he was a "theatrical man". The foursome began the evening at a beachfront speakeasy in the Wollaston section of nearby Quincy, just a few blocks from Phaneuf's former home on The Strand.

It was almost two thirty when they arrived at the Pickwick Club. Both couples headed for the dance floor as soon as the orchestra began to play "Twelfth Street Rag". Shepard and his girlfriend returned to their table when the dance ended while Phaneuf and Dixon remained on the floor. A woman who survived told reporters the next day she happened to look in their direction just as the floor gave way. "They just dropped straight down and disappeared," she said.

Shepard and his girlfriend fared a lot better. They had the good luck to be on a section of floor that tilted downward but didn't fall all the way to the basement, and they reached the street after they climbed through a ground floor window.

Firefighters discovered another victim only a short distance from where Dixon and Phaneuf were found. The facial features of thirty-three-year-old Ella Calley, a waitress at the club, were crushed beyond recognition, and authorities had to base their tentative identification on the recollection of a survivor who described the dress that Calley was wearing. The pockets of that dress still bulged with the tip money she had earned throughout the evening.

Boston mayor James Michael Curley came to the site around midnight and, after a brief consultation with Fire Commissioner Glynn, he told an aide to ask for help from the region's rapid transit system, the Boston Elevated Street Railway Company, and from the New England Telephone and Telegraph Company. The transit company sent about one hundred men from its construction division, while the telephone company furnished three large cranes.

Curley had no sooner left when a group of several police officers arrived. They had gone off duty at midnight, and most of them were drawn by curiosity rather than a desire to help. Eventually there were so many off-duty police officers milling around that Superintendent Michael Crowley had to step in and tell them to either help with the search effort or go home.

At one thirty Sunday morning, firemen uncovered another body, that of a man about thirty. It raised the tally of known dead to thirteen. A short time later, more excitement broke out. The Grand Garden restaurant was still open and doing a good business when a waiter happened to look up and see someone sneaking up the stairway to the third floor. None of the businesses on the upper floors were open at that hour, and he mentioned it to his boss. The manager walked downstairs and told a policeman at the barricades. Patrolmen Gerald McCarthy and William Loomis hurried over to the building to investigate. There were telltale signs of forced entry at a clothing store on the third floor, and the two officers burst in with their guns drawn. Four men ran through the darkened room toward the fire escape, but three of them stopped short when McCarthy shouted for them to halt. The fourth man managed to make it through the window and started to run along the fire escape. McCarthy once again ordered him to stop. When he kept on running, McCarthy took aim and fired three shots. One of them struck the fleeing man in the arm just as he was about to start down the fire escape stairs. A few ambulances still waited alongside the wreckage, and the police used one of them to transport him to Boston City Hospital where he was identified as William Robson of nearby Malden, Massachusetts. Robson had gained some local acclaim a few years earlier during his short career as a professional lightweight boxer. "Bill" Robson was somewhat embarrassed when one of his first bouts ended with him lying flat on his back on the canvas as the referee stood over him and counted to ten. When it happened a second time, Robson decided to call it quits. He hung up his gloves and retired from the ring with a not-very-impressive two and five record, and then took a job as a driver with the Malden Health Department. He was married and had two children, but he and his wife had recently separated. Robson tried to convince the police that he and his companions had broken into the clothing store just to get a better look at the fallen building.

While search operations continued without letup throughout the night, officials at police headquarters wrestled with the problem of how to cope with what promised to be a huge crowd of spectators the next day. The combination of a holiday weekend and a weather forecast that called for Sunday to be a gorgeous summer day with high temperatures in the low eighties was all but certain to attract hundreds, and perhaps even thousands. The police commissioner decided to take no chances. He sent sixty additional officers to help control the anticipated crowds.

| SIX |

A blanket of low, gray clouds all but blocked the first light of dawn on Sunday, but the sun broke out around ten o'clock, and the afternoon turned out to be an almost picture-perfect, mid-summer day. The Salvation Army opened a temporary canteen in a vacant storefront that morning to serve coffee, donuts, and sandwiches to the men who continued to comb the wreckage. Two blocks away, Rev. Philip J. O'Donnell celebrated Sunday mass at Saint James Church on Harrison Avenue. O'Donnell asked his congregation to pray for the victims, and then launched into a brutal attack on the numerous speakeasies and nightclubs in his parish. He called the collapse "a warning from the Almighty", and he said establishments like the Pickwick Club were enticements to crime, despoilers of young women, and an absolute curse on the City of Boston.

O'Donnell returned to the collapse site after mass, and spoke with a reporter from the *Boston Advertiser*. The veteran prelate could have been quoting right from Mayor Curley's playbook

Boston Sunday Post
July 5, 1925

when he told the reporter that blame for the disaster must rest squarely on the shoulders of the Massachusetts Secretary of State because his office granted a license to the Pickwick Club. He didn't stop there, and proceeded to tear into Prohibition itself, which he blamed on fanatics who forced their wills upon people born with wills of their own. He added that he was sure all Catholic clergymen shared his views. That may or may not have been true, but Mayor Curley would have agreed with his outspoken, anti-Prohibition stance. Curley hated Prohibition with a passion, and he never passed up an opportunity to savage the unpopular edict—and its backers. Jack Beatty, author of *The Rascal King*, a celebrated biography of the four-term Boston mayor, says four thousand speakeasies openly flourished in Boston at the height of Prohibition. Four of them were on the same block as police headquarters.

A 400-foot-long section of Beach Street remained cordoned off

Chapter Six

Hundreds of spectators gathered at the intersection of
Harrison Ave. and Beach St. on Sunday.

Boston Traveler
July 6, 1925

between Washington Street and Harrison Avenue. The intersection at Washington Street was somewhat closer to the fallen
building. So many spectators had gathered behind the barricades
by late morning that the police had to divert traffic onto nearby
Tremont Street. Officials knew that tempers would flare and the
situation might well get out of hand if people at the rear of the
crowd began to push their way toward the front. As a precaution,
the police moved spectators along so everyone could get a chance
to look. Most people willingly followed the directions, but a
thirty-five-year-old Roslindale man insisted on taking a longer

look. The police finally had to arrest him after he repeatedly ignored a policeman's order to move on.

While the vast majority of the spectators were orderly and well behaved, a few people still tried to con their way past the police barricades to get a better view. Some tried to convince the police they were workers. Others said they feared a friend or relative might still be trapped in the wreckage. Police officers politely suggested they check with officials at Boston City Hospital or the Southern Mortuary. Occasionally one or two young girls tried to charm their way past the rope barricades, but the police turned them away with a smile and a gentle rebuke. The worst offenders, however, were off-duty firefighters and out-of-town police officers who thought their badge would entitle them to a closer look. The men at the barricades thanked them for coming, but graciously told them they already had enough help. The police did make one exception that day—they let a New York man approach closer to the fallen building.

Nathan Stern was sitting at home in his apartment in Brooklyn on Saturday afternoon when the telephone rang. Inspector Leahy of the New York City Police was on the line, and he asked if he could speak with Mrs. Stern. When Stern said his wife had gone to Boston a few days earlier to visit a friend, Leahy told him he might have bad news. A building had collapsed in downtown Boston the night before. It housed a private club, and the Boston Police were afraid his wife might have been inside. Her brown Hudson sedan was parked directly across the street from the collapsed building. It hadn't moved since the first firefighters arrived on the scene almost twelve hours earlier.

Stern hurried over to Grand Central Station where trains for Boston departed every hour. It was almost five o'clock on Sunday morning when he showed up at the collapse site. He told a policeman at the barricade that he had gone to the apartment where his wife was staying, but her girlfriend had no news. He also went to Boston City Hospital and the Southern Mortuary, but neither place could give him any information. A police sergeant overheard the conversation, and he lifted the rope and told Stern he could watch the search efforts from a doorway on the opposite side of the street, but he cautioned him not to approach any closer.

Patrolman George Snell walked down Beach Street a few hours later with an armload of coats and jackets that firefighters found in the rubble. Stern asked if he could take a look. "Go ahead, buddy," Snell replied. Stern took one look at a woman's black, fur-trimmed cape, and began to choke up. "It's hers," he said. The Brooklyn man returned to the doorway and maintained his silent vigil for a while longer, and then walked back to the barricade at Washington Street where he spoke with a policeman for a few minutes, and then left. Firefighters found Mrs. Stern's body just inside the collapsed staircase three hours later. The *Boston Advertiser* described the recovery scene: "They carried it over the tangled mass of timbers with the pitiful shreds of her salmon-colored party dress flapping in the breeze." The popular tabloid's concocted story about the dress flapping in the breeze was pure fiction. Rescue workers made sure that every victim's body was completely shielded from view before they began to remove it from the ruins.

The police went to the apartment on Commonwealth Avenue where his wife had been staying and gave Stern the bad news. He identified the body at the Southern Mortuary that afternoon, and told attendants he would make arrangements to return it to Brooklyn. None of the New York newspapers mentioned her funeral or burial.

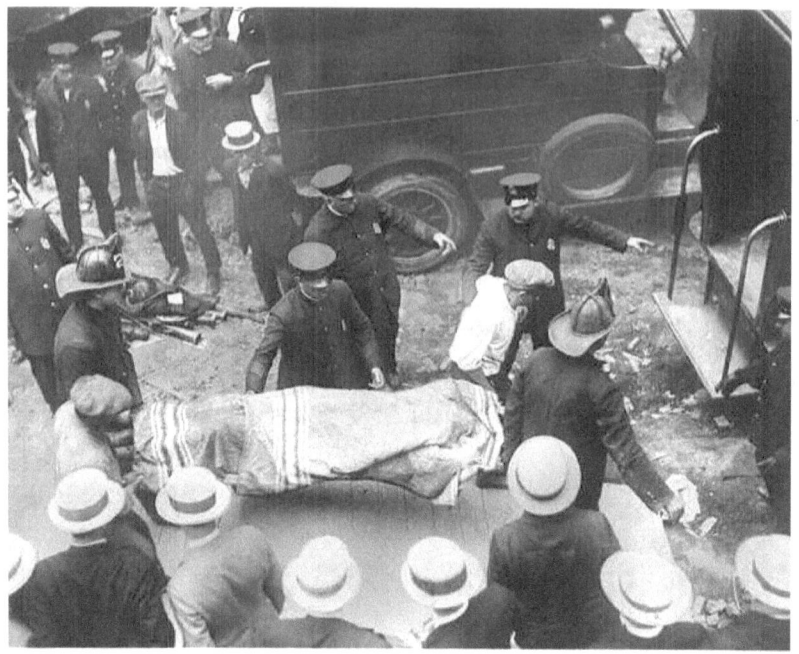

Firefighters remove a body from the Pickwick Club ruins Sunday afternoon.

Mrs. Stern was the unquestioned mystery woman of the Pickwick Club collapse. She went to the club that night with a friend named Madeline Curtis who later told reporters it was about quarter of three, or maybe a bit afterward, when they decided to leave. "I walked down the stairs, but Dora stopped to talk with some people we knew. I waited outside at the foot of the stairs for a few moments, and then I walked across the street to where Dora had parked her car. Then I heard a terrible crash. That's all I remember. I must have fainted."

Chapter Six

Curtis never said how long she remained at the crash site, but at some point, she left the scene and took a taxi back to her apartment on Commonwealth Avenue without telling anyone that her friend hadn't made it out of the building. Several hours later, the name *Doris Curtis* made its first appearance in a published list of the missing and feared dead. It marked the beginning of what turned out to be a deliberate, concerted effort to hide the victim's true identity.

The United Press broadcast a news report early Saturday evening that said rescue workers had located Doris Curtis's body that afternoon, and removed it from the wreckage. Several Sunday newspapers reported that she lived on Commonwealth Avenue, and sometimes used the name Doris Stearns. They identified her father as Edward DeRocher of nearby Arlington, and said he rushed to his daughter's apartment as soon as he heard the news. Boston newspapers quoted DeRocher as saying the family had formerly lived in Brooklyn. He added that his daughter still hoped for a career in motion pictures. One newspaper said that Curtis was believed to be engaged to victim Paul Halleran.

None of those statements were true. There wasn't anyone named Doris Curtis inside the club that night. Madeline Curtis was there, but she escaped without injury. The victim's real name was Dora Stern. She didn't live on Commonwealth Avenue, or anywhere else in Boston. She didn't even live in Massachusetts. Edward DeRocher was not her father. She and Paul Halleran didn't know one another. Firefighters eventually found her body buried in the rubble, but the discovery came more than fifteen hours after the United Press sent out their erroneous report.

By Sunday afternoon, the national wire services were reporting her last name as Stern, but they couldn't agree on her first name. Some called her Dora; others called her Doris. They did agree that she was twenty-seven years old, and lived at 69 Sumner Avenue in Brooklyn. Her husband Charles was a linoleum salesman. Boston reporters who covered the collapse site on Sunday had a different story. They claimed her husband's first name was Nathan, not Charles. Mr. Stern's first name wasn't the only subject of confusion. Newspapers couldn't agree on why his wife happened to be in Boston. The July 6 edition of her hometown newspaper, the *Brooklyn Daily Eagle*, carried two conflicting reports on the very same page. One said that she and her husband had homes at 69 Sumner Avenue in Brooklyn and at 728 Commonwealth Avenue in Boston where she operated a beauty parlor; the other said she had gone to Boston on vacation two days earlier, and was staying with a friend who lived on Commonwealth Avenue.

New York began to take its 1925 state census on June 1, only a few weeks before the Pickwick Club disaster. The enumeration lists the residents of 69 Sumner Avenue in Brooklyn as forty-five-year-old Sam Levy, his thirty-year-old wife Esther, and their two children. Sam worked as a chauffeur. It doesn't show any Brooklyn resident named Doris Stern whose age was even close to twenty-seven, but it does list a twenty-two-year-old, Russian-born immigrant named Dora Stern who lived at 565 Jerome Street with her husband Nathan and their two small children. Nathan wasn't a linoleum salesman, though. He worked as a printer, and the house on Jerome Street was four miles from Sumner Avenue. The Esther Levy who lived on Sumner Avenue was Dora's older sister.

The brown Hudson with New York license plates wasn't the only car on Beach Street that hadn't moved since the first rescue workers arrived on the scene. The police traced the second one to a Roxbury man named Frank Carra. He came to the door when a Boston patrolman rang the bell at his Warren Street

Nathan and Dora Stern.

home. Carra said he let a friend named Carl Paulson borrow the car the night before. Paulson was able to get the night off from work, and he wanted to go out on the town to celebrate the holiday. Carra told the policeman that Paulson hadn't been in touch with him since he drove off in the car.

The Paulson family's agonizing wait came to a sad end at one fifteen Sunday morning when rescue workers removed the badly crushed body of twenty-four-year-old Carl Paulson Jr. from the wreckage. They identified it from the driver's license they found in his pants pocket.

Carl lived with his mother and father on the first floor of a neat, two-family home at 15 Greenville Street in Roxbury. His sister Natalie and her husband lived on the second floor. Carl Sr. was a self-employed wallpaper hanger who came to the US from Sweden when he was three years old. His wife Catherine was a native of Ireland, and emigrated when she was fifteen. She worked in a downtown millinery store. Natalie Paulson joined her mother in the shop when she graduated from high school; Carl Jr. went to work there when he graduated from Mechanic Arts High School a few years later. Carl wasn't terribly keen about working in the stockroom of a ladies' hat shop, and he left after a few years and went to work with his father as a paperhanger. Natalie's husband drove a taxicab for a living, and he was able to get his young brother-in-law a part time job with the same company. By the summer of 1925, Carl was working with his father during the day, and driving a cab for Town Taxi at night.

Catherine Paulson went to the Southern Mortuary on Sunday, but officials wouldn't let her see her son's body. They did give her a list of the items they found in his pockets. One of them was a pair of rosary beads. Mrs. Paulson told the attendant she had given them to Carl as a present when he received the sacrament

Chapter Six

A small crowd lingered outside the Southern Mortuary on Sunday, awaiting news of their missing friends and loved ones.

Boston Post
July 7, 1925

of confirmation in grammar school. He always carried them with him, and she asked if she could have them. Catherine Paulson was devastated when the attendant said no. "We might need them for identification," he explained.

Mrs. Paulson was one of many anxiety-stricken people who made their way in and out of the Southern Mortuary that day. The grim building was located right next door to Boston City Hospital on Albany Street, and at one point Sunday afternoon seven hearses waited outside. For some, the visit was a necessary formality—they came to identify the remains of a loved one and sign a release so a funeral director could remove the body. For others, like the two teenage boys who hadn't heard from their friend John McLaughlin and feared he might have gone to the Pickwick Club, or Louis Vara who hoped to get news of his brother Frank, or the two girls from the West End who wondered if anyone knew the whereabouts of their friend William Grossman, the agonizing, uncertain wait would have to continue a while longer.

On Sunday afternoon, the Boston Police released a partial list of the injured victims who remained hospitalized:

Blanche Kent, 25, 41 Mystic Street, Medford; fractured spine and collarbone

Mary McDougall, 20, 505 Columbus Avenue, Boston; fractured spine, multiple cuts and abrasions of the body

Catherine Walker, 25, 17 Anita Terrace, Roxbury; foot injury, multiple cuts and abrasions of the body

Jacob Rosenberg, 31, US Coast Guard Cutter *Mojave*; fractured spine, compound fracture of left leg

Edward Whalen, 22, 78 East Brookline Street, South End; laceration of left leg

Frank Castelone, 26, 69 Hale Street, Hyde Park; on the danger list at Boston City Hospital; fractured skull

James Corso, 29, 53 Jones Street, West Haven, Connecticut; contusions and abrasions of the body

Edward F. Doyle, 32, 10 Antrim Street, East Boston; Boston Fire Department; collapsed from exhaustion while he helped at the rescue site

Edward LaGroff, 20, 7 Bradford Terrace, Everett; cuts and abrasions on face, hands, and legs

Rita Carlson, 20, 25 Auburn Street, Cambridge; on the danger list at Boston City Hospital; scalp partially torn off, multiple contusions and abrasions of the body

Ethel Conlon, 21, 185 West Boylston Street, Worcester; abrasions on both knees, lacerations on right foot

John Heffernan, 45, 4 Graylock Road, Allston; compound fracture of right leg, lacerated forehead and contusions of the body

Edna Price, 35, 303 Dudley Street, Roxbury; cuts on hands

Max Mulmat, 33, 24 Homestead Street, Roxbury; on the danger list at Boston City Hospital; contusions and abrasions of right hip, lacerated scalp, and possible fractured jaw

Richard Lovejoy, 20, 28 Sherman Street, Everett; dislocated right collarbone

Oreste Cheba, 22, 44 Porter Street, South End; lacerated nose, dislocated left shoulder, contusions and abrasions of the body

Rocco Scarparto, 20, 34 London Street, East Boston; Pickwick Club doorman; injured leg

Harris Hirshberg, 49, 45 Monmouth Street, East Boston; Pickwick Club waiter; shock

The number of confirmed dead continued to climb as the day went on. So did the number of mistakes in published news reports. By nightfall, the list included the names Alice Nixon of New York City and Charles Smith of Providence, Rhode Island, along with two Boston men—J. Lanza, and Serge Penta. The next day the two Boston men had somehow become one—J. Lanza, alias Serge Penta, age twenty-five. James Lanza and Serge Penta must have been puzzled when they saw their names on the victim list since neither man was anywhere near the Pickwick Club when it collapsed. The two men were the co-owners of Penta and Lanza, a barbershop on Hanover Street in Boston's North End. When firefighters pulled victim Frank Vara from the wreckage, they found a card from the barbershop in his pocket. How the two proprietors ended up on the list of known dead remains a mystery, as does the inclusion of Alice Nixon and Charles Smith. Neither one was known to be in the club that night.

The *Boston American* said authorities identified the twenty-eighth body that firefighters pulled from the ruins as Lawrence Nugent of 40 Fenwood Road in Boston. Mr. Nugent may or may not have been in the club that night, but if he was, he escaped without injury. The *American* also said that well-known Boston and Chicago cabaret singer Trudy Ainsworth was missing and feared dead in the collapse. Miss Ainsworth hadn't gone to the Pickwick Club. The *Boston Post* claimed that Patrolman Frank Callahan had dragged Tommy Conroy from the club less than two minutes before the collapse, and was holding him at a patrol box when the building fell. Callahan took Conroy into custody more than an hour earlier after Conroy attacked him as he attempted to make an arrest.

Boston's Sunday newspapers published three conflicting accounts of Arthur McNeil's harrowing escape from the building. The *Herald* printed the thirty-one-year-old Jamaica Plain man's account verbatim: "We heard an awful cracking sound. The floor swayed, and three of our party went tumbling down into the wreckage [...] I found myself standing near the entrance to the stairway next to the girl I was with. We managed to escape down the stairs." The *Post* gave a similar account of McNeil's flight, but it implied that he was alone. According to the *Post*, his companion was still missing. No one had seen her since the collapse. The *Sunday Advertiser* didn't even mention her. The *Advertiser* told its readers McNeil couldn't recall how he managed to get out. "He was dancing when the warning shudder came," it reported. "The next thing he remembered was standing outside in the street."

Newspapers throughout the US and Canada carried a wire service report that claimed the Pickwick Club building was right next to a forty-foot-deep excavation. The excavation was sixteen feet deep. A Canadian paper speculated that a bomb might have wrecked the Pickwick Club.

Edith Jordan's heroic struggle caught everyone's attention, and it's no surprise that some reporters couldn't resist the temptation to embellish it. One wire service story had Mrs. Jordan raise herself on one elbow just as hospital attendants carried her from the ambulance and gasp, "I'm all right. See, I'm all right. Tell my husband I'm all right." The story went on to say, "then she sank back, and her eyes closed in death." It was all make believe. The hospital barred everyone except essential workers from areas that were anywhere near the emergency department that day.

Monday's *Boston Advertiser* nearly doubled the count of the known dead. A front-page article said rescue workers had removed thirty-nine bodies from the Pickwick Club shambles, while the banner headline at the top of the page claimed that forty more were still in the ruins.

Newspapers weren't the only ones who made embarrassing mistakes. Elizabeth Hallahan was just starting to cook Sunday breakfast in her home on Linwood Avenue in Melrose when she heard the doorbell ring. A Melrose police officer was outside on the porch, and he told her as gently as he could that officials believed her twenty-one-year-old son Ralph was dead. Firemen had found his body in the Pickwick Club wreckage during the night, and the Boston police wanted a family member to come to the Southern Mortuary and make a positive identification.

"Ralph is upstairs in his bedroom, sound asleep," the puzzled woman replied.

What Mrs. Hallahan said was true. Her son was nowhere near the Pickwick Club on Friday night. For some reason a Malden man named Francis McLean had a piece of paper in his pocket with Hallahan's name on it. McLean's body was the one that firemen recovered.

McLean was one of six young men who had traveled into Boston on Friday night with plans to see a show, and then return to Malden and watch a bonfire. The show ran late and they missed their train, so they decided to go to the Pickwick Club instead. McLean had never been there before. All six were still inside when the building collapsed. Two of them died in the wreckage, another suffered serious injuries.

Francis McLean was the youngest of eight children. He was born in Chelsea, but his family moved to Malden three years later after the Great Chelsea Fire of April 1908 destroyed their home. His father had been a carpenter in his native Canada, and he followed that trade when he came to the US. A few years later, however, he decided to go into business for himself as a demolition contractor. McLean joined his father in the business after he graduated from high school.

His parents began to worry when he didn't come home on Friday night, and when one of his friends stopped by the house early Saturday morning and told them what had happened,

Chapter Six

Annie McLean took the train to Boston. She waited behind the barricade all day, hoping and praying that rescue workers would find her son alive.

The revelation that two of their fellow officers had lost their lives in the collapse sent shock waves throughout the ranks of the Boston Police Department. Lieutenant Benjamin Alexander was one of the most popular men on the force—a man people today would call a *cop's cop*. The forty-two-year-old lieutenant inspector and father of six had stopped by the club a short time before the collapse, hoping that he might be able to apprehend a suspect the police were looking for in connection with a recent robbery at a downtown jewelry store.

Patrolman Paul Halleran was not on duty at the time, although some newspapers mistakenly claimed he was inside the club on a paid detail. Halleran was in the Pickwick Club for the same reason almost everyone else was there—he stopped in to have a drink on his way home from work. Halleran was thirty-three years old, and a six-year veteran of the Boston Police Department. He had seen combat in France during the First World War while he served with the 101st Field Artillery Battalion of the Massachusetts National Guard. One of his fellow soldiers in the 101st was a private from Cambridge named Walter Brennan. When the war ended, Brennan moved to California and embarked on an acting career that brought him three Academy Awards. Halleran returned home to Brookline, a well-to-do community adjacent to Boston. A few months later, he married his long-time girlfriend, Anna Chisholm, and they moved into an apartment on Inwood Street in Dorchester. The new Mrs. Halleran worked as a salesclerk.

On September 9, 1919, an event took place that had a profound impact on Halleran's future—almost three quarters of the members of the Boston Police Department went on strike, seeking the right to unionize. That night, several mobs roamed the streets, smashed windows, and looted storefront displays. The next morning, Governor Calvin Coolidge called out the National Guard. A shootout in South Boston a few hours later claimed two lives, and a riot in Scollay Square that afternoon left another man dead.

Police Commissioner Edwin Curtis was dead set against the idea of police officers joining a union—especially one with ties to a national organization like the American Federation of Labor. After four days of lawlessness, he had had enough. He fired the 1,100 strikers and announced plans to replace them with new hires. Mayor Andrew Peters opposed the move, but Curtis had the support of Governor Coolidge. Most newspapers, both local and national, backed Curtis, and often described the strikers as deserters and traitors.

The Boston Police Strike propelled Coolidge into national prominence. Newspapers across the country printed his response to a telegram from labor leader Samuel Gompers that placed the blame on Commissioner Curtis. Coolidge wrote, "There is no right to strike against the public safety by anyone, anywhere, anytime." A year later, he won the Republican nomination for vice president. He and presidential candidate Warren G. Harding went on to win the election by a landslide.

Halleran was one of those hired as replacement officers. Commissioner Curtis had promised that the department would give preference to unemployed veterans, and while Halleran was a veteran, he was not unemployed. He went back to work at his old job with a local grocery store only a few weeks after his return from France.

He was working out of Division Four on Lagrange Street

Chapter Six

Two members of the Boston Police Department perished in the Pickwick Club collapse. Lieutenant Inspector Benjamin Alexander (left) was on duty that night. Patrolman Paul Halleran was not. He had just finished his shift in Roxbury, and stopped in for a drink on his way home.

when he was called to the Pickwick Club on March 23, 1925 to investigate a reported stabbing. That was the time he had to back away from the angry crowd that prevented him from making an arrest, and seek help from another officer. Two months later, Halleran transferred from Lagrange Street to Division Nine on Dudley Street in Roxbury.

His holiday eve shift ended at two o'clock that Fourth of July morning. His wife had made plans to leave for a long-awaited, two-week vacation in New Hampshire in a few hours, and he wanted to be home in time to say goodbye, but there was still enough time to stop at the Pickwick for a drink—maybe two. Anna Halleran wasn't the least bit concerned that he hadn't come home to see her off. She assumed that something had come up, and she left for New Hampshire as planned.

Another name on the list saddened sports fans. Rescue workers found former professional boxer Neddo Flanagan's badly crushed body thirty hours after the collapse. It also bore several burn marks, apparently caused by contact with live wires. The twenty-nine-year-old lifelong Malden resident's real name was Edward, but almost everyone knew him as *Neddo*. The one time a newspaper called him Edward was in connection with an incident he would have been happy to forget. On October 2, 1923, a *Boston Globe* headline proclaimed:

BACK TO NATURE STUNT
EXPENSIVE FOR FLANAGAN

The article went on to state that some of Flanagan's friends had dropped him off on a highway in Danvers, Massachusetts the night before, clad only in what the newspaper called "Joe Knowles garb". Joe Knowles had captured the attention of Bostonians a decade earlier when he stripped off his clothes and walked into the Maine woods naked, determined to find out if he could survive for two months without any type of tools. Before he turned his back on civilization, however, Knowles had struck an agreement with his employer, the financially strapped *Boston Post*. The newspaper gave him an undisclosed sum in return for exclusive rights to his stories. For eight weeks, the *Post* kept his name before their readers, and printed the journal entries he wrote on birch bark. Knowles had become something of a local celebrity by the time he emerged from the woods, and the *Post's*

Local boxers Frank Tillo (left), and Edward "Neddo" Flanagan lost their lives in the Pickwick Club collapse.

circulation had more than doubled!

The Danvers police didn't take kindly to Flanagan's stunt, and they charged him with disorderly conduct and drunkenness. A Salem district court judge fined him twenty-five dollars, and then tacked on another thirty dollars to cover the cost of the damage he caused while he struggled during his arrest. The police claimed he snapped the chain on his handcuffs, broke the rear window of a patrol wagon, and tore a police officer's uniform to shreds.

Flanagan had gained some acclaim throughout the Boston area—first as a welterweight, and then as a light heavyweight boxer. He fought ninety-four rounds in a fourteen-fight career that ran from February 1921 to August 1924. After his retirement from the ring, he took a job as a lineman with the New England Telephone and Telegraph Company. He was out of work when he went to the Pickwick Club that night with his friend and fellow Malden resident David Yaffee. His job had come to an abrupt end a few weeks earlier when the telephone company let him go without notice. Yaffee was decidedly reticent after the collapse. The only information he disclosed was that he was on the dance floor when the building began to fall, and Flanagan was at a table with friends.

"The little hero of Boston night life," was how the *Boston Post* described Johnny Duffy when they told their readers the popular hotel, cafe, and dance hall entertainer had lost his life in the collapse. Like Alexander, the thirty-year-old Duffy was a family man, and had two small children. The youngest was only two weeks old. His wife left the hospital just a few days before the crash, and was staying with a friend in Cohasset while she recuperated.

Mr. Originality, as he liked to call himself, often sang at local dance halls like Rougan's in Charlestown, and the Hibernian and the Intercolonial in Roxbury. He also served as a combination emcee and vocalist at benefits and testimonials. Firefighters discovered his badly crushed body shortly before ten o'clock on Sunday night—forty-three hours after the collapse. The whispered words "They found Johnny," quickly spread from the ruins to a small group of his friends and fans who had maintained an around-the-clock vigil at the site, hoping and praying that Duffy had somehow miraculously survived.

The most heartbreaking news that day had to have been the disclosure that a Roxbury widow named Nora Sullivan lost both of her young daughters in the collapse. The family was originally from Cambridge, but they had lived in Roxbury for several years.

Chapter Six

Nora's daughter Mary was the first to strike out on her own when she married a man named William McEachern. Wedding bells rang once again two years later when Lillian married a truck driver named John McIsaac. Sadly, neither marriage lasted. Lillian had been married less than two years when her husband died suddenly, leaving her with an infant child. She and the baby moved back to her mother's apartment on Blanchard Street. Mary and her husband broke up a short time later, and she and her two small children also moved back in with her mother.

People cope with adversity in different ways, and neither Mary nor Lillian was the type to sit around the house and brood about it. Two of their friends stopped by after supper on July 3, and the four girls went out to see a holiday eve bonfire. Mary told her mother they would be home by one o'clock. Nora happened to wake up around three o'clock, and she was surprised to find that her daughters hadn't returned home. She had a nagging feeling that something was wrong, and she decided to stay up. Four o'clock came and went, and there was still no word from either Mary or Lillian. She grew more and more upset as each minute passed. At five o'clock, the doorbell rang. One of the girls who went out with her daughters was in the vestibule outside the front door. She tried, but she couldn't hold back her tears as she told Nora they watched the bonfire, but then decided to go downtown to the Pickwick Club. All four were inside when the building collapsed. The girl said she searched for Mary and Lillian for over an hour, but no one at the site had seen either girl.

Arthur McNeil's recollection of the events just before the collapse left little hope that either girl had survived. McNeil said Mary and Lillian were at a table near the wall, and he caught sight of them as they tumbled into the pitch-black hole. He told a reporter the next day, "they didn't have a chance."

The discovery of Johnny Duffy's body raised the count of known dead to thirty-nine. A few hours later, someone spotted a man's hand sticking out from some rubble in a trench near where the weakened sidewall had fallen. Firefighters had to dig for nearly four hours before they reached what turned out to be the badly mangled bodies of three men and a woman.

The woman was forty-one-year-old Clara Frederick of West Roxbury. Her two younger sisters had managed to break through the police barrier Sunday afternoon, and they almost reached the edge of the wreckage before officers could overtake them. They explained that their sister had gone to the club Friday night, and neither of them had heard from her. She wasn't at Boston City Hospital, and the desk clerk at the Southern Mortuary couldn't find a record of anyone with that name. The police brought them back to the barricade and said they were sorry, but all the two women could do was wait.

Francis Driscoll, a prominent labor leader in Boston, was one of the three men. Firemen identified his body by the blue union membership card he carried in his wallet. Massive chunks of bricks and masonry had crushed the other two bodies to the point where their facial features were no longer recognizable. A *Boston Post* reporter thought their identification might well prove impossible. It took a while, but the authorities eventually identified them as twenty-three-year-old Thomas McManus and twenty-seven-year-old Charles Whalen. They lived in the same rooming house in South Boston. The four bodies were the last ones removed from the ruins. When an ambulance carried the last one away, Boston Fire Commissioner Theodore Glynn decided it was finally time to go home. He had been at the scene for nearly forty-eight hours.

Chapter Six

A chance discovery a few hours later raised fears that yet another body might lay buried deep in the wreckage. A workman was searching through the debris when he found a wallet that belonged to a Wollaston man named Frank Jones. Those fears quickly vanished when a *Boston Globe* reporter rang the bell at the Jones home on Beach Street, and Jones came to the door. He said someone had stolen his wallet in downtown Boston several weeks earlier. How it ended up in the Pickwick Club ruins remains a mystery.

DEATHTRAP

| SEVEN |

The battle of blame raged on throughout the entire weekend, and almost every verbal taunt emanated from city hall. Most of them took aim at the Republican-controlled Massachusetts State House. Mayor Curley's carefully crafted statement set the tone for his administration's response. It accused the state of tying the city's hands, leaving it powerless to exert any type of control over the club, or the building, or the size of the crowd. Boston Police Captain Herbert Goodwin issued his own prepared statement a few hours later. Goodwin said, in effect, "Don't blame me." The Beach Street location fell under his jurisdiction as the commanding officer of Division Four on Lagrange Street. He made it a point to let everyone know that the Commonwealth of Massachusetts had granted the club's charter—not the City of Boston. According to Goodwin, the people at the state house issued that charter without even consulting the Boston Police Department. He acknowledged that his men had raided the club at least four times, but he said they spotted liquor only once. A man later came forward and admitted it belonged to him. He paid a fifty-dollar fine to settle the matter. Goodwin was mistaken. The man didn't come forward, he was arrested at the scene. The fine was $100, which is the equivalent of about $1,600 today, and it was Federal agents who made the arrest. The Boston Police weren't even there. Goodwin went on to claim the police found no evidence of any violations during their other three "visits", as he called them, and he said his men assured him that no one but a cardholding member could gain admission. The police had no control over the dancing, he added, since it was a state-chartered club.

Fire Chief Daniel Sennott also waded into the fray on Sunday when he told reporters that blame for the collapse should most likely rest on the club's managers. Sennott suspected they had allowed too many patrons inside the premises.

On Monday, the people at the state house began to fight back, and when they did, they hit hard. Massachusetts Secretary of State Frederick Cook was the most vocal. Cook was furious at the way city officials were trying to shift the blame for the collapse onto his office, and he didn't mince any words letting people know what he thought. He released a statement on Monday that read in part: "Any attempt to divert responsibility for continued occupancy of an unsafe building to the office of the Secretary of State because the building was supposed to be occupied by a chartered corporation is not only ridiculous, but dastardly. This office has absolutely no connection with the matter."

Cook said his office had no record of any Pickwick Club, Inc., but it had issued a charter to an organization called the Commercial Men's Club, Inc. at the same address in March 1924. Nine months later, the Commercial Men's Club submitted an application to change the corporation's name to the Pickwick

Club, Inc., but someone in Cook's office sent the paperwork back for correction when they noticed that the application did not state how many officers had voted for the change. The club failed to return the corrected application, so the state had no "official" record of the proposed new name. Even so, the club still filed papers at the Commissioner of Corporations and Taxation's office on February 2, 1925, that notified them that the Pickwick Club, Inc. had elected a new slate of officers. Cook didn't say whether anyone in his office responded.

Cook directed the brunt of his anger at Captain Goodwin. He said Goodwin was very much mistaken when he claimed that state officials never sought input from the Boston Police before they granted the charter. His prepared statement read:

"On March 13, 1924, the Commissioner of Corporations and Taxation forwarded the (Commercial Men's Club) application to the police commissioner for the City of Boston for an investigation of the proposed incorporators. The police commissioner replied five days later, and he said a Boston Police investigation found that none of the incorporators were involved in selling intoxicating liquor, or maintained places used for illegal gaming, or were engaged in any other unlawful activity. Since the police report was favorable, the Commissioner of Corporations and Taxation issued a charter on March 20, 1924."

Cook wasn't finished with Goodwin. He told reporters that after he learned about the repeated, flagrant violations at the Pickwick Club, he decided to ask Goodwin and Police Commissioner Wilson to meet with him at his office to hear their thoughts about the possibility of revoking the club's charter. Goodwin admitted that his men had raided the club several times, but he was very much mistaken when he told Cook the courts had never handed down a conviction. He also apparently neglected to mention anything about the federal raid in January. In any event, after listening to what Goodwin and Wilson had to say, Cook decided to let the matter drop.

Massachusetts Commissioner of Public Safety General Alfred Foote released his own highly critical report on Monday afternoon. It placed the full blame for the collapse on the Boston Building Commission, and its top official, John Mahoney. Governor Calvin Coolidge named Foote to his post in 1919, shortly after the decorated officer returned from France where he commanded the 104th Infantry Regiment. Among his battlefield awards were the French Government's Legion of Honor, and the American Distinguished Service Medal.

Foote said the building commissioner's office should have conducted a thorough structural investigation before they granted a permit to repair the fire damage. They should have conducted a second structural investigation when the excavation work next door went below the foundation of the Pickwick Club building. Had these inspections taken place, he said, he couldn't understand why the city building inspector didn't notice the structural weaknesses. The city should have immediately ordered the premises vacated, and closed the street. He cited the various laws that placed the responsibility for inspection on the mayor of Boston and the city's building commissioner. Those two men, along with the inspector, had ample authority to take whatever action they deemed necessary to protect the public against this catastrophe. Foote concluded his report by acknowledging that no one could expect the commissioner to keep track of every single issue, but he said the individual members of the inspection staff should have done so.

Monday was not one of John Mahoney's better days. First, there was General Foote's scathing report that placed the entire blame for the collapse squarely on his department. Then there was the embarrassing revelation that one of his inspectors had checked the building only two days before the collapse, but failed to find anything wrong. By Monday, it was front-page news throughout the country. Mahoney also had to back down and admit that the statement he helped draft on Saturday was incorrect. He did, in fact, have the authority to close the building, but he added that he had never heard of the Pickwick Club until it collapsed, and claimed he was unfamiliar with what he termed, "so-called night life festivities."

Governor Alvan Fuller had spent the weekend at his summer home in Rye Beach, New Hampshire, and he stopped by the collapse site on Monday morning while on his way to the state house. He was six months into his first two-year term as governor at the time. His opponent in that bitterly fought gubernatorial race was none other than the current mayor of Boston, James Michael Curley, and there was little love lost between the two.

Curley had resorted to his favored "us vs. them" political strategy throughout the entire race, and he relentlessly branded his wealthy opponent as a privileged aristocrat who was insensitive to the needs of the working class. For some reason, he also tried to turn the campaign into a religious, Catholic vs. Protestant contest, and he persisted with that questionable tactic long after the Fuller camp publicized that fact that Fuller's wife was a Catholic, and that he was a longtime, generous supporter of Catholic charities.

The Ku Klux Klan happened to be in the midst a brief, but vocal resurgence at the time, and they expanded their hate-filled rhetoric to encompass Catholics, Jews, and foreigners. They feared their latest targets were gaining too much influence in government, higher education, and law enforcement. The Klan was particularly active in central Massachusetts, and on several occasions, people leaving a hall or auditorium at the close of a Curley rally in that part of the state encountered the terrifying sight of a crucifix fully enveloped in flames on a nearby hillside. The message was clear—don't cast your vote for the Catholic Curley. When a prominent Republican named Elijah Adlow questioned why every burning cross seemed to coincide with a Curley rally, the veteran Boston mayor fired back, saying the only time a Jew goes into politics is when he doesn't have what it takes to succeed in business. The callous comment infuriated Jewish voters, many of whom retaliated by throwing their support behind Fuller. When the final results came in, they showed that Fuller had won by a landslide, capturing nearly sixty percent of the vote. Curley admitted many years later that it was his own campaign workers, and not the Klan, who had torched the fiery crosses. They hoped to galvanize the anti-Klan forces into throwing their support behind the Boston mayor.

Fuller had come a long way from his humble, blue-collar origins. The forty-seven-year-old governor's first job was in a rubber factory, and he repaired bicycles in his spare time. By 1925, he had become one of the wealthiest men in America, and owned what his biography called, "the world's most successful auto dealership." The state was in the midst of a serious budget crisis when he took office, and he refused to accept a salary for the four years he served.

Fuller held an impromptu news conference at the State House that afternoon. He knew the Suffolk County district attorney had promised to have a grand jury look into the collapse, and he told reporters he had instructed Attorney General Jay Benton to provide him with a daily report on the jury's progress. He also told them Benton had assigned Assistant Attorney

General Lewis Goldberg to the investigation, with instructions to make sure he was present in the grand jury room when every witness testified.

"Frankly, I don't care if the Pickwick Club sold alcohol," the governor said, "or even allowed gambling. Those are minor issues. The most pressing point in question is to determine whether or not any negligence has occurred." He ended the news conference by promising that the attorney general would step in and take whatever legal action he deemed necessary if the investigation should uncover evidence of wrongdoing, and Suffolk County officials failed to prosecute.

The *Boston Evening Globe* ran an editorial on Monday that lambasted public officials for trying to pass the buck. It began by comparing two recent tragedies: an earthquake in Santa Barbara, and a nightclub collapse in Boston. The former was unavoidable, they noted, while the latter was inexcusable. Two days had already passed, and the public still had no clear-cut explanation as to why the misfortune occurred. The only agreement among officials was that the blame must lie with someone else. The city government points in the direction of the state house, they wrote, and the state government points back at city hall. The exhibition of buck-passing was without equal, the *Globe* said. "Why was it possible to use an undeniably ramshackle building for semipublic purposes?" they asked. "Why was it not condemned?"

The Boston American was more vocal in its criticism, calling the collapse "utterly indefensible". It went on to say the columns of Boston's newspapers were "overburdened with the excuses, explanations, and countercharges of a frightened officialdom". Under the headline "Fix the Blame for Boston's Most Disgraceful Disaster," the *American* concluded, "Only the

A cartoon in the *Boston Post* chided officials for trying to pin the blame on others.

The Boston Post
July 7, 1925

veteran buck passers of a crooked administration will have the impudence to suggest an excuse ... only those who have been made cowardly by the gnawing of a guilty conscience will attempt an alibi."

The next day the mayor came under fire from State Representative Bernard Ginsberg of Dorchester who told reporters, "It is pitiful to find the mayor of Boston blame state officials, the police department, and the whole world except himself. This is purely a political alibi. The charge by His Honor the Mayor that the state issued the charter may be characterized in Kipling's language as 'an empty kettle that makes the most noise'."

Two days later, the *Globe* once again blasted officials. Until the disaster occurred, they said, nobody bothered to learn whether the club operated in accordance with the law or not. "Everybody explains that it was up to someone else."

The *Boston American* also had more to say as it grumbled about the jellyfish, incompetents, and crooks who were counting on what they hoped would be the short memory of the general public. Any assumption that the people of Massachusetts could be intimidated into forgetting this crime, the *American* stated, would be a fatuous insult to their intelligence. It ended by calling for a purge of each and every public servant whose presence on the payroll is a menace to life and property.

The deluge of false news reports reached its peak on Monday. Some of those stories, like the *Boston Post's* account of twenty-two-year-old Johnnie Scales, were simply the result of carelessness. Firefighters removed the Roxbury man's body from the rubble on Saturday morning, only a few hours after the collapse. The *Post* included his name and photograph in their tally of the confirmed dead on Monday, but a headline on an inside page claimed he was the only vocalist in the club to survive.

William Randolph Hearst owned two wire services in 1925. Universal Service provided news reports to the morning newspapers while the International News Service served the evening papers. The former invariably took top honors when it came to sending out false news reports. Monday, July 6, was one of their banner days. Among the stories they reported that day was the fictitious account a man whom they called Bishop. It claimed the police shot and wounded him as he attempted to enter the floor directly above the Pickwick Club. He supposedly told the police that he had heard one of the victims had an $800 stash in his wallet, and he planned to steal the money. The story went on to say that firefighters later found the unidentified man's body, and the $800, wedged into a tight space between the club's ceiling and the floor above. Whoever concocted that preposterous story obviously hadn't seen any of the numerous news photographs that showed the extent of the devastation.

Another news item that Universal Service sent out that day told the incredible tale of John Sullivan, a demolition worker from South Boston, who allegedly made not one, but two almost-miraculous discoveries. While he probed the depths of the ruins, he supposedly came upon a subterranean chamber that had somehow managed to survive unscathed under the countless tons of debris.

According to the wire service, what he discovered brought amazement to his "dust filled eyes." Seated around a table with their heads bowed were the bodies of four men, their hands outspread before them. On the floor next to them was a gallon can of alcohol. The faint light that filtered down from above revealed a striking scene. Their playing cards lay face up on the table. "It was the showdown," the report stated, "but death had taken a hand in the game." A few feet away, a woman's body was on the floor, "crumpled in death." Even though several dozen rescue workers were on the scene at the time, Mr. Sullivan allegedly carried each body from the wreckage by himself, one body at a time. The reporter who fabricated the story apparently didn't realize that several inches of fetid, stagnant water covered the entire basement floor. It splashed down from the upper stories during the violent thunderstorms a few days earlier.

Mr. Sullivan wasn't quite finished. According to the dispatch, he descended into the rubble once again, where he discovered yet another body that was "stiff and cold in death." The report continued, "It was that of a fighting man crouched in a battle pose with his fists tightly clenched. His left arm was raised in a defensive pose, while his right arm was drawn back, ready to deliver a punishing blow. His cauliflower ear left little doubt—the man was a professional boxer."

Newspaper readers throughout the US and Canada must have scratched their heads in utter amazement when they came upon another dispatch from Universal Service on Monday. That report claimed that rescue workers spotted a man's feet protruding from under a piece of rubble on Sunday afternoon, but it was obvious he was dead. Several workers grabbed hold of his feet and ankles, and began to pull and tug. Ever so slowly, inch-by-inch, the corpse emerged. Five feet of it came out from the wreckage, then six feet, and then seven feet. When workers finally freed the elongated man from the twisted mass, he measured nine feet long! The falling debris had snared his head and feet, according to the report, and pulled every bone from its socket.

The carelessness, exaggeration, and sensationalism that marked much of the news reporting had begun to taper off by

Tuesday, but the final edition of that day's *Boston Advertiser* carried a prominent article on the front page that was pure fiction. The *Advertiser* said Inspector Dennnessy of the homicide squad was probing the disaster to determine if the victims had been murdered due to criminal negligence. There isn't a court in the nation, on either the state or federal level, that equates criminal negligence with murder. They didn't do it then, and they don't do it now. A murder charge requires proof that the defendant intended to kill.

A fanciful rumor began to spread throughout the city soon after the collapse. By Tuesday, some newspapers were treating it as though it were true. According to the rumor, several well-heeled Boston gamblers had gathered to play a high-stakes poker game in a former private dining room on the fire-damaged third floor while the holiday eve merry makers continued to celebrate in the Pickwick Club just below. The game was still going on when the floor gave way from beneath them. As the unfortunate men tumbled into the abyss, their winnings fluttered down onto the street like a shower of confetti. Another version had the cards drift down onto the street, but the jackpot ended up buried somewhere deep in the rubble where it awaited some lucky finder. It was all make-believe, but many a rescue worker probably kept his eye peeled, just in case.

Another rumor that made the rounds at the time didn't sit very well with the people at city hall. That one began to circulate soon after officials acknowledged that a Boston Building Department inspector had checked the Beach Street property only two days before it collapsed. According to the rumor, the building's dilapidated condition so frightened him that he rushed back to his office and told his superiors the old structure could fall at any moment. City officials decided to revoke the building's occupancy permit right away, but someone with political clout managed to delay the enforcement for a few days. That would allow the Pickwick Club to reap a windfall profit from the large holiday eve crowd that was sure to attend on Friday night. It was completely untrue but, in 1920s Boston, it wasn't nearly as far-fetched as the story of the nine-foot man.

DEATHTRAP

| EIGHT |

While officials at the Massachusetts State House were getting ready to launch their barrage of counterattacks on Monday morning, a clerk at the Newton District Court called out Frank Tillo's name. There was no response, so he shouted the name a second time. It was a legal formality—everyone in the courthouse knew Tillo had lost his life in the Pickwick Club collapse. He wasn't the only victim whose untimely death cheated the justice system. Twenty-eight-year-old Charles DeCostis of the South End was also awaiting trial that night.

His troubles with the law began three years earlier when he introduced his friend George Scisco to Paul Tapoozian, the owner of a Newton shoe store. Scisco told Tapoozian he was in deep trouble. He had incurred a large gambling debt a few months earlier that he wasn't able to pay. In desperation, he borrowed the money from a Boston loan shark. It was time to repay the loan, but he didn't have the ready cash. After giving the shoe store owner a frightening description of the consequences he faced if he couldn't make good on the money he borrowed, he offered to part with three diamonds for only half of their retail value. He told Tapoozian he was welcome to have them appraised by any jeweler he chose. The appraisal showed the gems were worth far more than the $950 Scisco was seeking. Tapoozian withdrew the money from his bank and walked away with his prize purchase. A few days later, he decided it might be a good idea to get a second appraisal.

"These things are fake, completely worthless," the puzzled jeweler said. "They are just pieces of glass."

Scisco had switched packages while Tapoozian was inside the bank. The Newton merchant left the jeweler's shop and hurried to the police station. The Middlesex County District Attorney's office brought the evidence they had gathered before a grand jury that, in turn, returned two indictments for larceny; one was against Scisco, the other against DeCostis. Scisco got word of his indictment, and fled before the authorities could take him into custody. The prosecutors wanted to try both men simultaneously. There was no point in going ahead without Scisco, and they postponed the trial indefinitely. Scisco's flight ended when the New York City police apprehended him a year after the Pickwick Club disaster. He fought the extradition order, but the authorities succeeded in bringing him back to Cambridge where he went on trial in October 1926. Paul Tapoozian testified that DeCostis had introduced him to Scisco. The jury returned a guilty verdict a few days before Christmas, and Judge William Burns sentenced Scisco to five years in the old Charlestown State Prison. He told Scisco he would have handed him a longer sentence if the law allowed it. "It was as deliberate a swindle as was ever staged," he said.

Thirty-five-year-old William "Toots" Murray of Somerville was another one of the victims who had had a run in with the law. He made headlines a year earlier when a grand jury indicted him after he allegedly set off a gas bomb inside the Rhode Island State Senate chamber. The "stink bomb" incident, and the legislative maneuver that followed, made Rhode Island the laughing stock of the nation. The chain of events that led up to the bizarre affair began two years earlier with the 1922 state election. When the final results came in, the tally showed that Republicans had lost their longstanding control of the Rhode Island Senate. With forty-nine Republicans, forty-eight Democrats, and three Independents holding Senate seats, neither party could push through their favored legislation. The state's top two constitutional officers were Democrats, however, and that negated the Republican's one-vote advantage in the Senate. Governor William Flynn had veto power over any legislation the Senate might pass. Lieutenant Governor Felix Toupin was an even more formidable foe. As lieutenant governor, he was also the presiding officer of the Senate, a position that not only gave him control over what bills came up for a vote, but also allowed him to recognize or ignore anyone who wished to speak. Toupin used those powers to block passage of any legislation that Democrats opposed. Frustrated Republicans retaliated by routinely voting against any Democrat-sponsored legislation. The session was deadlocked from the very first day, and several important pieces of legislation, including an appropriations bill to fund state institutions and pay state employees, languished in limbo. It was partisan politics at its very worst. As long as Toupin was present, the Democrats held control of the Senate. If he were absent, however, Republicans could take over the chair. Toupin proved equal to the task, and he rarely missed a day at the Senate chamber. Tempers began to flare as the months went by, and several senators began to hurl insults back and forth. Some of them reportedly even came to blows.

The situation continued to deteriorate, and Democrats eventually brought in several men to more or less act as bodyguards for Toupin. Republicans suspected the men might be carrying blackjacks, and they felt intimidated by their presence. GOP chairman William Pelkey decided to level the playing field, and he sought help from John Toomey, a prominent Rhode Island gambler. The next day, several sinister-looking men from the neighboring state of Massachusetts were in the Senate chamber, ready to protect the Republicans should trouble break out.

By June 19, everyone's nerves were near the breaking point. Democrats had been pushing for a constitutional convention; Republicans opposed the move. Toupin decided to stage a filibuster, hoping that enough Republicans would grow bored and leave the chamber, thus giving Democrats the opportunity to pass the bill. Toupin had been on the rostrum for nearly two full days that morning, reading page after page from the *Encyclopaedia Britannica*. A local restaurant delivered his food, and Democrats even brought in a portable commode so he could relieve himself without having to leave the Senate chamber. A barber was giving Toupin a shave when Murray allegedly approached the two men and tossed a canister filled with bromine toward them. Republicans were sure the foul-smelling gas would drive Toupin from the room and give them a chance to take over the chair and end the filibuster. It didn't happen. Toupin seized the barber's towel and used it as a facemask while almost everyone else either ran for the doors or became ill. The Lieutenant Governor suddenly saw a rare opportunity. He tried to resume the session, knowing that with enough Republicans absent, Democrats would be able to carry the vote. Republican senators foiled Toupin's plan by refusing to reenter the chamber, thus denying Democrats the quorum they needed. An outraged Toupin then swore out arrest warrants against the Republicans for failure to perform their elected duty. Before anyone could serve those warrants, every Republican senator had fled the state and taken refuge in the small town of Rutland, Massachusetts. Toupin could not muster a quorum without the missing senators, and the legislative session eventually ground to a halt. The fiasco made newspaper headlines across the country.

Some people failed to see any humor in the situation. On August 4, 1924, a grand jury returned conspiracy indictments against Pelkey, Toomey, and Murray for their role in the attack against Toupin. Rhode Island newspapers put their own spin on Murray. The state's largest Republican-leaning newspaper called him a Boston sportsman, while its Democratic rivals branded him a hoodlum and a thug. Two months later Judge Jerome Hahn dropped the charges against the three men after Assistant Attorney General George Hurley admitted that the state's star witness had gone missing. Prosecutors had no idea where he was.

Another victim also had a well-publicized brush with the law a few years earlier. Burt Chapman made headlines in November 1921 when postal investigators took him into custody just as he was about to leave the country, and charged him with being an accessory in a mail truck robbery. That theft occurred almost nine months earlier in Oakland, California when three bandits held up a US mail truck and made off with six pouches of registered mail. Postal investigators soon determined that the stolen mailbags contained negotiable securities worth about $50,000.

The first of those stolen securities surfaced in Boston three months later when someone sold $10,000 worth of them to legendary Boston racketeer Charles "King" Solomon. Investigators were sure the seller was Burt Chapman, and they placed both men under surveillance. They were still gathering evidence when they learned Chapman was about to set sail from New York. Agents descended on the liner *Aquitania* and arrested him only minutes before the ship was due to cast off. Postal investigators arrested Charles Solomon in Boston the same day. Being convinced of someone's guilt is one thing; being able to prove it is something else, and postal authorities simply didn't have the solid evidence prosecutors needed to ensure a conviction. The government reluctantly decided to drop the charges against the two men a few weeks later.

Chapman was born Abraham Kaplan in Russia in 1893. He was eight years old when he moved to Chelsea, Massachusetts with his mother. His father had come to America a few years earlier and found work as a junk dealer. In 1910, the younger Kaplan worked as a packer in an envelope factory. Soon afterward, he changed his name to Burt Chapman and found work as an automobile salesman. He fought in France with a New York National Guard regiment during the First World War.

Ida Chapman happened to be in downtown Boston on Friday night, July 3, and she bumped into her brother outside a parking garage on Stuart Street, just a few blocks from the Pickwick Club. He didn't mention where he was going, but he told her he was planning on having a good time.

A curious incident took place in Roxbury District Court on Monday morning at about the same time the clerk in Newton called out Frank Tillo's name. Two girls from Manchester, Connecticut were in the courtroom to answer charges after their arrest early Saturday morning. Charlotte Dexter and Ada Goodwin had come to Boston to celebrate the Fourth, and the twenty-one-year-old visitors were doing so with a vengeance. Around one thirty Saturday morning, they decided to go to the Pickwick Club with two young men they had met a few hours earlier. The four were on their way to the club when they were involved in some sort of fracas at the intersection of Huntington

Chapter Eight

Avenue and Forsyth Street. The police didn't say what happened, but Patrolman Patrick Gilmore took the two girls into custody and charged them with disorderly conduct. The men continued on to the Pickwick Club without them. When Dexter and Goodwin spotted Officer Gilmore in the courtroom on Monday, they rushed over and hugged him while they thanked him repeatedly for saving their lives.

If the Fates had been kind to Dexter and Goodwin, they were decidedly cruel to a twenty-year-old, recent arrival from Cape Breton, Nova Scotia. The thought of going to the Pickwick Club never crossed Mary McDougall's mind as she got dressed for a night-before-the-Fourth party. The appointed time came and went, but the young man who invited her never called. McDougall grew more and more upset as the realization slowly sunk in that her young friend had jilted her. She finally decided she had waited long enough. "Who needs him?" McDougall probably said to herself as she picked up the phone and called her friend Mary Evans to suggest the two girls go out on the town on their own. They had the bad luck to choose the Pickwick Club.

Mary Evans was standing near the door with a man named Fairbanks when the loud cracking noise exploded throughout the room. She told a reporter the next day, "I saw a long, jagged crack appear in the wall on the side opposite the door. I thought at first the sound was fireworks, but the moment I spied that crack in the wall I knew something terrible was happening. Then there was an awful crash, and the lights went out, and there was more screaming. Mr. Fairbanks and I dashed down the stairway while the building started to fall behind us. All this happened in an instant. [...] I feel really sorry for poor Mary McDougall. She was at a table on the opposite side of the room from the door and had no chance to escape. I saw her later at the hospital. She told me that when the floor went down, she landed on someone's lap, and then passed out. She can't remember anything about being rescued, and she didn't regain consciousness until she was in the ambulance on the way to the hospital." Mary McDougall suffered a fractured spine and multiple contusions.

Mary Moore hadn't planned on going to the Pickwick Club that night either. The twenty-nine-year-old manicurist was already in bed when two friends rang her doorbell a little after midnight. They were on their way to the club, and they thought she might want to join them. Her friends must have been quite persuasive because she got dressed and went out with them.

Mary and her husband had separated six or seven years earlier, shortly after the birth of their second son. The Pickwick Club was one of her favorite nightspots. Her two friends went there on occasion, but not nearly as often as Mary. Clara Frederick was unmarried, and still lived with her parents and sisters in an attractive, single-family home in West Roxbury, a residential neighborhood on the outskirts of Boston. She made eyeglass cases at a small company in Jamaica Plain. Esther Wilson and her husband lived almost right around the corner from Mary's apartment. Before she left that night, Wilson asked her husband to drop by the club at three thirty and give her a ride home.

Frank Wilson was dumbfounded when he showed up and found the building in ruins. By that time, hundreds of spectators had gathered, and Wilson ran back and forth through the crowd, as he kept shouting his wife's name. There was no response. Esther and her two friends were helplessly pinned under tons of rubble at the bottom of the excavation next door. It took firefighters almost thirty-six hours to find the bodies of Esther

Chapter Eight

Wilson and Mary Moore. They carried Clara Frederick's badly crushed body from the wreckage several hours later.

Contemporary newspapers were incorrect when they claimed the three women were friends from childhood. There was too big a disparity in their ages. Mary Moore was only five years old, and Esther Wilson was still a toddler romping around her parents' apartment when Clara Frederick walked up on stage and received her high school diploma.

*   *   *

Crowds continued to gather at the site on Monday as workmen carried on their search efforts. One spectator was so absorbed in looking at the wreckage that he failed to see the curbstone, and tumbled headfirst into the gutter. He came to rest with his head leaning against the rear wheel of an ambulance. The attendant helped him inside and took him to the hospital where doctors treated him for a fractured wrist.

The men searching the wreckage were under strict orders to turn in anything of value they came across. Two of them happened to look up just in time to see a coworker reach down, grab something, and stuff it into his pocket. They walked over to Sergeant Joseph McDonough and reported what they had seen. McDonough called the man to one side and asked him to empty his pockets. He took out his wallet, which contained two dollars, but when he took another fourteen dollars from his pants pocket, McDonough placed him under arrest. At the Lagrange Street Station, officers found another fifteen dollars tucked inside the waistband of his underpants.

Forty-nine-year-old Angelo Cook of Everett went on trial in Suffolk County Municipal Court two weeks later. He admitted that he took the money, but he insisted he did so only to safeguard it until he could turn it over to the police. Judge James Parmenter didn't believe a word he said. Even though Cook had no police record, was married, had several children, and owned his own home, Parmenter sentenced him to three months in the Deer Island House of Correction.

Mayor Curley also stopped by on Monday to see how things were going. Chief Sennott assured him there was no chance of finding any more bodies. Before he left, the mayor told Sennott he wanted every bit of the old building removed. "I don't want anything left here at all," he said, "not even one single brick." Later that afternoon, Curley requested a $25,000 appropriation from the City Council to cover the cost of clearing the site. The Council approved his request without argument.

There weren't very many bricks left to remove at the time of Curley's visit. The back wall was down, and only the small sections of the second, third, and fourth floors that still clung to the sidewall closest to Washington Street awaited the wreckers. It was on that unreachable little spot of the second floor that Billy Glennon and the others found themselves stranded. A roll top desk and a piano were up there, and salvaging the desk was the first order of business. Investigators had no idea what secrets it might hold, and they wanted keep the contents under lock and key in case something inside should prove useful. It turned out to be a wise decision, even though an examination of the desk later failed to turn up anything of importance. While workmen were dismantling the third floor, part of it broke loose and crashed down onto the second floor. It would have reduced the desk to splinters if the investigators hadn't removed it.

A little while later, two men climbed out onto the second floor and gave what was left of the piano a vigorous shove that sent it tumbling down onto the debris below. The men then broke a hole in the floor, ran a heavy steel cable through it, and hitched it to the steam shovel. It took a few tugs, but that section of the floor broke loose and fell. The next section turned out to be more of a challenge. The steam shovel tugged and tugged, but the floor refused to budge. It took the added help of a heavy truck pulling at a second cable before the last of the second floor crashed down, bringing with it a large artificial potted plant and a torrent of bottles and glassware. One small section of the fourth floor was all that remained, but it soon yielded to the combined tugs of the steam shovel and the truck. A short time later, someone lifted a chunk of rubble and spotted a piece of blue woolen fabric underneath, raising fears that another body might lie buried down there. Once again, rescue workers tore into the debris, but all they found was a man's suit jacket.

The possibility that the back wall might collapse had kept firemen from checking the kitchen in the back corner of the basement. It was the last unsearched part of the building. When they finally reached it, they found the floor covered with ankle-deep, stagnant water. Although there was little likelihood that anyone was in the kitchen at the time of the collapse, or anywhere else in the basement for that matter, firefighters still had to be sure.

The kitchen had been there since Arthur Dreyfus renovated the old warehouse in 1905, and installed a dumbwaiter to carry meals to the first-floor restaurant, the second-floor banquet room, and the private dining rooms on the third floor. When Dreyfus closed his hotel in 1920, the kitchen went unused for almost five years until the Greenwich Village Café opened. While the new restaurant displaced the Pickwick Club from its ground floor location, it did provide one unexpected benefit. The owners were more than willing to prepare meals for Pickwick Club patrons, and send them upstairs in the dumb waiter. The April fire put an end to that little convenience, and it turned the process of feeding a hungry customer into a rather convoluted procedure. The waiter took the customer's order, and then went downstairs and told the doorman. He, in turn, called the order in to the St. Regis, or some other nearby restaurant. The restaurant delivered the food to the Pickwick Club, and the doorman summoned the waiter. He or she came downstairs, picked up the order, and carried it upstairs to the waiting customer. The club understandably tried to discourage patrons from ordering food after the Greenwich Village Cafe closed, and the menu choices became somewhat more limited—salads, cold sandwiches, and desserts.

As expected, the search of the kitchen proved fruitless.

* * *

Many, but not all, of the victims had been identified by Monday, and that day's newspapers carried descriptions of two others that rescue workers discovered the day before. One read, "Man, five feet, seven inches, light brown hair, black two-piece suit, white pencil-stripe shirt, black bow tie with red spots, black socks, low brown shoes, black belt with brown buckle." The other read, "Man, five feet, eight inches, long brown hair with pompadour, gray soft worsted two-piece suit, lavender shirt, red and white diagonal stripe bow tie, black stripe belt, and low black patent leather shoes." Authorities later identified the second body as that of Stuart Henderson, a thirty-six-year-old Milton resident.

Along with reporting the latest developments from Beach Street, Monday's papers also carried a stinging indictment from the Suffolk County Medical Examiner. Timothy Leary was highly critical of the initial rescue efforts, which he called "disorganized". Leary also faulted the fire department for not having the proper equipment to lift the fallen timbers and debris. He had nothing but praise, however, for the Boston Elevated Street Railway and the Edison Electric Illuminating Company for the prompt and effective help they provided.

Newspapers were anxious to print every bit of information about the Pickwick Club they could get their hands on—with one exception. Only one Boston paper named the owner of the garage under construction next door, and that appears to be unintentional. The *Boston American* carried an interview with Boston building inspector James Hendrick in its July 6 edition, during which he mentioned that steam shovels had been working on the new Jordan Marsh garage site on the adjoining lot. It's easy to see why the local papers were reluctant to identify the garage owner. Jordan Marsh & Company was New England's largest department store at the time, and a major advertiser in every Boston newspaper.

DEATHTRAP

| NINE |

Anyone who glanced at Monday morning's *Boston Globe* couldn't help but spot the eye-catching headline over a prominent, front-page article:

LEAPING OF DANCERS CAUSED COLLAPSE

The story featured a lengthy interview with Frank Decker, the thirty-one-year-old Melrose man who claimed he was pounding on the door to get back in when the building began to shake. Decker described his narrow escape, and said he had left the club a few minutes earlier to go downstairs to the street to get a breath of fresh air. When he returned, he found the door was locked and there was no sign of the doorman, so he began to kick the door to get someone's attention. He was still kicking and pounding the door when the upper floors began to fall. Decker said he fled down the stairs, but as soon as he reached the sidewalk, he thought of the girl he had been dancing with a short time earlier. He turned around and started back up, only to see a crowd of panic-stricken people coming down, heading right toward him. Decker had no choice but to turn around and run. Even if he had made it to the top of the stairs, it would have been too late to help Mary Moore. Firefighters discovered the twenty-nine-year-old Roxbury woman's body thirty-six hours later. It was near the bottom of the excavation next door, almost sixteen feet below the sidewalk.

Decker told the reporter it was the "leaping of dancers" that brought the building down. "Imagine the force of fifty couples leaping up and down in unison," he said. "The heavy tramping set the floor swaying, then it cracked. The dancers, hilarious and gay, were leaping about vigorously. As the dance neared its close, the orchestra speeded up the rhythm and the dancers moved faster and faster. They jumped higher and higher."

Decker said he was surprised that any of the patrons inside were able to follow him down the stairs. The latch on the second-floor door was extremely difficult to open, and he had never succeeded on the first try. "A person unfamiliar with the lock would have to manipulate it several minutes before he could open it," Decker added.

The next day's *Boston Herald* carried an interview with Pickwick Club waiter Harold Shaw that corroborated much, but not all, of what Decker said. Shaw told the reporter he had gone upstairs to use the restroom, and was on his way back down when he heard a loud, cracking sound. "The noise caused me to stop short on the stairway," he said, "and then the whole building began to move. Frank Decker came running down the stairway behind me. At that moment there was a tremendous roar, and a mass of crumbling masonry came rolling down the stairs. The dust choked and partly blinded us. I made a frantic effort to open the door, but a crowd was trying to work the lock from the inside. Suddenly all the lights went out, and the people inside began to scream and shout. Decker and I then leaped down the remaining stairs and reached the street door."

Chapter Nine

Shaw told the *Herald* reporter he was sure the locked door hampered escape efforts. Unless a person was familiar with the lock's operation, it would be pointless to try to open the door. Even some of the employees had a hard time opening it, he said. The only one who could open the door easily was the regular doorman, but he had stepped away from his post. In order to unlock the door, a person had to first turn the knob to the left, and then turn it to the right. Shaw went on to say the lock served a dual purpose—it prevented undesirable guests from entering the club, and it hindered any unexpected visits from the police or federal prohibition agents.

*   *   *

Suffolk County District Attorney Thomas O'Brien was true to his word when he told reporters he would convene a grand jury investigation to look into the collapse, possibly as early as Monday. The investigation got underway on Monday morning, July 6, in the six-story, German Renaissance-style granite courthouse in Pemberton Square, just as O'Brien had promised. Nineteen jurors, all men, would sift through the evidence and decide whether or not to hand down criminal indictments. It wasn't until 1950 that Massachusetts allowed women to sit on juries, and even then, state law allowed a woman to request exclusion if she suspected any testimony might prove embarrassing.

An unusual chain of events preceded O'Brien being appointed Suffolk County District Attorney. He was thirty-seven years old when Governor Channing Cox named him to the post in February 1922 after the Massachusetts Supreme Judicial Court removed his predecessor from office following his conviction on multiple counts of blackmail and extortion. The court also barred Joseph Pelletier from being able to practice law in

Massachusetts a short time later. If anyone thought those embarrassing episodes would put a damper on Pelletier's political plans, they were very much mistaken. Three weeks after his disbarment made front-page headlines in the Boston newspapers, Pelletier announced plans to run for re-election. He claimed there was no reason why a district attorney had to be able to practice law. He beat O'Brien by a wide margin in that September's Democratic primary, but O'Brien had taken the unusual precaution of entering his name in the Republican primary as well. He won that contest easily, and went on to defeat Pelletier in the November election by an almost two-to-one margin.

Although court officers barred everyone but witnesses from entering the grand jury room, no one prevented reporters from waiting outside in the corridor to see who showed up to testify. Newspapers printed the names and, in many cases, photographs of those witnesses. Some of them were more than happy to speak with anyone from the press. The Boston dailies also disclosed the names and addresses of the grand jurors. The *Boston Advertiser* even had them pose for a group photograph.

O'Brien wanted the jurors to take a close look at what was left of the Pickwick Club before they began to hear testimony. It was almost noon when two bailiffs with their traditional white staffs led the nineteen men past the police barricades and into the wreckage. Police Commissioner Herbert Wilson joined Captain Ainsley Armstrong of the Criminal Investigation Bureau in giving them an overview, and then Fire Chief Sennott and Commissioner Glynn described the rescue and recovery operations in detail.

Chapter Nine

District Attorney Thomas O'Brien leads the Suffolk County grand jurors on their inspection tour of the Pickwick Club ruins.

©*New York Daily News Archive*/ Contributor Getty Images
Used with permission

The jurors stopped for a leisurely lunch on their way back to the courthouse, and they didn't return to Pemberton Square until midafternoon. By that time a number of witnesses had arrived, and were waiting to testify. One of them was a well-known celebrity.

Harry Houdini, the noted escape artist, was there at the invitation of the district attorney. Houdini had become something of a zealot in his efforts to expose fake mediums and spiritualists, and it was in that capacity that O'Brien had requested his help with an ongoing investigation of several séance parlors in Boston. Houdini had to wait like every other witness while the grand jurors journeyed to the collapse site, and he made no attempt to hide his growing displeasure at the delay. O'Brien was all apologies when he returned with the jurors, and he called Houdini right away. When the New York man left the grand jury room, Tom O'Brien turned his attention to the Pickwick Club collapse.

Pickwick Club treasurer Timothy Barry had his lawyer with him when he showed up at the courthouse that afternoon. Reporters greeted him with a barrage of questions, but his attorney stepped in and told them Barry wished to make a statement. Barry took out a piece of paper and read the following:

"We were given permission by Mr. Bloomberg of 6 Beach Street, from whom we secured our lease, to return and occupy the second floor during the first part of April, following a fire in the building. We had no control over any part of the building but the second floor, and we are ready, willing, and anxious to assist the authorities in any way we can."

When Barry finished, the reporters once again began to pepper him with questions. This time, his attorney didn't try to stop him from answering. At one point, Barry said the only revenue he took home from the club was the markup he received from selling ten-cent bottles of ginger ale for fifty cents. "The waiters make more in tips than I make selling ginger ale," he added.

One of the reporters asked him if he had any comment on Frank Decker's remarks in that morning's *Globe*. Not surprisingly, he took strong exception to everything Decker had said. Barry assured the reporter that both the first and the second-floor door locks were simple to operate. The street door had a deadbolt that was easy to pull. The door on the second floor had a slot for a key on the outside, and a knob on the inside. There was nothing tricky about it at all. Anyone could open it.

Barry said he obtained the building owner's permission before he went ahead and installed the trap door. He hired a professional carpenter who assured him that it conformed to the city's building codes. He had no idea the building was unsafe, he said, and he reminded them that a city inspector checked it only a few days earlier and said everything was OK. Barry was so sure his club was operating on the up-and-up that he invited J. Frank Chase, the firebrand secretary of the Watch and Ward Society, to stop by anytime and see for himself. The members of Chase's organization considered themselves Boston's unofficial censors, and they made the phrase *Banned in Boston* world famous. Chase declined the offer, but he told Barry his agents had already visited the club. Judging by the comments he made a few months earlier at a State House hearing, his agents weren't especially thrilled with what they found. Hootchie-kootchie dancing and drinking liquor were the main attractions at clubs like the Pickwick, according to Chase.

Hyman Bloomberg didn't hesitate to answer the questions reporters posed while he sat in the corridor as he waited to testify. He made it a point to remind everyone that he merely leased the building from the estate of Albert Rosenthal. "It was the estate that hired the contractor to repair the roof, not me," Bloomberg said, "and no one from the estate got in touch with me before they made their decision."

Boston building inspector James Hendrick also had a few words to say. He admitted that he inspected the building two days before the collapse, but he assured the reporters that he didn't spot anything that caused him to think it was unsafe. He didn't see any reason to shore the building from outside because the Charles R. Gow Company had put a substantial concrete base under the foundation. Hendrick said they were right up there with the best structure support firms in the United States.

Several other witnesses appeared on Monday afternoon. Massachusetts Secretary of State Frederick Cook and Massachusetts Tax Commissioner Henry Long gave testimony, as did Boston Fire Chief Daniel Sennott, and Suffolk County Medical Examiner Dr. Timothy Leary. Sergeant John Montague and Patrolman Neal McDevitt of the Boston Police Department also testified that afternoon, as did three Pickwick Club employees—orchestra leader Billy Glennon, waiter Harris "Mike" Hirshberg, and doorman George Callahan.

The jury took a one and a half-hour break for dinner, and then returned to the courthouse. Building inspector Hendrick was the first witness to testify after the dinner break. He was inside the grand jury room for ninety minutes. Architect George Funk, who designed the replacement roof, testified next for almost an hour. Boston Building Commissioner John Mahoney followed him into the grand jury room. Someone from Mahoney's office showed up a short time later with what many reporters incorrectly assumed were building plans. Mahoney later admitted that no one in his office could locate any drawings or plans for the old building. It was twenty minutes to twelve when Mahoney finished testifying. O'Brien adjourned the proceedings and told the jurors, and a handful of witnesses who were still waiting to testify, to return at nine thirty the next morning.

Pickwick Club waiter Mike Hirshberg was the lead-off witness when the grand jurors went back to work Tuesday morning. His testimony marked the beginning of what turned out to be another twelve-hour, marathon session. He had appeared before the grand jury on Monday afternoon, but the district attorney wanted him to return and answer more questions. There must have been quite a few, because he was inside the grand jury room for almost an hour.

Louis Epple looked quite dapper and relaxed in his light-weight summer suit, straw hat, and bow tie when he arrived at the courthouse. As usual, he had a cigar in his mouth. When the affable secretary of the Boston Licensing Commission left the grand jury room, he couldn't wait to add his name to the ever-growing *don't-blame-me* list. His office had never issued a license of any type to the Pickwick Club, he told reporters, and therefore neither he, nor anyone who worked for him, had any responsibility for the collapse. All his office did was issue licenses to individuals and business firms who applied for them. That's all they did. They weren't responsible for enforcing compliance. That was the police department's job.

It didn't take Boston Police Commissioner Herbert Wilson long to respond to Epple's comments. "The Pickwick Club didn't have a common victualer's license because it didn't need one," he told a reporter that afternoon. "It didn't need a license any more than the Harvard Club, or the Somerset Club, or the Algonquin Club, or any other club of good standing. If it had been open to the general public, it would have been a different matter but, by securing the status of a club, it avoided regulations which might have been inconvenient for an all-night dancing and drinking club." He went on to say that as far as he was concerned, the inner recesses of the Pickwick Club were every bit as inviolate as those other clubs. "The police had no authority on the Pickwick Club premises," he added.

Several years ago, the landmark Copley Plaza Hotel in Boston advertised its five-star dining room as a "bastion of Edwardian elegance". The phrase also paints a perfect picture of the sedate, ultra-exclusive, Back Bay enclaves that Wilson likened to the Pickwick Club. His comparison is rather strange to say the least, for there was nothing dignified or exclusive about the little speakeasy on the edge of Chinatown; there was nothing elegant about its second- floor location in a fire-damaged building with a trap door to drain the rainfall that flooded the dance floor after every storm; there was nothing genteel about its rough and tumble clientele. A person has to wonder what Wilson was thinking when he said its premises were "inviolate," especially since his men had raided the club several times.

Boston's top cop was fifty-five years old at the time of the collapse, and three years into his term as the city's police commissioner. Wilson had one notable shortcoming when he started his new job—he had no experience in law enforcement. He had spent almost thirty years in the city's engineering department before Mayor Curley's predecessor appointed him building commissioner in 1919. He had also served brief terms as a state senator and state representative. He resigned from the building commissioner's post when Governor Channing Cox named him police commissioner in September 1922. Today, the mayor makes that appointment.

Twenty-two-year-old Mildred McGilvary of Revere was the next witness to take the stand when Louis Epple left the grand jury room. The attractive brunette had to take two days off from her job as a "bow tier" [sic] in a local candy factory to comply with her summons. Like Timothy Barry, she arrived at the Suffolk County Courthouse on Monday afternoon as directed, and then waited outside the grand jury room until nearly midnight, only to have a court officer tell her to come back in the morning. McGilvary looked particularly stylish when she returned on Tuesday, clad in a bright, short sleeve, knee-length summer dress, and a large cloche hat decorated with feathers. The *Boston Herald* said she was dressed, "as if she wished to be ready sartorially to step into any setting, from a dance to a conference. She was very young," the *Herald* continued, "and her face lacked expression, but her eyes were constantly calculating as they roved about the masculine forces contemplating her covertly or openly."

McGilvary didn't mind speaking with reporters while she waited to testify. She told them it was her first visit to the club. "I just got up to dance," she said, "when the lights went out. I rushed to the door with several men and women in front of me, but they all disappeared as the building caved in beneath them with a resounding roar. I was catapulted over their heads as they went down, and for a moment I was in space until I landed in a heap. Where I landed, I don't know. Someone grabbed me by the leg and pulled me to safety. I was at the club with two girlfriends whose names I won't mention because they may not wish it known. They escaped, too."

Unfortunately, her run of incredibly good luck was about to come to an abrupt end. McGilvary was riding through Boston's North End in the front passenger seat of an automobile later that afternoon when a line of violent thunderstorms swept through the city. A Back Bay man named John Smith was behind the wheel. Smith's windshield wipers couldn't keep up with the windswept, driving rain, and he failed to see that there was a massive support beam of an elevated railway directly in front of him as he turned from Hanover onto Commercial Street. He drove right into it and demolished the front end of his car. Smith escaped with minor injuries, but McGilvary suffered multiple contusions when the impact threw her face first into the windshield. A

Mildred McGilvary, a short time after she left the Suffolk County grand jury room.

Boston Post
July 7, 1925

passerby helped her into a nearby store where someone called an ambulance. After doctors at the Haymarket Relief Station treated her injuries, McGilvary checked herself out against their advice, and took a taxi home.

A few more witnesses testified after McGilvary left the grand jury room that morning. Pickwick Club busboy Earl Davis was one of them, as was John Pultz, the owner of the construction company that was building the garage. An agent from the Massachusetts Industrial Accident Board also showed up at the courthouse on Tuesday, and told the district attorney that Barry had failed to notify the board of the number of dead and injured as required by law. Barry refused to speak with the man, and suggested he contact the club's attorney to arrange for an extension.

The outside temperature had climbed to ninety-five degrees by the time the jurors returned from lunch. Air conditioning was still several years away, and the fans inside the sweltering courthouse did little to alleviate the oppressive heat and humidity. Joseph Tomasello, the contractor who dug the excavation next to the Pickwick Club, and Martin Kane, a concrete inspector for the City of Boston, testified on Tuesday afternoon, but the star witness was Pickwick Club treasurer Timothy Barry. After waiting all day, he finally entered the grand jury room in midafternoon, but he came out a short time later in tears. Reporters said he sat in the corridor with his head buried in his hands while he shook visibly. He was sufficiently composed to go back inside an hour later, but he left when the jurors took a break for supper. Barry went back into the grand jury room a third time when the jurors returned, but he emerged from the room in tears once again a short time later, and left the courthouse. He gave no further testimony.

DEATHTRAP

| TEN |

The large, round thermometer that perched above the front entrance to Thompson's Restaurant registered a pleasant seventy-five-degrees at nine o'clock Tuesday morning. That thermometer had become something of a downtown landmark over the years, and the front page of the *Boston Globe* always gave the previous day's morning, noon, and afternoon temperatures "as indicated by the thermometer at Thompson's." O'Brien's grand jurors had already left their homes by that time, as had hundreds of grief-stricken people who were heading to churches and funeral homes throughout the city and the nearby suburbs to pay their final respects to friends, neighbors, and relatives who lost their lives in the Pickwick Club collapse. Many of them doubtlessly hoped the weather forecasters were wrong when they predicted the day would turn out to be a scorcher, with high temperatures soaring well into the nineties.

While fourteen funerals were scheduled for Tuesday, two

other victims had already been laid to rest the day before. Twenty-eight more funerals would be held over the course of the next few days in Massachusetts, New Hampshire, New York, Canada, and Texas.

The first funeral service was for thirty-one-year-old William Grossman. It took place on Monday afternoon at the Jewish Cemetery in Woburn. The West End bachelor worked as a traveling salesman for a furniture manufacturer, and he had returned home from an extended business trip on July 2. The next night he went to the Pickwick Club for a get-together with some of the friends he hadn't seen since he left. Grossman had managed a bowling alley before the war, but he quit that job to enlist in the Navy. He went to work for the furniture company a short time after his discharge.

Grossman lived with his parents and siblings on Allen Street, just around the corner from Chamber Street where actor Leonard Nimoy was born six years later. No trace of that neighborhood exists today. Bulldozers flattened a large swath of the West End in the late 1950s as part of a controversial urban renewal project that displaced 2,700 working class families in order to build six luxury, high rise buildings that contained a mere 427 apartments. Top city officials threw their full support behind the proposal, and they cut back on street cleanings and trash pickups to bolster their claim that the neighborhood was an eyesore. The promised affordable housing for those who faced eviction was just that—a promise, and nothing more. Nothing ever came of it, and few if any displaced residents ever returned to their former neighborhood. Today, the once-vibrant West End is little more than an almost forgotten, secluded refuge with virtually no stores or restaurants. The only people who have reason to venture there are the handful of well-to-do residents.

Chapter Ten

William Cochrane's funeral service also took place on Monday afternoon. The twenty-two-year-old delivery truck driver stopped by the club with five of his friends Friday night after they missed their train back to Malden. His body was interred at the Glenwood Cemetery in Everett following a brief service at the Robinson Memorial Church in Malden.

Many of the funeral services for Pickwick Club victims were quiet and low-key; a few were just the opposite. The service for Mae Lawson, the Brookline woman who went to the club with John Owen, was especially subdued.

Mae was born Mary Drew in 1896 in the old industrial city of Dover, New Hampshire, but her family moved thirty-five miles north to the small lakeside community of Wolfeboro when she was still in high school. Wolfeboro has long boasted of being America's first summer resort. Her father had taken a job there as a supervisor in a local sawmill. The Manchester, NH *Union Leader* reported that she later returned to Dover, but left the city once again when she married a man named Lawson in 1922. They separated two years later.

Mae took the breakup particularly hard. Her younger sister Marguerite was sure that a change of scene would work wonders, and she urged Mae to come to Massachusetts and share her apartment in Brookline. Mae thought about it for a while, and then said yes. In April, she moved in with Marguerite in a red brick, bow-front townhouse on Beals Street, just a few doors down from where former president John F. Kennedy was born a few years earlier. Brookline is the second-most-populous town in Massachusetts, and the north end, where Marguerite lived, is one of the most densely populated areas in the United States.

The first lists of the confirmed dead included the name *Peggy*

Lawson. It was an obvious composite of Marguerite's nickname and Mae's married surname, but how the two became linked together remains a mystery. Peggy had gone away for the holiday weekend, and no one answered the bell when the police came to her home on Beals Street. That's why they had to ask Mae's mother to travel down from Dover on Sunday and identify the body. The rest of the family arrived in Boston the next day. None of them had anything to say when questioned by reporters.

The family also chose to forgo the traditional newspaper obituary. Mae's unannounced funeral mass was celebrated at Saint Aidan Roman Catholic Church in Brookline on Tuesday morning with only her immediate family members in attendance. The family later held a private burial service in New Saint Mary Cemetery in Dover. The name on the brown marble headstone reads Mary E. Drew Lawson.

While Mae Lawson's funeral was quiet and low-key, Frank Tillo's was nothing short of a public spectacle. Friends and fans sent so many floral arrangements that it took three flower cars to carry them to the cemetery. The large crowd of people who came to his funeral mass not only filled every seat in Sacred Heart Church in Boston's North Square, but they spilled out past the sidewalk and onto the ancient, narrow street where they partially blocked traffic. Moon Street and North Square date back to 1649, only nineteen years after the first English settlers arrived in Boston. It is the city's oldest neighborhood. The home of famed patriot Paul Revere is only one hundred feet down the street from Sacred Heart Church.

The bereaved weren't the only ones who gathered outside the church. The Boston-based Napoli Band lined up on the sidewalk, and they broke out into a mournful funeral dirge when pallbearers appeared carrying Tillo's steel gray casket. Nearly fifty automobiles joined the funeral procession in its seven-mile journey to Saint Michael Cemetery in Forest Hills. Once again, the Napoli Band played funeral hymns before and after the brief graveside prayer service.

Tillo left his parents and five sisters. Although he grew up on Fleet Street in Boston's North End, and always maintained close ties to that neighborhood, he lived in nearby Chelsea at the time of his death. The name Frank Tillo was an alias. Newspapers gave several variations of what they claimed was his real name, but his death certificate bears the name Alfred Terrino.

Another funeral mass for a Pickwick Club victim also took place at Sacred Heart Church that same day. Frank Vara's was in the morning, four hours before Frank Tillo's afternoon mass. Vara was the West End man who lost his grip on his wife's hand as they pushed their way toward the door. The floor gave way beneath his feet before he could reach the stairs, and he tumbled to his death amid the tons of debris that crashed down from the upper floors. It was a tragic end to a long-awaited night on the town for the young couple who had been married less than a year.

Frank Theodore Vara was born in Ariana, Italy in August 1899, and arrived in Boston two months later. His parents opened a small fruit store on Prince Street in Boston's North End, and he went to work there when he left school. By the time he married in 1924, he had given up his job in the store and found work as a truck driver. Vara and his wife settled on Leverett Street in Boston's West End, but then moved to nearby Billerica Street a few months later. Neither street exists today. Along with dozens of other streets, they were bulldozed during the 1950s West End redevelopment project.

A brief prayer service at his parents' home on Prince Street preceded Vara's requiem funeral mass. The *Boston Globe* remarked that the funeral cortege was unusually large. Vara's burial also took place at Saint Michael Cemetery in Forest Hills where a large, elaborate granite monument marks his gravesite.

One other Pickwick Club victim was buried at Saint Michael Cemetery that day. The graveside service for thirty-five-year-old Pauline DeLucca took place that morning, following her funeral at the Langone Funeral Home on Hanover Street in the North End, and a requiem mass at nearby Saint Stephen Church.

Mrs. DeLucca was born Pauline LaVie in Quebec in 1890. Like thousands of her fellow French-speaking *Quebecois*, she left home as soon as her schooling was over and came to New England, hoping to find work in one of the region's numerous textile mills. In Pauline's case, the destination was Lowell, Massachusetts where she joined her sister who lived on Grafton Street. She married Frank DeLucca in 1912 and they settled in East Boston, close to his job in a local laundry. Twelve years later, they moved to a larger apartment on Worcester Square in Boston's South End. By that time, the once-fashionable neighborhood had fallen into decline, and most of its elegant townhouses had transitioned into tenement houses.

If there was one passion that Pauline and Frank did not share, it was dancing. Pauline had a fondness for dancing that went back to her high school days in Quebec. She was quite good at it, and onlookers couldn't help but notice how graceful she looked on the dance floor. Her husband, on the other hand, felt awkward and uncomfortable every time he got up to dance. Sometime early on in their thirteen years of married life, the DeLuccas came to an understanding. He wouldn't object if she wanted to go dancing with her girlfriends, and she wouldn't insist that he tag along. It was an arrangement that worked out quite well—until that fateful Fourth of July eve. Frank DeLucca was home on Friday night when one of his wife's girlfriends called and said she was going dancing. She wondered if Pauline wanted to join her. For some reason, Pauline neglected to tell him where her friend planned to go.

"My wife loved to dance," DeLucca told a reporter from the *Boston Traveler.* "I knew she was going dancing, although I didn't know she was going there."

Firefighters found Pauline DeLucca's body on Sunday. She left her husband, her father in Quebec, and three sisters in Lowell. She and Frank had no children.

While mourners were gathering at the Langone Funeral Home for Pauline DeLucca's funeral, Neddo Flanagan's close friends and relatives were making their way to Avon Street in Malden, six miles away. Flanagan's brief, closed-casket service took place at his mother's house. At the conclusion, a detachment of Marines escorted the body to the nearby Immaculate Conception Church for a high mass of requiem, and then to Malden's Holy Cross Cemetery where Flanagan was interred with full military honors. He was one of four Pickwick Club victims who were buried at Holy Cross Cemetery that day.

The *Boston Herald* used the words "very pretty" to describe Loretta Keegan. The thirty-six-year-old Cambridge woman was an interesting, fun-loving person from a decidedly colorful family. For starters, her name wasn't Loretta, but no one ever called her anything else. She wasn't a native-born American either, but only her immediate family was privy to that little secret.

Little Bridget Keegan was a few months shy of her first birthday when she left Ireland in 1889 and came to America with her parents and her older sister. The family settled into a predominately Irish, working-class neighborhood in East Cambridge, Massachusetts. When it came time for the Keegans to provide information for the 1900 US Census, they said Bridget was eleven years old, and a student in grammar school. They reported her birthplace as Ireland. Ten years later, another Federal census taker came to the house. By that time, Bridget was old enough to answer the questions herself. She told the person her first name was Loretta, and she said she was born in Massachusetts. She never used the name Bridget again.

She held a number of different jobs over the years, but she had a habit of quitting as soon as the warm weather arrived, and usually spent the summer months working as a waitress in a resort area.

Sometime during the early 1920s, Loretta and two of her sisters moved into the first floor of a two-family home in West Cambridge. Their sister Elizabeth had recently purchased the house, and she and her husband thought it would be nice to have family living downstairs rather than strangers. Elizabeth's husband was an up-and-coming boxing manager and promoter named Johnny Buckley. The Keegan girls hadn't been living in the house very long when Buckley spotted a young heavyweight who was about to be discharged from the Navy. He liked what he saw, and he soon had the young fighter under contract. The ink on that contract had barely dried when Buckley decided to change his new boxer's name. Lithuanian-American Joseph Zukauskas became all-American Jack Sharkey.

For some reason, Loretta decided to forego working as a

Chapter Ten

waitress as the summer of 1925 drew near, and she kept her job as a sales clerk with the long-established Boston department store Houghton & Dutton.

Contemporary newspapers didn't say how she spent the early part of the night before the Fourth, but they did note that she was in her living room with some friends when someone suggested going to the Pickwick Club. It sounded like a great idea, and she invited her younger sister to join them.

"It's too late. It's almost one o'clock," Sadie Keegan protested.

Loretta wasn't surprised to hear her sister decline the invitation. Sarah Keegan—Sadie to her family and close friends—had long disapproved of Loretta's frequent "nightclubbing", as she put it, and she made no attempt to hide her feelings. Turning down the invitation almost certainly saved Sadie Keegan's life. Two hours later, her older sister was lying dead under a massive beam—her torso snapped back at her waist at an almost ninety-degree angle.

Loretta Keegan's funeral mass was celebrated on Tuesday morning, July 7, at Saint Peter Church in Cambridge, only a few blocks from her home. Burial was at Holy Cross Cemetery in Malden.

The Keegan family was back in the news four weeks later when Cambridge police responded to a report of an early morning disturbance on Windsor Street. There they found an unruly crowd celebrating the wedding of Francis Duggan, a divorced, thirty-four-year-old meat cutter, and Ellen Keegan, Loretta's twenty-seven-year-old sister. They also found an Everett dentist, Dr. Lester Schreiber, suffering from a broken arm. Schreiber told the police he accidentally tripped and fell down the stairs. "You know how things sometimes happen at wedding receptions," he said. The police were convinced he was lying. Someone had deliberately hurled him down a flight of stairs, but no one at the party was willing to identify whoever it was.

Ellen Keegan's new husband had his own brush with the law a few years earlier when a Middlesex County grand jury indicted him and his ex-wife Theresa on charges of conspiracy to commit larceny. Prosecutors eventually dropped the charges, but a grand jury later returned additional indictments against Mrs. Duggan and several others, including former Middlesex County District Attorney William J. Corcoran. The defendants allegedly conspired on several occasions to lure wealthy men into compromising situations that left them open to blackmail. Some of those named in the indictments pled guilty and agreed to testify for the prosecution. The others went on trial in Middlesex County Superior Court, and the heated clashes between the current prosecutor and his predecessor made front-page news on an almost-daily basis.

The jury eventually returned guilty verdicts against every defendant. They appealed their convictions on numerous grounds, including race prejudice by the jury—a puzzling move since the defendants and eleven of the twelve jurors were white. They felt their attorneys should have excluded the sole black juror because he would be predisposed to convict a white defendant. The Supreme Judicial Court spent almost a year reviewing the trial transcripts, and then upheld the convictions. On hearing the news, Mrs. Duggan fled to her native Canada. She was hiding in Montreal the day her ex-husband married Ellen Keegan.

Meanwhile, Johnny Buckley was doing quite well. As Jack Sharkey's star began to rise in the boxing world, Buckley's income kept pace. He and Elizabeth sold their two-family home in Cambridge and moved to an attractive new home in the Brighton

Chapter Ten

section of Boston. They were even able to afford a live-in maid.

Sharkey went on to win the world heavyweight crown from Max Schmelling in a controversial split decision in 1932, but lost it the following year to Italian heavyweight Primo Carnera in a contest many still believe was fixed. After five uninspiring rounds, Sharkey suddenly fell to the canvas from what some of the more cynical sportswriters called a "shadow punch". Several people seated close to ringside swore Carnera's glove hadn't touched him. Jack Anderson, in his book *The Legality of Boxing: a Punch Drunk Love*, said everything about that fight smelled badly, and the smell continued to cling to Sharkey and Buckley's reputations for some time afterward.

Sharkey fought a few more bouts, and then quit boxing after Joe Louis pummeled him in 1936. Buckley went on to manage two more champions: 1930s middleweight champion Lou Brouillard, and Paul Pender, who retired from the ring in 1963 while still holding the world middleweight championship title. Buckley's success as a manager would later earn him a listing in the World Boxing Hall of Fame.

Edith Jordan had very little in common with the impulsive, fun-loving Loretta Keegan. She was born Edith McBurnie in the western Massachusetts city of Holyoke, and grew up in nearby Springfield. She was working in a candy factory when she married John Jordan in 1922, and they moved to East Boston soon afterward. Two years later, they moved again, this time to a duplex home in Somerville. It was closer to Arlington, where John worked as a steamfitter for a plumbing and heating contractor.

The Jordans went to the Pickwick Club with three friends that night. Jordan told reporters his wife had been dancing the

Charleston with another woman, and they were still on the dance floor when it gave way. He also slid into the wreckage, but he escaped with only cuts and bruises. An ambulance brought him to Boston City Hospital, but he had to wait while doctors and nurses treated those with more serious injuries. He was still waiting when Edith arrived by ambulance after her dramatic rescue. No one realized that the two were husband and wife, and by the time someone made the connection and summoned him, it was too late.

Edith was laid to rest in a white casket, dressed in her wedding gown. Almost 200 people climbed the steep granite steps of Saint Joseph Church in Somerville to attend her funeral mass on Tuesday. Afterward, the procession travelled to Holy Cross Cemetery in Malden for burial. Edith Jordan had no living relatives other than her husband.

The funeral for another Somerville victim also took place that morning. Even though William Murray, of the Rhode Island *stink bomb* affair, lived in West Somerville, his family arranged to have his funeral mass celebrated ten miles away at Saint Joseph Church in Roxbury. Like Neddo Flanagan, Loretta Keegan, and Edith Jordan, he also was buried at Holy Cross Cemetery in Malden.

Nineteen-year-old John McLaughlin's sudden death was the second blow to strike his family within a short time. His father passed away a few months earlier. Margaret McLaughlin couldn't hold back her tears when she spoke with a reporter in the family's small apartment in Boston's South End the day after the collapse. She said John was "the sunshine of the family, a good boy, and a model son." She told the reporter that he spent most evenings at

Chapter Ten

home, practicing the saxophone.

John was born in Boston on November 23, 1905, making him the youngest victim. He spent one year at Boston English High School, and then dropped out to go to work for a downtown catering company. He and his friend Eddie Whalen stopped at the Pickwick Club with a few other young people after watching a bonfire in South Boston. It was McLaughlin's first visit to the club, and he wasn't particularly keen about going, but he finally agreed to stop in "for just one".

His funeral mass was celebrated on Tuesday morning at the family's parish church, Boston's Cathedral of the Holy Cross. Burial was at Mount Benedict Cemetery in West Roxbury.

The funeral for Joseph Phaneuf, the oldest of the forty-four victims, took place a few hours later. A large delegation from the Fraternal Order of Elks attended his prayer service at Boston's Crosby Funeral Home. Burial was at Mount Hope Cemetery in Mattapan.

A brief service was held that afternoon at the John Burns Funeral Home in Cambridge for thirty-six-year-old Stuart Henderson. The New Brunswick native was only twelve when he left home to stay with his older sister in Portsmouth, New Hampshire. He married sixteen-year-old Florence Bowker of nearby York Harbor, Maine six years later. Two and a half years after she and Henderson exchanged wedding vows, Florence was dead—a victim of diphtheria. Her death certificate lists her marital status as single and, like her headstone in Portsmouth's Harmony Grove Cemetery, it gives only her maiden name.

After a brief trip back to Canada, Henderson returned to the US in September 1918 with his second wife, Lolita. They settled in Cambridge where he found work as a creamery checker. A year later he applied for US citizenship. Lolita was twenty-seven when she died in Cambridge in September 1922, leaving Henderson widowed once again.

By early 1925, he had moved to Milton, Massachusetts where he bought a one-half interest in a dairy farm. Like millions of others, he wanted to celebrate the night before the Fourth, and he set out after work with two other men—his business partner and the man's brother. When the others decided they wanted to go swimming, Henderson returned home, changed his clothes, and drove into Boston where he eventually came to the Pickwick Club. Rescue workers found his body Sunday night, more than forty hours after the collapse.

The *Boston Traveler* said his burial took place in the Loyalist Cemetery in Saint John, New Brunswick, "not far from his home." Henderson had lived on Cliff Street in Saint John at one time, and the cemetery is only a quarter of a mile away, but the cemetery's website casts considerable doubt on the *Traveler's* claim. It states that the cemetery closed for burials in 1848, some seventy-seven years before the Pickwick Club disaster.

For seventeen-year-old Dan Glavin, that night before the Fourth had been something of a rite of passage. He had graduated from high school a few weeks earlier, and it was the first time his parents allowed him to go into downtown Boston at night with just his friends, and no adult supervision. By three o'clock, they had long since run out of interesting things to do, and the four young men from Dorchester decided to go home. One of them suggested stopping in Chinatown on the way and grab a bite to eat. They had no sooner started out when a passerby told them the Pickwick Club building had collapsed. The news hit Glavin

Chapter Ten

like a punch in the stomach. His oldest brother Patrick was a waiter at the Pickwick, and Dan knew he was working that night. Glavin began running toward Beach Street as fast as he could. The scene that greeted him when he arrived was the same one that confronted Frank Wilson fifteen minutes later when he came to give his wife a ride home. The old building was in ruins, people were shouting and screaming, sirens pierced the air as additional ambulances and pieces of firefighting apparatus drew near, and the police were struggling to move everyone back away from the tottering wall on Beach Street.

It was easy to spot those who had been inside the club—they tended to be better dressed than the crowd of spectators that was swelling by the minute, and many of them looked stunned as though they still couldn't grasp what had happened. Glavin couldn't see any sign of his brother, and his frantic shouts brought no reply. Unbeknownst to his younger brother, the elder Glavin was buried under fifteen feet of rubble. It took firefighters nearly thirty-six hours to locate his body.

Patrick Glavin was born and raised in South Boston, where he picked up the nickname *Boston Red*. After graduating from high school, he embarked on the same career path that hundreds of South Boston residents had already followed—he went to work for South Boston's own Gillette Safety Razor Company.

A few years later, he married and moved to an apartment on Beacon Hill, but he still commuted back to South Boston every day. By 1925, the marriage was over, and so was the job at Gillette. He had moved back with his family in Dorchester, and was working as a machinist. He also took a part-time job waiting on tables at the Pickwick Club.

His funeral took place at the family home on Tuesday morning, and was followed by a funeral mass at Saint Matthew Church

Pickwick Club victims clockwise, from top left: Carl Paulson, Patrick Glavin, Stuart Henderson, Johnny Duffy.

Chapter Ten

in Dorchester. Burial was at New Calvary Cemetery in Mattapan.

A number of Jimmy Glennon's friends came to the family home on Marcella Street in Roxbury on Tuesday morning to pay their respects to the popular club manager. Afterward, they made their way to All Saints' Church in Jamaica Plain for Glennon's funeral mass. Burial was at Mount Benedict Cemetery in West Roxbury. Jimmy's younger brother Billy was one of the pallbearers, as was his friend Lester Fogg who was awaiting trial for the Lever Brother payroll robbery two months earlier.

Five days after Glennon's funeral, two cars pulled up outside the Fourth Presbyterian Church in South Boston where another funeral service was taking place. This one was for a fifty-six-year-old man named Robert Allen. Inside the nondescript vehicles were five plain-clothes inspectors from the Cambridge Police Department. When the mourners filed out of the white, clapboard building and returned to their cars, the newcomers discreetly joined the rear of the twenty-car funeral procession. They followed it for six miles until they arrived at Hall Cemetery in West Quincy. The men from Cambridge stood in the background and tried to blend in with the grieving friends and relatives until the graveside service was over, and then they quickly moved in and took Allen's thirty-two-year-old son John into custody. His mother and his sister nearly collapsed when they saw the police put him into handcuffs. As the astonished mourners looked on in disbelief, the Cambridge inspectors whisked Allen into one of their cars and sped from the cemetery. They brought him to Station Two in Central Square, and booked him on a charge of masterminding the Lever Brothers payroll theft. The detectives noted that he bore an uncanny resemblance to Lester Fogg. The district attorney's office dropped all charges against Fogg a few days later.

Allen went on trial for the Lever Brothers payroll heist in September. The jury returned a guilty verdict, and Middlesex County Superior Court Judge George Flynn sentenced him to life in prison. Allen's lawyer filed an appeal, but the full bench of the Massachusetts Supreme Judicial Court upheld the conviction, and Judge Flynn's lifetime sentence. Fogg later filed a damage suit against the First National Bank of Boston. He claimed that it was their employee's mistaken identification that caused his false arrest and imprisonment.

Like many of the Pickwick Club victims, Benjamin Alexander would have been all but forgotten by now if it weren't for one thing. The forty-two-year-old Boston Police lieutenant-inspector died in the line of duty at the Pickwick Club that night, guaranteeing him a place of honor every time police officers gather to pay homage to their fallen comrades.

Benjamin, or *Benny* as he was generally called, was born in New York City in 1883, but grew up in Boston's South End. He joined the Boston Fire Department in 1909, beginning what might have been the shortest firefighting career on record. He resigned after only three weeks on the job when the Boston Police Department offered him an appointment to the force.

The new recruit was a talented athlete as well as amateur boxer, and he soon won a place as a starting infielder on the department's baseball team. He transferred to the Bureau of Criminal Investigation in 1914; eight years later the department promoted him to lieutenant-inspector. Pickpockets were a particular pet peeve with Alexander. Many an out-of-town "dip" who came to Boston hoping to make a score at a convention or some other large gathering was startled when he heard the affable detective greet him by name. After receiving a friendly pat on the shoulder and a bit of sage advice, the visitor invariably returned to his hotel and packed his bags.

Alexander was one of five Boston inspectors who traveled to suburban Woburn one night in late May 1925, only a few weeks before his death. They were investigating the $60,000 theft of imported tweed from a Boston wholesaler. With help from the Woburn Police, they found the stolen cloth stashed in the attic of the prime suspect's home in a remote part of that city. The Woburn Police took the owner into custody, and the Boston men remained in the house to see if anyone stopped by. At two thirty in the morning, they were just about ready to call it a night when a car pulled into the long driveway. Three men got out and started to walk toward the house. The police were able to take two of them into custody, but the third broke free and led Alexander and another inspector on a wild, half-mile long chase through bushes and brambles before he outdistanced them in the almost pitch-black woods.

Benjamin Alexander was tenacious in chasing down clues, and that tenacity brought him to the Pickwick Club that fateful night, just a short time before the collapse. He had gone there with the hope that he might spot a man named Arthur Best, a suspect in a recent diamond theft from a downtown Boston jewelry store. His wife wasn't particularly worried when he didn't come home that evening. Police work often kept him out all night. It wasn't until he failed to show up for roll call on Saturday morning that his fellow officers became alarmed.

Alexander lived with his wife Fannie and their six children in a six-family apartment building in Dorchester. The youngest child was only two. Hundreds of people—Boston police officers, city and state officials, and police officers from many surrounding communities—came to the house on Tuesday afternoon to pay their respects and attend his funeral service. Six of his fellow inspectors served as pallbearers, and an honor guard of six ranking police officials and forty-eight patrolmen accompanied his body on the sixteen-mile trip to the Pride of Boston Cemetery in Woburn. One person who attended the funeral service said afterward that every room in Alexander's house was crammed with floral displays sent by police departments throughout the country. The family reportedly received so many that Mrs. Alexander had to ask her neighbors to take some.

* * *

Benjamin Alexander's family, friends, and fellow officers were on their way home from the graveside service in Woburn when the first of three violent thunderstorms tore through eastern Massachusetts that afternoon. It struck at the worst possible time—just after five o'clock, as thousands of commuters were starting their journey home. The next day's newspapers said the storms were the worst the region had seen in more than fifty years.

Twenty-four-year-old Arthur White was riding home from work on his motorcycle, and had gotten as far as Somerville when the storm approached. Every few seconds, another jagged bolt of lightning tore through the ominous, pitch-black sky up ahead, and each resounding clap of thunder was louder than the one before. For a few moments, White may have thought that he just might make it. If he could get across the Wellington Bridge over the Mystic River, and then turn right onto the Revere Beach Parkway before the storm's fury hit, the wind and the rain would pass behind him. Unfortunately, he was a bit too late. The first sheets of rain began to pummel the roadway just as he started across the bridge. As soon as he reached the Medford side, he pulled over and sought shelter under the protective canopy of a huge oak tree. White never saw the blinding flash a minute or two later; he never heard the ear-splitting, crackling sizzle. The young Lynn man died instantly when a powerful lightning bolt split the tree's trunk in half.

Tony Mullus dashed across James Street in Worcester in the midst of a violent, windswept downpour, and ran right in front of an oncoming streetcar. He slipped and fell face first on the tracks. The driver couldn't stop in time, and the trolley's front wheels decapitated the thirty-two-year-old Worcester man.

Lightning bolts struck seven streetcars in Boston and its nearby suburbs that night. Six of them were packed with home-bound commuters. Miraculously, no one was injured. In Malden, passengers had to wade through waist-deep water after the deluge disabled another streetcar. Brookline High School, Cambridge City Hall, and St. Paul's A.M.E. Church in Cambridge were among the numerous buildings that suffered lightning damage. Lightning also struck the central fire station in Lexington, setting the building on fire and disabling the town-wide alarm system. The storm also knocked out power to most of the town of Swampscott, leaving President Calvin Coolidge and the other occupants of that year's summer White House in the dark for nearly an hour. In downtown Boston, Mildred McGilvary's boyfriend smashed his car into a support beam for an elevated railway, while over on Beach Street, a mile and a half away, all work at the Pickwick Club site ground to an abrupt halt as spectators made a mad dash for shelter.

DEATHTRAP

ELEVEN

Fifty-five-year-old Adelina Caredo walked into the Southern Mortuary shortly before noon on Tuesday, accompanied by three members of her family. She told a guard at the front desk that an inspector from the New York Police Department had come to her home in Brooklyn the day before and said the Boston Police were all but certain that her nephew had died in the Pickwick Club collapse. They wanted someone from the family to make a positive identification, and claim the body. Mrs. Caredo burst into tears when an attendant pulled back the white sheet, and she looked down at the ashen face of thirty-three-year-old Gellato Lombardi. News reports said he lived at 16 Fleet Street in Boston's North End.

"Just last week he drove to Brooklyn in his Cadillac to see us," Mrs. Caredo told a reporter afterward. "His mother left Jerry in my hands when he was a little baby," she added, "and he has always been like a son to me. When we heard that one of the men who was missing had left his Cadillac outside the club, we knew it was him." Before she returned home, Mrs. Caredo arranged to have a local funeral home transport the body to Brooklyn for burial.

Boston newspapers had nothing further to say about Mr. Lombardi. His name does not appear in the *1925 Boston Directory*, nor is he listed as a Boston resident in the 1920 US Census. A search of the popular genealogy databases failed to find anyone in Massachusetts with his name, or a similar variation, during the first half of the 1920s. None of the local newspapers said anything about finding a Cadillac outside the club, nor did any of the wire services. New York newspapers made no mention of his funeral.

A man whom the newspapers identified as James Congdon proved to be even more elusive. The papers had little to say about him, only that he was fifty years old, he lived on North Bennett Street, he had once worked as a ship's cook, and he might have a sister who lived in suburban Norwood. None of them made any mention of his funeral service or burial. There is a good reason for the scarcity of information. While the mysterious Mr. Congdon left an easy-to-find paper trail as he made his way through life, much of it is riddled with inconsistencies and deliberate falsifications. In short, he was not fifty years old, or even close to it, and his name was not James Congdon.

His story begins with the 1880 US Census that listed Nova Scotia natives Charles and Ella Congdon as residents of Norwood, Massachusetts. The couple had no children. Their first son came into the world two years later, on February 22, 1882, but his name wasn't James, it was Ralph Kenneth Congdon. Ralph's sister Bertha was born five years later, in May 1887.

Chapter Eleven

Ralph grew up at the family home in Norwood, and then moved to the small city of Medford, Minnesota where his mother's brother owned a farm. Medford is about sixty miles south of Minneapolis. Farming didn't appeal to the young Massachusetts man, and he returned to his family in Norwood. The 1910 US Census said he was twenty-eight years old and single. He lived at home with his parents, and worked as a cook in a hotel.

Some people say that desperation is the driving force behind drastic change. Ralph Congdon must have been a very desperate man in the spring of 1914, because he left his comfortable family home and his secure job at the hotel quite abruptly, and took a position as a cook with the Eastern Steamship Line. When he filled out their application, he said his name was James Congdon. He also added eight years to his age, and claimed he was born in Norwood, Ireland, a small village near Waterford. He never used the name Ralph again.

Congdon had worked for the Eastern Steamship Line for only a few months when a nineteen-year-old student in Bosnia fired two shots at Archduke Franz Ferdinand and his wife, killing them instantly, and plunging Europe, and eventually America, into one of the deadliest conflicts in history. Fighting raged unchecked for nearly four years until the March 1918 Treaty of Brest ended hostilities on the Eastern Front, and allowed the German Army to move nearly a million men to the Western Front where they began a massive assault called "The Spring Offensive". Congress reacted to the new threat by expanding the pool of eligible draftees. The new directive required all men between the ages of thirty-one and forty-five to register. The Selective Service Act threatened registrants with stiff prison sentences if they falsified any answers, and that doubtlessly explains why Congdon took a lot fewer liberties with the truth when he registered for the draft than he did when he applied for a job with the steamship company. He lived in a rooming house on Kneeland Street in Boston at the time, and he falsely claimed his first name was James, but that was the extent of the fabrications. He said he worked for the Eastern Steamship Line as a ship's cook, and he gave the correct date and place of his birth. The questionnaire asked for the name of his closest relative. He furnished his sister Bertha's name, and her address in Norwood.

Congdon had to answer more questions eighteen months later when the time came to provide information for the 1920 US Census. He gave his correct address, occupation, and birthplace; everything else he said was untrue. Once again, he gave a false first name, he added seven years to his age, and he lied about his parents' birthplace, saying they were both born in Ireland. When his sister answered the same questionnaire, she said her mother and father were born in Canada.

A few months later, he left his lodgings on Kneeland Street and moved into a rooming house on North Bennet Street in Boston's North End, not far from the waterfront.

Congdon's seafaring career came to an abrupt end in the early months of 1925 when he took sick while on a voyage to Alaska. He had no choice but to return to Boston. Soon afterward, Timothy Barry offered him a job as a cashier at the Pickwick Club. He worked there for only a few months, and left sometime in mid-June. The separation must have been amicable, because Barry called him and asked if he could come in and wait on tables the night before the Fourth. Congdon said yes. That decision cost him his life.

The body of forty-three-year-old Ralph Kenneth Congdon lies alongside his parents in the Highland Cemetery in his

Chapter Eleven

hometown of Norwood, Massachusetts. The inscription on the monument gives his correct name and birth year.

*   *   *

The demolition crew had already removed much of the soil from around the concrete support piers before Tuesday afternoon's thunderstorms brought all work to an abrupt halt. Several people had begun to grow quite interested in those piers. Tom O'Brien was one of them. He delayed the start of Wednesday's grand jury testimony so he could send the jurors over to the collapse site where they could take a closer look.

The jurors had no sooner completed their examination and started back to the courthouse when Mayor Curley arrived, accompanied by Fire Commissioner Theodore Glynn and Building Commissioner John Mahoney. Two other men were with them—Professor Edward Miller of the Massachusetts Institute of Technology, and Guy Emerson, a consulting engineer that Tom O'Brien had hired. No one knew for sure what direction the grand jury probe might take, but it was a safe bet it would focus primarily on determining if anyone's criminal negligence had caused the collapse. Many people thought it was equally important to find out how a five-story building could fall without warning in the middle of the night. Several members of the Boston City Council shared that view, and they were concerned about the cloak of secrecy that envelops all grand jury proceedings. Some councilors thought the panel should hold its own public hearings, but the city's assistant corporation counsel told them they did not have the authority to conduct such a probe.

As Mayor of Boston, Curley had the authority to conduct any type of investigation he wanted, and he sought help from Samuel

Stratton, the President of the Massachusetts Institute of Technology. Stratton agreed, and he assigned Professor Miller to the task. Miller was the chair of the Department of Mechanical Engineering, and he had played a large part in expanding the department's testing laboratories. He was eager to take a close look at the concrete footings, and he requested a one-hundred-pound sample from each of the seven underpinnings. Emerson wasn't keen on bringing another engineering consultant onboard, and the two men got into a heated argument. Curley listened for a while, and then gave the go ahead to remove the samples and deliver them to Miller's lab.

Emerson later complained, "I don't see why the city should be so interested in calling for outside experts to examine the foundation unless it's because some people like to bask in the spotlight of publicity."

Curley fired back: "The City of Boston has no desire to shield any individual, and this independent investigation, conducted by eminent professors representing the Massachusetts Institute of Technology, has a two-fold purpose: first, the determination of the probable cause of the disaster, and second, the adoption of such measures that may be necessary to prevent a recurrence." Contemporary newspapers never disclosed whether those eminent professors ever submitted a report. If they did, the Curley administration kept it under close wraps. To this day, the cause of the collapse officially remains unknown.

While the grand jurors were examining the concrete underpinnings at Beach Street, an investigator from O'Brien's office was hard at work at the city dump in Dorchester. Anyone who saw Joseph Cheever that day would have realized that he was a man on a mission. Somewhere, amidst the countless tons of rubble that trucks had carted over from the collapse site, was the infamous door with the trick lock that several patrons had mentioned. Cheever was determined to find it, even though it was akin to looking for the proverbial needle in a haystack. The door might well have been splintered beyond recognition. His dogged determination finally paid off. He found the door, and it was still in one piece. But, instead of clearing up any mysteries, Cheever's discovery only added to them. Someone had removed a metal plate from the bottom of the door quite recently, and it was apparent that there had been an electric deadbolt behind that plate. It too was missing, as was the faceplate and inside knob of the lock that Frank Decker and Harold Shaw found hard to operate. O'Brien had to admit he had no idea where or when the tampering took place. Pickwick Club treasurer Timothy Barry never mentioned an electric lock when reporters questioned him about the door the day before.

Harry Haven, the architect who designed the garage next door to the Pickwick Club, was the first witness O'Brien called after the jurors returned from their tour of the collapse site. Chief Inspector Edward Roemer of the Boston Building Department followed him. Patrolman Frank Callahan and demolition contractor Thomas Elston also testified before the jurors, as did John Goff, the carpenter who walked off the roof repair job, convinced that the former warehouse could fall at any moment. Like several other witnesses, Goff was quite willing to speak with reporters while he waited his turn. His former boss Nathan Fritz arrived later, to testify at the evening session. Not surprisingly, he denied every one of Goff's allegations when he spoke with reporters.

Wednesday was a busy day at Tom O'Brien's office. An inspector from the state attorney general's office stopped by with a man named Guy Seaborne. The *Boston Traveler* described him as "an expert on floor and roof construction." Seaborne told O'Brien's investigators he walked past the Pickwick Club building on July 1, and he could not help but notice that the sidewall didn't look right.

He said he happened to pass by the building again two days later, and looked up at the sidewall once again. He walked over to a construction worker and told him , "That building is going to fall."

"What happened then?" an investigator asked.

"He told me to go to hell."

O'Brien had someone in his office bring Seaborne to the grand jury room. What the Roxbury man told the jurors is anyone's guess, but one thing is certain—he was not an expert on floor and roof construction as the *Traveler* claimed. The *1925 Boston Directory* listed his occupation as a sign painter.

Most of the witnesses who testified before the grand jury came voluntarily, in response to a telephone call. The district attorney's office had to deliver an official summons to those whom they were not able to reach by phone. Nat Clark, one of the three principals of the former ground floor Greenwich Village Cafe, chose to decline the phone request, and the district attorney had to send a court officer to Clark's home in nearby Nantasket with a summons that commanded him to appear. Getting the other two owners of the defunct restaurant to testify proved to be every bit as challenging. The person who answered the phone at Michael Ward's home said he was on vacation, and they had no idea where he had gone, or when he planned to return. John Glynn's wife claimed that he too was on vacation, but she promised to try to reach him. Glynn contacted the district attorney's office several hours later and he assured them he would come in the next day. Ward finally called O'Brien's office the next day. He said he was not on vacation as the person who answered the phone at his home had claimed, and he was not trying to evade a summons.

*   *   *

Fourteen more victims were laid to rest on Wednesday. Eight of those funerals took place in a small, four-square-mile section of the city called Roxbury. The saddest one without doubt was the funeral of Nora Sullivan's daughters Mary McEachern and Lillian McIsaac. Nora was devastated by their deaths, and her anguish only increased when the funeral director told her that her long-time parish church would not be able to accommodate her daughters' double-funeral mass. Saint Joseph already had four funerals scheduled that day, and two of them were for Pickwick Club victims. The pastor said they simply could not handle any more. Mary and Lillian's funeral mass would have to take place at some other Catholic church.

The service began at the Crosby Funeral Home, and was followed by a funeral mass at the nearby Saint Patrick Church on Dudley Street. Nora began to collapse when she saw pallbearers carrying the two caskets, one behind the other, up the steps and into the church. Two men had to rush over to keep her from falling. When the mass was over, pallbearers once again carried the two caskets down the center aisle, one behind the other. Hundreds of spectators gathered in silence outside the church to watch the two hearses pull away as they left for Cambridge Cemetery where Mary and Lillian were buried side-by-side.

Carl Paulson's family were heartbroken when they encountered the same problem that Nora Sullivan did. Saint Joseph was also their parish church, but with so many funerals scheduled for Wednesday, the earliest a priest at Saint Joseph could celebrate a mass for Carl would be on Thursday morning. The Paulsons would have to find another church, or wait until Thursday. They chose to wait. Carl's funeral service still took place on Wednesday afternoon at his home on Greenville Street, but without a mass. The cab that he usually drove, with his chauffeur cap resting on the center of the hood, led the funeral procession on its trip to Saint Joseph for a brief prayer service. Two uniformed cab drivers walked alongside it. At the conclusion, the procession brought Carl's body to Evergreen Cemetery in Brighton for burial. His funeral mass was celebrated at Saint Joseph the next morning.

Pickwick Club victims Johnnie Scales and Margaret Murphy were among the four people whose funeral masses were celebrated at Saint Joseph on Wednesday morning. In addition to being a talented vocalist, Scales was also a *frisco dancer*, an energetic style of solo dancing that combined exaggerated, high-stepping struts with shuffles and turns. It took its name after vaudeville entertainer Joe Frisco, who often wore a derby hat and smoked a cigar while performing his routine on stage. Scales was one of the four vocalists who entertained the crowd with a rendition of "West of the Great Divide" shortly before the crash. The twenty-two-year-old Roxbury man had been married for only a year, and had just started a new job as a sales clerk at a men's clothing store in Boston. He and his wife lived with her family on Spring Terrace. Scales was buried at Saint Joseph Cemetery in West Roxbury.

Margaret Murphy loved to dance and, like Pauline DeLucca,

went to the club with one of her girlfriends that night while her husband stayed home. The two women arrived shortly after midnight. They decided to leave when the orchestra began to play "Twelfth Street Rag", but Margaret changed her mind and lingered just a bit too long. She was on her way to the cloakroom when the floor collapsed. Her friend had already gotten her wrap, and was standing at the door. She escaped unharmed. William Murphy identified his wife's body the next day. The twenty-nine-year-old lifelong Roxbury resident was buried at Mount Benedict Cemetery in West Roxbury.

There was a time when grieving friends and relatives didn't have to travel to cemeteries like Mount Benedict after attending a funeral mass at Saint Joseph. The parish had its own cemetery, right behind the church. It opened in 1847, only two years after the church's dedication, and it closed in 1866 when it ran out of space for burials. That little cemetery would one day become yet another major embarrassment to the already beleaguered Archdiocese of Boston.

For nearly a century, the term "Saint Joseph parishioner" was almost synonymous with "Irish Catholic". The racial makeup of the neighborhood began to change after the Second World War, and attendance at Saint Joseph dwindled as more and more parishioners migrated to the suburbs. The Archdiocese closed the church in the 1980s, and sold the property in 2002. Four years later, a construction crew was doing excavation work on the site when they uncovered human remains. All work stopped while investigators probed the surrounding area and found several more bodies.

Flustered church officials confessed they had no idea that the property had once been used for burials when they offered it for sale, and they could not explain how the old, long-forgotten cemetery eventually became a parish playground and picnic area. A broken piece of headstone engraved "County Donegal, Ireland" that was found years earlier was the only relic that linked it to a burial ground. The Archdiocese hired a Rhode Island firm to exhume the remains and reinter them in Calvary Cemetery in Waltham. By the time they finished, they had moved 1,238 bodies along with personal artifacts, parts of coffins, and broken headstones. The old parish cemetery had no affiliation with the newer and much larger Saint Joseph Cemetery in West Roxbury. It was just a coincidence that they shared the same name.

Two other Pickwick Club vocalists were buried on Wednesday. Like his good friend James "Bubba" Murray of Dorchester, twenty-three-year-old John Murphy had a good voice and an outgoing personality, and he enjoyed getting up in front of an audience to sing a song or two. He and Murray went to the club that night with two friends from Jamaica Plain—Arthur McNeil, and a man that the newspapers identified only by the surname "Campbell". The four men spent the earlier part of the evening at the John Eliot Club in Roxbury with Murphy's older brother Joseph, and then headed for the Pickwick Club around one thirty when Joe Murphy decided to call it a night. McNeil later said there were seven people at their table in the club—the four men, along with Mary McEachern, her sister Lillian McIsaac, and a married woman whose identity he refused to divulge. "Her husband has no idea she was there," he told a reporter the next day, "and no one need know her name." The mysterious Mr. Campbell was also married, and refused to speak with reporters. McNeil and the unidentified woman ran for the stairs as soon as the floor began to sway. They made it to the street, but McNeil suffered a minor leg injury. Campbell escaped without a scratch.

Chapter Eleven

Lillian McIsaac, Mary McEachern, and Bubba Murray were at a table close to the wall that fell, and they didn't stand a chance. John Murphy had left the table a few minutes earlier. McNeil remembered seeing him with two young women in the back of the hall moments before the crash, and that raised hopes for a while that he might have survived. Those hopes were shattered when rescue workers found his body deep in the ruins the next day. McNeil and Campbell tentatively identified it based on a description of his clothing. Daniel Murphy made that identification positive when he viewed his son's body at the Southern Mortuary early Monday morning.

Murphy's funeral began with a few brief prayers at the family home in the Mission Hill section of Roxbury. His funeral mass followed at Mission Church, a twin-spired structure at the base of the hill. With nearly 1,300 seats, it is one of the largest churches in the archdiocese. What began as a local nickname has become the commonly accepted name for the imposing structure. Today, very few Bostonians know that its official name is Basilica of Our Lady of Perpetual Help.

The church occupies the site of the former home of General Henry Dearborn, a distinguished veteran of the American Revolution who later served as the Secretary of War under President Thomas Jefferson. The city of Dearborn, Michigan is named in his honor.

The *Boston Globe* reported that several hundred people attended Murphy's funeral mass. Many of them were friends from the Pickwick Club. Interment followed at Saint Joseph Cemetery in West Roxbury.

The families of the Pickwick Club victims handled sorrow in different ways. Some wanted to share every memory of their loved one's life; others needed to spend time by themselves. The family of John Murphy's twenty-eight-year-old friend and fellow-vocalist James "Bubba" Murray fell in the latter group. The only information that contemporary newspapers revealed, other than the sparse details in his small death notice, was that he was a salesperson, he went to the Pickwick Club with Murphy, and his wife spent all day Saturday at the site of the collapse. Census records and street directories tell us his parents were from Northern Ireland, his father died a month after Murray's eighth birthday, and he and his wife lived with his mother in Dorchester. Murray's funeral mass at Saint Margaret Church followed a brief funeral service at the family home. Burial was at Holy Cross Cemetery in Malden.

While Murphy's friends, relatives, and neighbors were attending his mass at Mission Church, another group of mourners gathered for twenty-six-year-old Esther Wilson's funeral mass at the much smaller Saint Mary of the Angels church on Columbus Avenue in Roxbury, a mile and a half away. Funeral services for her two companions also took place that day. Mary Moore's service was held at the Crosby Chapel in Roxbury, and was followed by a requiem mass at All Saints Church in Jamaica Plain. Frank Decker, the Melrose man who danced with her only minutes before the collapse, served as a pallbearer. Esther and Mary were both interred at Saint Joseph Cemetery in West Roxbury. Services for Clara Frederick took place that morning at the J.S. Waterman Chapel in Kenmore Square with only a few family members and close friends in attendance. Burial was at Mount Hope Cemetery in Mattapan.

Patrolman Paul Halleran's funeral began with services at his home in Dorchester. An honor guard of forty police officers accompanied the hearse as it led a long procession to nearby Saint Peter Church for a high mass of requiem. Afterward, the procession traveled to New Calvary Cemetery in Mattapan. When the echo of the last of the three volleys fired by the fifteen-member Boston Police rifle squad faded, two Army sergeants removed the flag from Halloran's casket, folded it into a neat triangle, and presented it to his widow. The service ended with a lone bugler playing "Taps".

Thirty-four-year-old Michael Cheffalo's funeral mass was celebrated at Saint Leonard church in the North End on Wednesday. He lived with his parents on Fleet Street, just around the corner. His fiancé had spotted what she thought was his name in a Sunday newspaper's list of the known dead, but the spelling was different. "I know it's probably Michael," Helen Christman told the attendant at the Southern Mortuary that afternoon, "but the name says Cefalo and that's not how he spells his name. He told me he was going to the Pickwick Club, and if I can see him, I'd know for sure." The attendant was sympathetic, but he said he could not allow her to view the body. The dead man's brother had already made a positive identification.

Bartholomew O'Donnell had to work late that Fourth of July Eve. The twenty-five-year-old South End resident was a property man at the Schubert Theater, and Arthur Hammerstein's block-buster musical hit *Rose Marie* had played to yet another full house. The show's advertisements proclaimed it "the biggest musical hit ever produced in America." It not only ran longer than most stage performances at the time, but the elaborate sets and costumes meant extra work for O'Donnell and the other members of the backstage crew. It was almost midnight before he was able to leave the theater and join three friends who were waiting outside.

He had managed to get the rest of the weekend off, and he and his friends planned to set out early the next morning on a long-awaited, two-night camping trip to suburban Sharon. Even so, there was still time to squeeze in a little holiday-eve enjoyment before going home. They grabbed a bite to eat, and then headed over to the Pickwick Club for some dancing. The four young men were still inside when the building began to shake. Three of them managed to reach the stairs before the floor gave way; O'Donnell wasn't quite that lucky. Rescue workers pulled his body from the bottom of the wreckage on Sunday afternoon.

O'Donnell was born on Warrenton Street in the heart of Boston's Theater District, a few doors away from where the Charles Playhouse stands today. After graduating from Boston English High School, he went to work for the Boston and Albany Railroad as a plumber's assistant, but he left a year later to take a job as a stagehand with the Boston Opera House. He stayed there for four years, and then moved to the nearby Schubert Theater, and a new job as a property man.

His funeral took place at the family home on Saint Charles Street in the South End on Wednesday morning. Thirty members of the Stagehands Union escorted his body to Saint James Church on Harrison Avenue for the funeral mass. The church was only two blocks from the collapse site. O'Donnell left his widowed mother, two brothers, and one sister. The quiet cul-de-sac where the O'Donnell family lived in the 1920s has become one of the most exclusive streets in Boston's South End. Real estate professionals say their circa-1875 apartment would fetch more than $3 million in today's marketplace.

Chapter Eleven

Twelve of the fifteen victim funerals that were held on Wednesday took place in Boston. Francis McLean's funeral mass was celebrated at Sacred Hearts Church in Malden. Burial was at the nearby Holy Cross Cemetery. Pickwick Club waitress Ella Calley's service took place on Wednesday afternoon at her mother's home in Danbury, New Hampshire. Burial was at the Homeland Cemetery in the nearby town of Bristol.

The newspapers had a lot to say about Calley, but almost everything they said was wrong. New Hampshire's largest newspaper, the *Union Leader*, even mistakenly called her by her roommate's last name when they reported the details of her funeral. The worst offender was the *Boston American*. Their July 6 article about Calley did manage to get her occupation right, but that was the only correct statement in the entire piece. Every other bit of information was the product of someone's imagination. They even misspelled her name. Under the headline "Little Angel Killed", the article said she was nineteen years old, and proud of the fact she had never touched a drop of intoxicating liquor in her life. The club's patrons knew her only as the little angel, the story claimed, and it went on to say she often counseled young girls about the pitfalls of nightclubbing, even as she served them alcoholic drinks. It ended by stating that officials identified her body right away. Once they had established her identity, they sent the body to the little apartment that she maintained for herself on Peterborough Street.

Ella Calley was, in fact, a thirty-three-year-old divorcee who was on a first name basis with all of the regular patrons. Rescue workers had a difficult time identifying her body because she carried no identification, and her facial features were smashed beyond recognition. A massive beam had crushed her head and much of her upper body. One newspaper said the beam nearly

Four victims of the Pickwick Club collapse. Clockwise from top left: Dora Stern, Edith Jordan, Mae Lawson, Ella Calley.

decapitated her. The *American* reporter obviously had no grasp of the facts when he told his readers that officials sent her body to her apartment. Rescuers sent each one of the bodies that were taken from the wreckage directly to the Southern Mortuary where they were held until a positive identification was made.

Ella was born in the small town of Hill in central New Hampshire in March 1892. Like most of the neighbors, her parents were farmers. By 1915, Calley had traded life on the farm for a factory job in Waltham, Massachusetts. Three years later, she married a man four years her junior in New York City. Charles Hoch was twenty-two, and worked as a hotel desk clerk.

By 1925, the marriage had failed and Ella was sharing an apartment in Boston's Back Bay with another waitress named Florence Moore. Moore often stopped by the Pickwick Club for a drink after she finished work at a downtown restaurant. She and Calley would then take a cab for the two-mile ride back to their apartment on Peterborough Street. Moore had gotten to know several of the regular Pickwick Club patrons, including a Cambridge girl named Rita Carlson. Carlson was sitting at a table with three men when Moore came into the club that night, and she invited Moore to join them. Ella Calley stopped by a few times and chatted for a moment or two.

Florence Moore spoke with a *Boston Herald* reporter the next day. "Some people were dancing, and others were throwing firecrackers around the place," she said. "There was a great clatter of noise. Then the wall just seemed to open up. I don't remember any sounds because there was so much noise inside. I made a dash for the door and didn't stop for anything. I know I'm hoping against hope that Ella is still alive. I can't see why she couldn't get out if I did. I only hope she did."

Moore's worst fears came true when firefighters found

Calley's body twenty-one hours after the collapse.

Rita Carlson later spoke about the collapse: "We were sitting at the table, watching the dancing and the merrymaking, when the crash came without any warning. There wasn't the least inkling of danger until the ceiling fell, and then the whole thing came down on top of my head. We were all hurled together and pressed down under a great weight. There was a long, long fall and then I struck something hard. I was lying on my back on top of one of the men, crushed down on him by a heavy timber. I have a horrible feeling that my weight might have suffocated him." When rescue workers finally reached Carlson, they found that the section of the ceiling that landed on her head had also torn off part of her scalp. An ambulance rushed her to Boston City Hospital where she remained on the critical list for several days.

Thirty-three-year-old Max Mulmat of Roxbury finally succumbed to his injuries at Boston City Hospital on Thursday morning. He had clung to life for five days with a fractured skull, a fractured jaw, and numerous internal injuries. The clandestine clerk's passing brought the death toll to forty-four. It climbed no higher. If Mulmat had stuck to his original plans, he would have been sound asleep somewhere in Ohio when the Pickwick Club building collapsed. He had made plans to take a train to Chicago on July 3, but he postponed his trip at the last minute so he could spend the holiday at home.

Mulmat was born in Newark, New Jersey on February 2, 1892, soon after his parents and two older sisters arrived in the United States from Russia. By the turn of the century, the family had moved to Boston's West End. A few years later, Charles Mulmat moved his family once again—this time to Roxbury where he bought a wholesale egg business. By 1920, Max was living at home with his parents and working as a chauffeur. Five years later he was still single and still lived at home, but his occupation had changed from chauffeur to broker. He was also the corporate clerk of the Pickwick Club—something none of the newspapers mentioned. Mulmat's funeral took place at his home in Roxbury on Thursday afternoon. His burial followed at the Jewish Cemetery in Woburn.

Services for three other victims also took place on Thursday. Johnny Duffy's funeral began at his brother's home on John A. Andrew Street in Jamaica Plain. A requiem mass followed at nearby Saint Thomas Aquinas Church. Boston Fire Commissioner Theodore Glynn was one of several hundred mourners who packed the church. Burial was at Saint Joseph Cemetery in West Roxbury.

Under the headline "Victim's Sister Meets Disaster Same Day", that morning's *Boston Advertiser* told its readers that Johnny's older sister went on trial for larceny in a Los Angeles courtroom the day before her brother plunged to his death. Prosecutors claimed the former Mary Duffy had passed several bad checks. The judge found her guilty, but let her off with a suspended sentence.

The fact that Duffy's friends were able to persuade the Mayor of Boston and the Governor of Massachusetts to take part in a charity baseball game to benefit the well-known entertainer's widow speaks volumes about "Mr. Originality's" popularity.

Arthur Graham was no stranger to the neighborhood around the Pickwick Club. The twenty-seven-year-old Jamaica Plain resident owned a small restaurant called South Cove Lunch that was just three blocks down the street. Graham was born in Dorchester, but his family moved to a neat little house on the shore of Sunset Lake in suburban Braintree when he was in grammar school. He bought the luncheonette soon after he returned to Boston after serving overseas in World War I. Delegations from both the Knights of Columbus and the Lodge of Elks came to his home on Thursday morning for his brief funeral service. A requiem mass followed at the nearby Church of Our Lady of Lourdes. Six of his fellow veterans served as pallbearers. Graham left his wife Veronica and a four-year-old son. Veronica Graham never remarried, and she continued to live in the same house on Kingsboro Park until her death forty-five years later. She was buried alongside her husband at Saint Joseph Cemetery in West Roxbury.

Mary Driscoll wasn't concerned when her forty-three-year-old brother Frank didn't return home Friday night. He often spent summer weekends at Nantasket Beach, a popular summer resort a few miles south of Boston, and she assumed he had gone down there for the holiday. Frank didn't say anything about going to Nantasket when he left earlier that evening, but he did mention that he planned to meet another union official at the Pickwick Club to talk about his upcoming trip to a labor conference on the West Coast. Driscoll was the business agent of the Plasterers & Cement Masons Union, and it was the union membership card in his wallet that helped firefighters identify his body when they pulled it from the rubble two days after the collapse.

Driscoll was born in South Boston, and later moved to Dorchester. He followed in his father's footsteps and went to work as a plasterer after he graduated from high school. Driscoll was an outspoken advocate of organized labor, and that zeal eventually secured him the position of business agent for his local union. He went on to win reelection six consecutive times. The most recent victory was only a few weeks before his death when he outpolled his opponent by a five-to-one margin.

A few months earlier, it looked like his career might be heading in a different direction. Boston Mayor James M. Curley nominated him to the vacant post of Superintendent of Public Buildings in December 1924, but the Civil Service Commission blocked the appointment. Driscoll later joined a special arbitration board that was attempting to avert a threatened strike by 30,000 unionized building trade workers in the Greater Boston area.

Driscoll's funeral mass was celebrated at Saint Joseph Church in Roxbury on Thursday morning.

A funeral director in the historic, oceanfront city of Salem had run into a problem on Thursday that was unlike any he had ever encountered—he had no idea whose body was lying in the casket in the front room of his funeral parlor. It was supposed to be a twenty-three-year-old Salem man named Thomas McManus but, at the moment, that was anything but certain. McManus had left the historic seafaring city a few years earlier and moved to a rooming house in South Boston. He had told some friends on Friday that he might go to the Pickwick Club that night. That was the last time any of them saw him. A police officer came to his rooming house on Wednesday and asked his roommate if he would mind coming to the Southern Mortuary for a few minutes. Firefighters had found a sweater on a badly crushed body, and they suspected it belonged to McManus. Harry Bainbridge told the officer he would be glad to go. He took one look at the sweater and said it was identical to the one McManus owned. A Boston Police official then called the McManus home in Salem and told Thomas's parents that officials were certain that the body in the morgue was their son. The family arranged for the Walter T. McDonald Funeral Home to bring the body back to Salem for burial. McDonald scheduled a funeral mass at nearby Saint James Roman Catholic Church on Friday morning, July 10.

Former prizefighter John "Buzzy" Mahoney was reading a Boston newspaper on Thursday when he spotted an article that said officials had positively identified the last two collapse victims: a man named Thomas McManus who was in his early twenties and was originally from Salem, and another man in his late twenties named Charles "Happy" Whalen. Both men lived in the same rooming house on West Broadway in South Boston.

"That's not right," Mahoney said to himself. He had bumped into McManus on a downtown street two days earlier, and the two men spoke for quite a while. Mahoney hurried to North Station and took a train to Salem, hoping to halt the proceedings. He told the funeral director that McManus was very much alive, and how he had spoken with him on Tuesday. He had no idea where McManus lived, but he knew McManus worked at Walton's Lunch on Washington Street in Boston. A call to the lunchroom confirmed that McManus had worked there earlier that day, but he had already gone home and was not due back for two more days. The people at the lunchroom weren't sure where he lived either. The situation grew more complicated when McManus's brother Joseph also questioned the identity. The funeral director refused to let him, or anyone else, see the body because of its condition. The massive blocks of masonry that crushed it destroyed all facial features, but officials at the Southern Mortuary noted the victim was five feet, seven inches tall with dark brown hair. McManus was sure his brother was shorter, and had medium brown hair. McDonald refused to go ahead with the funeral arrangements until every doubt about the dead man's identity was resolved. Several newspapers reported the incident, telling their readers the police were satisfied that McManus was alive and well, and the body in the funeral home was that of some unknown man.

The McManus family's hopes were dashed the next morning when police positively identified Thomas as the victim. Rescue workers had neglected to mention that they found a letter addressed to McManus's sister in Salem in the pocket of the dead man's trousers. A police officer then brought a family photo to Walton's Lunch, but none of the employees recognized Thomas. Harry Bainbridge, the roommate who had identified the sweater, came to Salem to try to help. The police refused to let him see the body, but they asked him if McManus had a peculiar mole on his shoulder. Bainbridge said he did, and his description matched a mole on the body at the funeral home.

The mix-up was caused by nothing more than an unfortunate coincidence. John Mahoney's friend just happened to have the same name as the Pickwick Club victim. Both men were approximately the same age, and both had moved from Salem to Boston to seek work. Neither man had kept in close touch with his family.

Funeral services for Tom McManus were held on Saturday, one day later than originally planned. Interment was in Saint Mary Cemetery in Salem.

While McManus's funeral services were taking place in Salem, friends and relatives of his good friend and roommate, Charles Whalen were gathering for his requiem mass at Saint Margaret Church in Dorchester, twenty-five miles to the south.

The two victims lived in the same South Boston rooming house, and were part of a group of four men who went downtown to celebrate the holiday. When two of them decided to go home, McManus and Whalen set out for the Pickwick Club. One newspaper said it was about two thirty when they arrived. Twenty minutes later, both men were dead.

Tom McManus was the youngest child in the family. He was born in Salem on February 18, 1902. His mother lost her ten-month battle with cancer when he was only six. Tom enlisted in the Army after he graduated from high school, and served for a while at Fort Banks in nearby Winthrop. He moved to Boston after his discharge and found work in the kitchen of a local school. Joseph McManus later told reporters that his younger brother "was not in the habit of keeping in communication with his folks, only dropping in on them at intervals."

Charles Whalen was born in South Boston on December 9, 1897, the youngest of Peter and Elizabeth Whalen's seven children. The Whalens were natives of St. John's, Newfoundland. Like McManus, he lost his mother at an early age. Charles was only two when she died. When his father passed away seven years later, his older brother Henry took over as head of the family.

Charles took a train to Canada in 1914, shortly after Great Britain declared war on Germany, and enlisted in the Canadian Expeditionary Forces. He lied when he told the recruiter he was born in Canada. Whalen served in the Canadian Army for four years, and then returned to his brother's home in Massachusetts when the war ended. He lived with his brother for a few years while he worked as a truck driver, and then decided to strike out on his own and move into the rooming house.

As family members and friends of McManus and Whalen were paying their final respects in Salem and Dorchester, Wayne Marr's body was enroute by train to his hometown of Dallas,

Chapter Eleven

Texas. Marr's commitment service took place in that city's Oak
Cliff Cemetery a few days later. The thirty-year-old Coast Guard
career man left his parents and a younger sister.

DEATHTRAP

| TWELVE |

Eighteen victims remained hospitalized on Thursday; seventeen of them were "resting comfortably," but Rita Carlson's name was still on the danger list. The Associated Press said she was near death, and not expected to survive. The twenty-year-old Cambridge woman surprised everyone. Three days after the news agency's somber prediction, Carlson was on her way home. Doctors had discharged her that morning, along with Edward LaGroff of Everett. That left just three victims still hospitalized—Frank Castelone of Hyde Park, Richard Lovejoy of Everett, and Coast Guardsman Jacob Rosenberg. Castelone was in Boston City Hospital; Lovejoy's family had arranged for his transfer to Everett Hospital, and Coast Guard officials moved Rosenberg to the nearby Chelsea Naval Hospital.

Rescue workers found a number of personal belongings as they probed the rubble. Authorities were able to identify many of them, but some proved all but impossible to trace. Among them were men and women's hats and coats, and a few handbags. One of the bags was made of black satin and contained, among other items, a torn piece of a paycheck stub issued by "H & D". Although the bag went unidentified at the time, it might well have belonged to Cambridge resident Loretta Keegan who worked at Houghton & Dutton, a long-established Boston department store. The bottom of another bag made of gray silk and decorated with steel beads was soaked with blood. The police brought every item they recovered to Station Four on Lagrange Street where, for several days, they remained spread out on a desk in a back room, awaiting owners who, in many cases, would never come to retrieve them.

While mourners paid their final respects, and searchers continued to probe the ever-shrinking pile of rubble, Tom O'Brien's grand jurors were still putting in marathon sessions as a steady parade of witnesses showed up to testify.

It was almost nine o'clock Friday evening when the last witness left the grand jury room. The jurors had spent more than forty hours over the course of four days listening to eighty-five people give testimony. The time had come to begin deliberations. They discussed the matter for the next two hours, and then left at quarter past eleven with instructions to return the next morning. Any hopes for a weekend break were out of the question. Tom O'Brien wanted indictments, and he wanted them quickly. That evening's edition of the *Boston Traveler* speculated that the district attorney would most likely seek a blanket indictment against everyone who had some connection with the case, and let a petit jury eliminate those who were not responsible. It turned out to be a prophetic prediction.

The nineteen jurors returned to the courthouse on Saturday

morning as instructed, but their deliberation would have to wait. The first order of business was to walk over to city hall and collect their jury duty pay.

With their paychecks in hand, the grand jurors resumed deliberation. Two hours later, they reached a decision. Jury foreman Arthur Downey presented Superior Court Judge Henry Lummus with nine bills of criminal indictment—each one for a single count of manslaughter in connection with the death of Patrolman Paul Halleran. Those named as defendants were:

George Funk, the architect who designed the new roof to replace the one damaged by the April fire.

Nathan Fritz, the contractor who constructed the new roof.

John L. Pultz, the president of the Pultz Construction Company, the firm that was building the garage next door to the Pickwick Club.

John M. Tobin, a superintendent employed by the Pultz Construction Company.

Lawrence Perkins, a supervisor employed by the Pultz Construction Company.

Edward W. Roemer, the chief district building inspector for the city of Boston.

James J. Hendrick, a district building inspector for the city of Boston.

Hyman Bloomberg, the lessee of the property at 6 Beach Street.

Timothy J. Barry, the treasurer of the Pickwick Club.

Barry, Funk, and Bloomberg arrived at the courthouse for their arraignment a few hours later. Each man pled not guilty, and posted $2,000 bail.

Judge Lummus had something he wanted to say before he

adjourned the court until Monday morning:

"In view of the fact that the trial of these cases is imminent, a word to the representatives of the press may not be amiss. Newspapers have been filled with rumors about this matter for the past week, with attempts to fix the blame for this catastrophe by headlines, discussions, editorials, and letters to the editors. Fairness to the Commonwealth, and the defendants, requires that everything beyond an uncolored and dispassionate report of judicial proceedings cease until the trial is concluded. In the presence of trial by jury, trial by newspaper must give way."

The remaining six defendants came to the courthouse on Monday morning for their arraignment. Each one pled not guilty and posted $2,000 bail. Some of them were still inside the building when they learned the grand jury had returned additional bills of indictment against all nine defendants, charging each one with four more counts of manslaughter. The jurors returned an additional charge against Timothy Barry—maintaining a common nuisance. They also handed down indictments against three other men: Nathan Ginsberg, the executor of the Rosenthal estate, Harry M. Haven, the president of Haven and Hopkins, the architects who drew the plans for the garage next door to the Pickwick Club, and Daniel Barry, the president of the Pickwick Club. They indicted Ginsberg and Haven on four counts of manslaughter, and indicted Barry on the charge of maintaining a common nuisance. In less than a week, the Pickwick Club had gone from what the city's police commissioner called "an inviolate establishment" to a common nuisance.

Ginsberg and Haven entered not guilty pleas at their July 15 arraignment and, like the other defendants, posted $2,000 bail. The Barry brothers didn't show up for their scheduled arraignment, and their attorney told the judge he had no explanation for their absence. Judge Lummus told him to make sure they were in court the next morning.

Any conversations that took place behind the closed doors of the grand jury room were kept secret, but it's safe to assume that, at some point, Tom O'Brien delved into the background of the people behind the Pickwick Club. Although the popular speakeasy attracted what many called "a criminal element," the officers and incorporators were ordinary people who led, for the most part, very uneventful lives. Club treasurer Timothy Barry was

The two Barry brothers. Timothy (left) was the Pickwick Club Treasurer. His younger brother Daniel held the office of President, but rarely set foot inside the club.

thirty-four years old, and he lived in a fashionable neighborhood in the Back Bay. He began his career as a clerk with the Boston and Albany Railroad, and then went to work for the post office. He left that job to open a billiard parlor on Tremont Street in the South End. His brother Dan was twenty-eight, and had been president for only four and a half months. He rarely set foot inside the club. Dan drove a taxicab by day, and spent his nights at home in South Boston with his wife and three children in a house that he shared with his widowed mother. Joshua Paine was the president of the Colonial Cold Storage Company in Provincetown. John Roth managed a restaurant. Edward Powers owned a tire store in South Boston. Louis Rosenfield and his brother were co-owners of a small garment factory that made pajamas and bathrobes. Max Pilder managed a furniture store. James Troy owned a newsstand in the Back Bay. Keron Clemens sold advertising space for a regional magazine. Francis Nevins sold woodworking machinery. Max Mulmat, the clerk of the corporation, worked at his father's wholesale egg business during the day. Charles Gluck, who supposedly lived at the Hotel Avery, managed to make it all the way through the turbulent decade of the Roaring Twenties without ever getting his name in a newspaper other than for his brief, three-week association with the Pickwick Club. His name doesn't appear in the *1925 Boston Directory*, nor does it show up as a Massachusetts resident in either the 1920 or 1930 US Census.

Paine was the only officer other than Mulmat to run afoul of the law. He was one of thirty defendants who went on trial in 1919, charged with price fixing at the Boston wholesale fish market. A jury acquitted thirteen of those defendants, but returned guilty verdicts against Paine and sixteen others. They appealed their convictions, and the cases dragged on for four years before the courts upheld the original verdict. Sherriff's deputies then took Paine and the others to the Deer Island House of Correction to serve their ten-month sentences.

Paine sold his interest in the Colonial Cold Storage Company a few years after the Pickwick Club collapse. His 1932 obituary said he was the manager of the Provincetown Inn, and a descendent of one of the oldest families on Cape Cod.

DEATHTRAP

| THIRTEEN |

The millstones of justice turn slowly, but they grind exceedingly fine.

T he well-known adage comes from Friedrich Von Logau's seventeenth-century poem "Retribution". In 1920s Boston, those millstones turned a lot faster. How finely they ground might well be subject to debate.

Judge Lummus wasted no time getting things underway. He ordered the prosecutor and the defense attorneys to attend a pre-trial conference that very afternoon, only a few hours after the grand jury handed down the second set of indictments. Tom O'Brien opened the proceedings by telling the group that Assistant District Attorney George Alpert would head the prosecution team. Alpert then announced that he planned to ignore the first set of indictments, and would try the defendants on the latest ones. No one in the room—at least none of the defense attorneys—was prepared for what he said next. Alpert asked the judge to set the trial date for Wednesday, July 22. That was only nine days away. That little bombshell set off a heated, two-hour squabble during which each and every defense counselor told Lummus he couldn't possibly prepare a proper defense in such a short time. Each one asked that the trial be delayed by anywhere from ten to thirty days. Joseph O'Connell, the defense counsel for James Hendrick, was particularly vocal. He said the court would be sacrificing the defendants on the altar of justice if it brought them to trial with such short notice. Elisha Greenhood, who represented Hyman Bloomberg, accused the court of trying to "railroad" the defendants.

The judge rejected every argument against the rush to trial, and denied every request for a postponement. If the defense lawyers thought things could not possibly get any worse, they were mistaken. Lummus set the trial's opening date for Monday, July 20. That was two days earlier than what Alpert had requested. The defense attorneys did gain one small victory—Lummus extended the time limit for filing dilatory pleas from four o'clock that afternoon until ten o'clock the following morning.

All but one of the defense attorneys were back in court the next morning to argue those pleas. Joseph O'Connell had been there the day before as counsel for James Hendrick, the Boston building inspector, but he had to make a hurried trip to New York for an emergency meeting several hours later. His brother James appeared in his place and requested additional time to file a plea. Judge Lummus extended the time limit from ten o'clock in the morning until four o'clock that afternoon.

Edward Roemer's defense counsel filed a motion to quash the manslaughter indictments. He told the court that the Boston police officer who escorted the grand jurors from the courthouse to the collapse site, and then to lunch at the Hotel Bellevue, made several arbitrary and subjective comments during the course of the journey. The officer's name was George McCaffrey, and he was on a temporary assignment with the Suffolk County District Attorney's office. Roemer's attorney felt McCaffrey's actions might have influenced the grand jurors, and violated the constitutional rights of every defendant. James Hendrick's attorney filed a similar motion, as did Samuel Rosenthal, the defense counsel for Hyman Bloomberg.

Albert Hurwitz filed a bill of particulars on behalf of Nathan Ginsberg that also covered defendants Bloomberg and Fritz. Hurwitz demanded the government state exactly where Paul Halleran was when the building collapsed. "We have a right to know," Hurwitz said. "He may have been there as a trespasser, or in the course of his duty, or as a chance visitor. We are accused of having killed him, and we don't even know where he was, or why he was there."

Defense attorneys also sought to have the cases tried individually rather than together, and the lawyers who represented John Pultz and Harry Haven told the court their clients wished to waive their right to a jury trial, and let a Superior Court judge decide their fate. Judge Lummus listened to every argument, and once again denied each one. The indictments would stand, and the defendants would be tried together before a jury as scheduled on Monday, July 20. The prosecution and the defense had less than six days to prepare for trial—and two of those days fell on a weekend.

The defense attorneys faced an enormous challenge. They couldn't present a unified or common defense since their clients, in many cases, didn't know one another, and each one had a different tie to the fallen building. In those precious few days, defense attorneys had to research similar cases, locate and hire consulting engineers and expert witnesses, and spend a considerable amount of time with their clients reviewing each and every action that might convey even the slightest hint of negligence.

At some point, Edward Roemer and James Hendrick realized they were the only defendants who were paying the attorney fees out of their own pockets. Everyone else was getting free legal counsel from their employer, or from the business they owned. The two Building Department employees thought the city should pick up the tab for their legal fees, but the mayor was hesitant. He was afraid someone could hold the city liable for damages in a subsequent civil suit if it provided legal counsel to an employee in a criminal trial, and the employee was found guilty. Boston Assistant Corporation Counsel Hale Power assured the mayor he had no reason to worry. Curley then went before the City Council and requested a $7,500 appropriation to defray Roemer and Hendrick's legal costs. One councilor asked the mayor why he didn't make use of the city's law department. Curley said the two men had acted quickly and hired attorneys on their own, and it might harm their defense efforts if they changed attorneys only a few days before the trial.

Many Bostonians thought the grand jurors had completed their investigation into the collapse when they handed down the additional bills of indictment on July 13. The jury was, in fact, still in session over at Pemberton Square, and the jurors continued to look into the collapse. Their investigation finally ended three days later when Tom O'Brien asked them to return bills of indictment against six more men:

Charles R. Gow, the titular head of the Charles R. Gow Company.

Chapter Thirteen

John H. Mahoney, the Building Commissioner of the City of Boston.

Joseph A. Tomasello, a subcontractor hired to excavate the foundation for the new garage.

Nathan Ginsberg, the executor of the estate of the Beach Street property's former owner. Ginsberg was already facing a manslaughter charge in connection with the death of Patrolman Paul Halleran.

Charles A. Leary, the general superintendent of the Charles R. Gow Company.

Charles E. Kendall, an engineer employed by Haven & Hopkins.

The jurors may have had second thoughts about having indicted seemingly almost everyone who had some link to the fallen building. After a short deliberation, they said no to every one of the additional indictment requests.

O'Brien's attempt to seek an indictment against Charles Gow is puzzling, since Gow had sold his business to the Raymond Concrete Pile Company three years earlier, and had all but severed his relationship with his former company.

Trial jurors in the 1920s didn't get anywhere near the advance warning that today's jurors do. On Saturday morning, July 18, just two days before the trial was to get underway, Assistant City Clerk Wilfred Doyle walked into the Boston City Council chambers where a special meeting was in progress. While City Councilor James Watson looked on, Doyle drew sixty names from a rotating drum. Each one was a male resident of Suffolk County, and they made up the jury pool for Monday's trial. Doyle then sent the names by messenger to the Suffolk County

Superior Criminal Court clerk. The next day, deputies fanned out across the county, delivering summonses by hand to every member of the jury pool. Courtroom observers couldn't remember the last time anyone served a summons on Sunday.

The jury selection process got underway on Monday morning. Finding twelve men who claimed to be unbiased proved to be quite a challenge. Almost every one of the prospective jurors said they had read about the collapse, and almost every one said it would be difficult for them to be open-minded and impartial. It was almost three o'clock before the prosecution and defense agreed on the last juror. Judge Lummus then adjourned the trial until Wednesday morning, but he told the jurors to report the next day as scheduled. He wanted them to visit the site of the collapse before they heard any testimony.

The trial got off to a chaotic start on Wednesday morning. The designated courtroom proved to be way too small. The jurors weren't affected—they had an enclosed jury box—but there wasn't enough space in the cramped chamber for twelve defendants, their attorneys, the prosecution team, court officials, reporters, and the handful of spectators who managed to squeeze in.

At one point, a court officer stepped into the room and said the trial would be moved to a larger courtroom down the hall. That led to a stampede along the corridor. The new courtroom was larger, but it was also bare. There wasn't a table or chair to be found anywhere in the room. A few minutes later, another court official appeared and told the crowd to go back to the original courtroom. It would have to make do, at least for the rest of the day. Several reporters said the room was so crowded that when an attorney wished to speak, he had to wait until others at the table moved their chairs so he could slide his chair back and stand.

Superior Court Associate Justice Henry Lummus (left), and
District Attorney Thomas O'Brien.

Judge Lummus opened the proceedings with a thirty-five-mi-
nute address to the jurors. He stressed the importance of disre-
garding personal feelings and public opinion, and he told them
they needed to concentrate on the evidence, and only on the evidence. It was quarter past eleven when he finished, and time for
the prosecution to make their opening statement. An assistant
district attorney usually handles the task, but Tom O'Brien decided to speak to the jurors himself. During the next twenty-five
minutes, he tried to link each defendant to the collapse.

He began by detailing the Beach Street property's convoluted
leasing and subleasing arrangement, and he described the roles
of Hyman Bloomberg and Nathan Ginsberg. The district attorney next described the April fire in detail, and he said defendants

Hendrick and Funk inspected the building soon afterward—Hendrick in his capacity as a city inspector, Funk while preparing drawings for a replacement roof. He said the Rosenthal estate hired defendant Nathan Fritz to rebuild the fire-damaged roof. He then moved on to the parking garage next door, and he linked four defendants to that project. Haven was the architect; Pultz was the contractor, and Tobin and Perkins were his employees. He told the jurors that taking down the two existing buildings had weakened the walls of three adjoining structures, and he said engineers recommended bracing the affected walls to make up for the lack of lateral support. O'Brien claimed that defendant Roemer was well aware of the Pickwick Club building's unstable condition at the time.

O'Brien didn't tell the jurors that Hyman Bloomberg had ambitious plans for the Pickwick Club building. In all probability, he wasn't even aware of those plans, but city records show that Bloomberg wanted to make several major changes to the building in the months that preceded the collapse. In October 1924, he sought permission to construct a new enclosed stairway from the third floor to the roof. The application noted that he intended to renovate the top three floors and use them for offices. He withdrew the application a few weeks later. He said he changed his mind, and decided against going forward with the project.

Bloomberg applied for another permit on February 27, 1925—just a few days after the Pickwick Club moved upstairs to the second floor. He wanted to remove a sixteen-foot partition and reposition it three feet away. The Building Department turned down his application on March 6. Their reason for rejection ends with an ominous, hand-written notation that never surfaced during the course of the criminal trial. The notation read,

Chapter Thirteen

"Is this to be used as a dance hall? If so, live load of party [wall] and exits are required." In other words, the Building Department said Bloomberg could not use the second floor as a dance hall until he satisfied the department that the party wall, the staircase, and the fire escape could support the weight of the occupants. None of the Boston newspapers reported the permit rejection or the ban on using the space as a dance hall. I spotted the penciled notation by chance while I was reviewing the building's numerous permit applications in the city archives. Nowhere is there any indication that Bloomberg ever complied with the Building Department's requirement.

Bloomberg was back at city hall a week later, seeking yet another building permit. He wanted to install a ten-passenger elevator to serve all five floors. The city granted the permit on March 20, 1925 but the fire that gutted the upper floors three weeks later put that project on an indefinite hold. Boston newspapers made no mention of Bloomberg's multiple building permit applications.

If anyone in the courtroom was beginning to feel the first pangs of hunger, they must have been gladdened when they heard the defense planned to forego the traditional opening statement. Any hopes for an early lunch break were dashed, however, when Judge Lummus told the prosecution to call their first witness. Boston Fire Department Chief Daniel Sennott rose and took the stand.

George Alpert began by asking several questions about the collapse. What time did the alarm come in? How long did it take the first piece of fire apparatus to reach Beach Street? How many firefighters and how many pieces of equipment responded? He then asked Sennott to step over to a scale model of the building and describe the scene in detail.

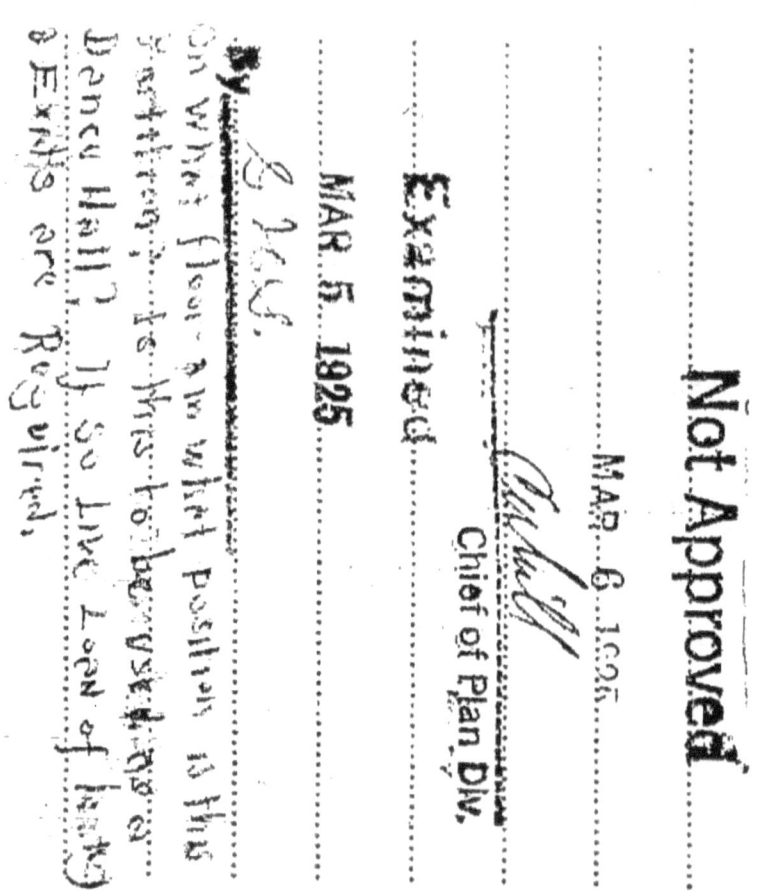

Boston Building Department's permit application refusal
that noted: "Is this to be used as a dance hall? If so, live load
of party [wall] and exits are required."

Chapter Thirteen

Judge Lummus interrupted him and said it was time to recess the proceedings. Sennott's description could wait until after lunch. He also told the prosecution team and the defense attorneys to stay behind for a few minutes. No one ever disclosed what transpired at that meeting, but it lasted for most of the noon recess. When the trial reconvened after lunch, the judge made an announcement—the jurors were to disregard any comments about the composition of the support piers or the condition of the wall that they may have heard during their visit to Beach Street the day before.

Sennott resumed his testimony, and used the scale model to point out various parts of the building, including the wall that leaned out over the sidewalk. He said he remained at the scene for almost twenty-four hours, until quarter of three Sunday morning. Alpert then asked about the April 13 fire. Sennott said it began on the third floor shortly after nine o'clock that night. The floor was unused except for two restrooms at one end of the corridor, and a tailor shop that occupied two of the former small, private dining rooms. The fourth and fifth floors were vacant. Sennott said it took about thirty minutes to extinguish the fire, but his men remained on the scene for another two hours.

When the assistant district attorney finally said "no further questions," the judge made another announcement. All cross-examinations were to take place in the order in which the defendants were listed. One by one, each defense attorney said he had no questions until it was Daniel J. Gallagher's turn. Gallagher was a former US Attorney for Massachusetts, and no stranger to controversy. His short stint as the state's top federal law enforcement official was marked by several allegations of misconduct. A few years earlier, Massachusetts prosecutors had named him an unindicted co-conspirator in a blackmail scandal that saw the state's highest court oust the district attorneys of Middlesex and Suffolk counties. Gallagher was in court that day as the defense counsel for John Tobin and Lawrence Perkins. He told the judge he was going to pass, but he might want to recall Sennott later. Lummus said no. "If you have any questions, ask them now. Otherwise it will cause undue confusion."

Gallagher walked over to the witness stand.

"How did the amount of damage stack up against the assessed value of the building as a percentage?" he asked

Alpert immediately jumped to his feet and shouted, "Objection. The question is irrelevant."

Lummus asked Gallagher what he hoped to determine by asking the question.

"There is an ordinance that states that a building has to be condemned and torn down if damage from a fire exceeds a certain percent of the value."

The judge overruled Alpert and told Sennott to answer the question.

"I don't know what the percentage was, but it wasn't anywhere near enough to condemn the building."

"How much water did you pour on the roof?"

"About 3,000 gallons, I imagine."

The prosecution and defense seemed obsessed with determining exactly how much water firefighters had poured on the building that night. The next day Alpert called no fewer than eleven of them to try and answer that question. When the last one stepped down that afternoon, the only thing prosecutors learned was that the eleven men had no idea how much water they used. While Chief Sennott thought it was about 3,000 gallons, some of his crew believed they used three times that much. Testimony in the days to come revealed that the water used to

Chapter Thirteen

fight the April fire played no part whatsoever in the building collapse, but Alpert's dogged determination to determine the exact amount suggests that prosecutors went to trial without having a clear understanding of why the building fell.

George Callahan took the stand after the last fireman returned to his seat. He was one of the club's two doormen who were on duty at the time of the collapse. Callahan was at the outside street door; Rocco Scarparto was at the upstairs door at the second floor landing. Callahan said he started work at eleven o'clock that night, and at least 150 people entered the club while he was at the front door. He couldn't say how many were still inside when the crash occurred. As to the crowd, they were "a good, agreeable class of people." There was dancing, he said, but no jumping. He also said he heard what sounded like firecrackers coming from inside the building. "One or two went off, then another one, and then one more. They sounded like two-inch cannon crackers."

Orchestra leader Billy Glennon testified next. He told Alpert he had worked at the club for eight months. He said the dance floor measured about fifteen by thirty-five feet, and had a linoleum covering. He guessed there were about forty tables in the room.

"Didn't you tell the grand jury there were close to sixty tables in the room that night?" Alpert asked.

"No, I did not."

Judge Lummus asked him how many people danced the last dance.

"Eight couples, possibly ten."

Glennon held fast to his low estimate of the number of dancers during the subsequent cross-examination. He told James Hendrick's defense counsel that normally only a few couples got up and danced. Most people remained at the tables.

Thomas Creed, the defense attorney for the Barry brothers, questioned him about the dancing that night. "There was nothing unusual about it," Glennon replied. "The music and the dancing were the same as any other night. There was no stamping or jumping in that last dance." Glennon said about 125 patrons were there earlier, but a few of them had left.

Waiter Harris "Mike" Hirshberg followed Glennon to the stand. He said there were only thirty-three tables in the room, but he placed a lot more people on the dance floor than Glennon did. He said he often saw as many as forty couples out there at the same time. As for the night of the collapse, Hirshberg said the dancing was ordinary ballroom dancing. "If it hadn't been, we would have stopped it," he added. Hirshberg thought there were between ninety and one hundred people in the club when the disaster struck, or about twice the normal crowd. He said the crowds had been running small recently.

Earl Davis was the club's busboy. He told Alpert the crowd had already begun to thin. There were perhaps 125 people in the club earlier in the evening; about 100 were still inside when the floor gave way.

Survivors who spoke with reporters the day after the collapse told a different story. All of them agreed the dance floor was crowded. Frank Decker said there were fifty couples on the floor, all of them leaping up and down in unison. Glennon's own trumpet player said he had never seen so many couples dancing. "Most people knew the song and liked to dance to it, and the dance space was packed," he added. None of the survivors mentioned "ballroom dancing". Anna McKee, the club's coatroom attendant, told a reporter from the *Boston Herald*, "Extra tables had been brought in that night, the crowd was so large. There were even tables in front of the bar."

Chapter Thirteen

It is apparent that someone had a few words with the employees before they testified—someone who was not happy to hear the mayor place the blame on overcrowding, or to read survivor claims that wild, energetic dancing had triggered the collapse. Perhaps it was someone who knew they were supposed to have verified that the party wall and the interior and exterior exits could support the weight of the crowd. One thing that employees and patrons did agree on, however, was that the Barry brothers were not in the club that night. Daniel Barry hadn't been there for almost two weeks.

The testimony had been rather humdrum until that point, despite a few skirmishes and the noticeable discrepancy between what the employees and the survivors claimed to remember. Courtroom observers didn't know it, but that was about to change. Alpert's next witness was Boston Building Commissioner John Mahoney, and two of his employees were on trial in that courtroom, charged with manslaughter for failing to spot the structural weaknesses that led to the collapse.

Alpert began by asking Mahoney about his background. The commissioner said he started working in the building department in 1892, and he held a variety of positions before he moved up to his current post in May 1921. Alpert then asked about defendant Roemer. Mahoney said he was the supervisor of construction, and a valuable member of the department. As supervisor of construction, he reviewed complaints from inspectors, checked soil conditions for load bearing ability, and he assigned concrete inspectors to building projects. Mahoney said that Roemer made frequent trips to New York to keep abreast of the latest developments in construction materials, and to conduct fire and water tests at Columbia University. He occasionally sat in on hearings in Mahoney's place when the commissioner was attending a convention. Mahoney added that those out-of-town trips were his only vacations.

"Have you referred to Mr. Roemer from time to time as the chief building inspector?" Alpert asked.

"I may have, to people who wouldn't understand what supervisor of construction means."

"Do any of Roemer's duties call for him to inspect buildings?"

"Yes, he may go with one of the inspectors. That is one of his duties."

"And what are Inspector Hendrick's duties?"

"Objection," shouted Joseph O'Connell, Hendrick's defense attorney. "His duties are clearly defined by statute."

"I think we would like to know what Mr. Hendrick does. Your objection is overruled," Lummus replied.

"He inspects buildings for alterations or new construction to see if they conform to statute," Mahoney said.

"Does he inspect both the inside and outside of buildings?"

"Objection," O'Connell shouted.

"Overruled," Lummus said.

"Yes, inside and outside."

O'Connell continued to object to almost every question that Alpert put to Mahoney, and Lummus overruled him every time. Sometimes he didn't even wait for O'Connell to finish stating the reason for his objection. The string of constant objections lasted until Mahoney's testimony moved on to the history of the building. He said his staff couldn't locate any plans or permits for the building's construction, but he was certain it was built sometime prior to 1871. When Mahoney finally stepped down, Judge Lummus recessed the trial for the weekend.

Chapter Thirteen

Demolition contractor Thomas Elston was the leadoff witness when the trial resumed on Monday morning. The prosecution focused most of their questions on the condition of the party wall (the sidewall of the Pickwick Club building that rested against the building next door). Elston said he thought it was structurally unsound. He told Alpert there had been five interior doorways between the two buildings. When his men began to brick up the openings, they discovered the sidewall of the Pickwick Club building was actually two walls—an eight-inch-thick outside wall and a twelve-inch-thick inside wall. There were no tie irons between them. Elston said he mentioned this to Harry Haven, the garage project architect. Haven asked him if his crew could bore a test hole through the two walls at ground level. When the test hole showed there were tie irons between the two walls at that level, Haven said he didn't think there would be any problem if they left the sidewall in place.

"Well, you'll have one hell of a time keeping it up if it isn't tied together," Elston remembered telling Haven.

Alpert recalled Commissioner Mahoney after Elston stepped down. The rest of the day's testimony dealt with the concrete underpinnings. Alpert questioned Mahoney at length about the need for them, and the techniques used to build them.

Elston was back on the witness stand the next day for cross-examination. Defense attorneys grilled him about his testimony the day before, and got him to admit several times that his recollection of events differed from what he had said previously. He told Daniel Gallagher that he was mistaken when he testified there was only an eighteen-inch difference in height between the five-story Pickwick Club building and the six-story building his firm was demolishing next door.

"You also told us yesterday there were no tie irons in the

Pickwick Club building above the first floor. Are you still positive, or was that a mistake too?"

Judge Lummus interrupted. "Mr. Elston does not have to tell the court he didn't make a mistake." He turned to Elston and said, "You can answer the question by saying whether or not you are still positive."

Elston said he was.

Defense counselors continued to question Elston's insistence that there were no tie rods in the doomed building above the first floor. When it came time for redirect, George Alpert asked him about the work he had done on the day of the collapse. The defense objected; Lummus again overruled them.

"I helped bring some bodies out, then I removed some debris and I pulled down the front wall."

"Did you see any tie irons in the debris?" Alpert asked.

"No."

Judge Lummus spoke up. "You weren't looking for tie irons, were you?"

"Yes, I was."

Joseph O'Connell asked, "Do you mean to tell us that while there were still dead bodies in the ruins, you were looking for tie rods?"

"Yes."

The subject of tie rods came up repeatedly during the course of the trial. Some witnesses swore they had seen them; others swore they could find no evidence of them. A quick look at the building's original plans would have put the matter to rest, but the Building Commission didn't have a copy of the plans on file. The matter was never resolved.

Charles Kendall took the witness stand when Elston stepped down. The Wollaston resident was a structural engineer employed by Haven & Hopkins. Much of his testimony dealt with the April fire. Kendall and Chief Sennott clearly didn't see eye-to-eye on the damage it caused. Sennott had told the court that while some of the beams were badly charred, the roof was strong enough to support several men. Kendall didn't agree. He testified that it was "very badly burned," and he said he could feel it sag when he walked on it.

"You weren't very enthusiastic about walking on it then?" Alpert asked.

Three defense attorneys rose to their feet to object, but they were laughing as they did so. Lummus told Kendall to answer the question.

"Not enthusiastic at all."

Kendall told the court the fire caused extensive damage to the upper two floors—especially the top floor. The blaze charred the staircase from the third to the fourth floor, and almost destroyed the one that led from the fourth to the fifth floor. The only things left were the two stringers. The flames burned the treads and risers almost completely away, and destroyed some of the floorboards.

Kendall said he met with Edward Roemer at City Hall on April 23 or 24—he couldn't remember the exact date—and told him his firm was constructing a garage next door to the fire-damaged building. He said he was concerned the fire had weakened its structural integrity, and wondered if someone could stop by and take a look. Roemer called James Hendrick and told him to inspect the building right away. Hendrick arrived about two hours later, and Kendall accompanied him while he spent about an hour examining both the inside and outside of the structure. When he finished, Hendrick told Kendall he thought it was safe, and there was no cause for worry.

Insurance appraiser Oliver Johnson's testimony corroborated Kendall's assessment of the fire damage. Johnson considered the building a total loss above the third floor. He told the court his big concern was the east-facing wall—the one that collapsed into the excavation next door. His impression was the wall was "wavy", but he wouldn't go so far as to say it was out-of-plumb.

"Did you tell Mr. Funk it was a terrible wall, and it would be quite a job to underpin it?" Alpert asked.

"I think I did."

Joseph O'Connell asked, "But you still passed this wall as structurally sound?"

"As far as fire damage was concerned, it was sound."

The prosecution called a surprise witness on Thursday. John O'Connor of Jamaica Plain was a retired concrete contractor. He testified that he happened to be on Beach Street in May when he noticed several cracks in the front wall of the Pickwick Club building. One ran from the top of a second story window up to the third story windowsill. Similar cracks ran from the third to the fourth floor, and from the fourth floor to the fifth. The cracks didn't break any of the bricks, they just separated them. O'Connor said he passed the building again on July 2, and noticed the cracks were somewhat wider. The stone lintel over a second story window was cracked right through. He went back to the site the next day and looked at the excavation next door. It was about fifty feet wide, and went down about five or six feet below the foundation. It was close enough to the Pickwick Club building that he could see the concrete piers. When it was his time for cross-examination, Joseph O'Connell asked, "Did you go down there as an idle curiosity seeker?"

"No. I was interested in how they were going to hold that

building up when they built the garage."

"When you first saw the cracks, did you think they made the building unsafe?"

"No."

"Did you consider it unsafe on July 2?"

"Yes."

"Did you say anything?"

"No."

"You thought the building was unsafe, but you didn't say anything?"

"There were inspectors there, and I didn't think it was any of my business."

The trial was already in its eleventh day, and the only hint of possible negligence to emerge was the revelation that Harry Haven ignored Elston's warning about the lack of bonding in the party wall. Some might say John O'Connor should have voiced his concerns, but he was not on trial. What's more, it was becoming apparent that prosecutors had no idea what caused the collapse. Without that knowledge, there was little hope they could convince the jurors of anyone's negligence. That was about to change as Alpert called his next witness.

DEATHTRAP

| FOURTEEN |

Martin Kane was sitting on a bench in the corridor outside the courtroom when a court officer opened the door and called his name. Kane was a long-time career employee of the City of Boston, and the testimony he was about to give marked a turning point in the proceedings. For the remainder of the trial, both prosecution and defense focused their attention almost exclusively on the Pickwick Club building's support piers.

The seventy-year-old East Boston man told Alpert that work on underpinning the Pickwick Club building began on May 16, and ended on May 25. Kane then described the process for constructing concrete support piers under a building, and went on to explain how construction workers mixed the concrete. They shoveled two wheelbarrows full of crushed rock, one wheelbarrow full of sand, and half a wheelbarrow full of cement into a machine that resembled a large rotating barrel, and then added water as the barrel rotated. When the mix reached the desired consistency, they poured it down a chute into a wooden form.

James Hendrick's attorney could hardly wait to begin his cross-examination. Joseph O'Connell began by reading a section of the Massachusetts law that mandates daily reports of concrete inspections.

"Did you make those reports every day?" he asked Kane.

"No. I made the reports when the job was finished."

"Did you swear to them?"

"Yes, I did," Kane answered, while he raised his right hand as though he wished to convince any skeptic that his reports contained nothing but the truth.

"Where are they now?"

"I don't know."

"How could you remember every detail if you didn't submit your reports until the job was finished?"

"I used the notes from my memorandum book." He reached into his pocket and produced the book.

Francis Garland, the defense counsel for Harry Haven, raised more questions about those reports during his cross-examination.

"Have some of those figures been changed since you submitted them?" he asked.

"I don't think they have been changed," Kane replied.

"Did you use two different pencils when you filled out a report?"

"No, absolutely not."

Garland then showed him entry after entry where someone had used two distinctly different pencils to enter the figures. Kane couldn't offer any explanation. Garland then passed each report to the jurors for their examination.

He went on to question Kane about the measurements in

those reports, especially the one concerning the sixth pier where the report stated the pier was two feet by ten feet. Kane looked at the report and told Garland the figures were wrong.

"Did you measure the pier, or did one of Gow's men?"

"I don't know where I got the measurement, but it's there."

"You realize those piers were supposed to be three feet wide, and if the bottom of that pier was only two feet wide, it wasn't laid according to the plan?"

"I know that."

"And you don't remember how you came up with the two-foot measurement?"

"I might have guessed."

Charles Leary followed Kane to the witness stand. Leary was the general manager of the Charles Gow Company, and he told Alpert that workers used what he called "a strong mixture" of sand and cement as they neared the foundation. It contained no gravel or stone. Once again, Garland was ready with some questions when it came time to cross-examine. He asked Leary if he read the contract between his employer and the Pultz Company.

"No. I referred it to Mr. White."

"Did you realize your firm was obliged to conform to the specifications of the contract?"

"Yes, of course I did."

Garland then showed him the plan for the piers and asked what the three-foot dimension meant.

"I don't know," Leary replied.

"It's the width of the pier, isn't it?"

"It doesn't say so."

"When you began this job, did you intend to make the piers only two feet wide?"

"Yes."

"Did you measure the piers after the collapse?"

"Yes."

"Were they three feet wide?"

"No, several of them were two feet, three inches wide."

Joseph O'Connell then took over the cross-examination. "What exactly is a 'Gow caisson'?" he asked. Leary told him it was a series of telescoping steel cylinders. Construction workers drove them into the ground, and then filled them with concrete.

"Did your company place Gow caissons under the Pickwick Club building?"

"No. The piers we built are called 'spread footings'."

"The proposal mentioned using Gow caissons, did it not?"

"I don't know. I worked from a plan, not from a proposal."

Clifford White, the Gow Company contract negotiator, took the stand next. He said the original proposal called for piers two feet by ten feet. Garland asked him if he read the section of the contract that specified the dimensions of the piers. White said no, he hadn't. Garland then handed him a copy of the contract and asked him to read the section in question. White took a quick look and then said he was apparently mistaken. The piers should have been three feet wide, not two feet.

"Are you familiar with the law that specifies that any alteration to the original plans must be submitted to the Boston Building Department?"

"Yes, I am."

"Did anyone in your organization tell the city that your company was not going to adhere to the three-foot specifications?"

"I don't know."

Daniel Gallagher had several more questions about the contract. When he asked White about some particular wording, White replied, "My job is to get new business. I didn't draw up the contract."

"Did you read it (the contract) before you sent it on for someone to sign?"

"I looked it over."

"Was there any reason," Gallagher asked him, "why it wasn't signed until June 1, a week after the work was completed?"

"Mr. Hart was out of town."

"Who took the responsibility of having the work go forward without a signed contract?"

White hesitated for some time before answering, "Mr. Leary did."

Alpert then called Lyton Hart, the vice president of the Gow Company. Hart admitted it was rather unusual to delay signing a contract until after the job was complete, but it was not unheard of. He assumed the contract he signed accurately described the work his company had already performed. No one in his organization told him otherwise.

Monday, August 3, marked the start of the third week of the trial. Charles Bliss of Whitcomb & Company was the principal witness that day. He spent a good part of his time on the stand describing the building's complex lease arrangement that required Hyman Bloomberg, the lessee, to pick up the cost of the monthly insurance premiums. Bliss said he met with Bloomberg on April 15, two days after the fire, and told him that Whitcomb considered the building unfit for occupancy. Bloomberg reminded him that he had already paid the rent for the entire month of April, and he told Bliss he wanted a refund from April 13, the day of the fire, to the end of the month. Bliss said no, Whitcomb would not issue a refund, but they would give him a credit that he could apply against a future rental payment.

During cross-examination by Thomas Creed, the defense counsel for the Barry brothers, Bliss told Creed he walked through the building after the fire.

"Did you spend any time on the second floor?"

"Yes."

"Was the Pickwick Club using that floor?"

"I suspected they might be."

"Did you notify any official of the Pickwick Club that the building was unfit for occupancy?"

"No."

"Did your rent collector tell you about the first of May that he had a talk with Timothy Barry?"

"I don't recall."

The prosecution introduced one other significant piece of evidence that day—a letter that Haven & Hopkins had sent to Whitcomb & Company. It contained a detailed description of the work they intended to do on the adjoining lot, and included the words, "we are taking every precaution necessary for the safety of the party wall." The letter bore defendant Harry Haven's signature.

The prosecution called several consulting engineers on Tuesday. One of them dropped a bombshell when he took the stand.

Guy Emerson's credentials read like he had just stepped from the pages of *Who's Who in Civil Engineering*. He graduated from MIT in 1890, and was a member of both the Boston and the American Societies of Civil Engineers. He designed the retaining walls of the nation's first subway tunnel under Tremont Street in Boston back in 1897. He went on to design tunnels throughout the US and Canada. He also happened to be an acquaintance of Charles Gow, the founder of the company that constructed the piers in question. In 1912, the two men served together on a commission that developed long-range plans to provide an adequate water supply to the city of Salem, Massachusetts.

"The collapse of the Pickwick Club building was due to a failure of the concrete piers under the foundation," he told the court. "Those piers failed due to a lack of lateral bracing on their easterly side." That was the side that faced the excavation next door. In non-technical language, Emerson said the wall collapsed because its support piers gave way and fell forward, and they were able to do that because the excavation work had removed the soil from in front of them. Without that soil, there was nothing to keep them in place. In two short sentences, Emerson exonerated his friend's business firm, and pinned the blame for the collapse on the people who were building the garage.

The judge allowed Emerson to proceed with his testimony despite outcries from several defense attorneys. Emerson went on to describe the soil under the piers as soft clay, and he said the vertical load on those piers was at least four tons per square foot.

Joseph O'Connell went on the warpath when it was his turn to cross-examine, and Lummus had to stop him several times. One time he told O'Connell his question was silly; another time he remarked, "I can answer that question myself." At one point, O'Connell asked Emerson, "If the cement that was used in building the piers varied in mixture, wouldn't the piers also vary in strength?" Lummus interrupted, "You don't need to question a witness to establish something like that."

Consulting engineer John DeWolfe of Winchester took the witness stand when the trial resumed on Wednesday. He agreed with Emerson that pressure from the building's easterly wall caused the piers to tip and that, in turn, caused to foundation to sag and bring down the entire wall. During cross-examination, Francis Garland questioned him about the vertical pressure on the concrete piers. DeWolfe agreed with Emerson that it was about four tons per square foot.

"What would the pressure be if the piers were three feet wide?" Garland asked.

"Two and two tenths tons."

Once again, Joseph O'Connell and Judge Lummus locked horns during O'Connell's cross-examination. At one point Lummus told O'Connell his question was ambiguous.

"The witness understood me," O'Connell said.

"I don't think he understood you any more than I did," Lummus replied.

"Your Honor's interruptions are not helping, and they are making my cross-examination very difficult."

"If your cross-examination was proper, you wouldn't be having trouble with me."

"I have had a lot of experience examining witnesses, and I believe I know what is proper", O'Connell replied.

DeWolfe was back on the stand the next day for more cross-examination. Daniel Gallagher had several questions about the concrete support piers. At one point, he asked DeWolfe about the ingredients in pier two. DeWolfe said the sand, gravel, and cement had not been thoroughly mixed. He went on to tell Gallagher that the concrete mixing machine was not large enough to hold all the material that was needed to make one complete pier, and the construction workers had to pour the concrete into the forms one batch at a time.

"Suppose they couldn't pour the second batch until the first had begun to set. You wouldn't expect a good union, would you?"

"Concrete will not bond if a set has been made."

Alpert called another consulting engineer that afternoon. Bion Bowman said he examined the piers on Sunday, and found that pier one was still practically vertical. The prosecutor asked him what he thought about the quality of the concrete. Bowman said it was "fair". Pier two was broken in half, and badly shattered. Piers three, four, and five were in a similar condition. Pier six was noticeably tilting forward, but not broken; pier seven, like pier one, was practically vertical. He told Alpert that excavating the soil from in front of the piers without having made some provision to brace them was both improper and unsafe.

Alpert called the final prosecution witness when the trial got underway on Friday morning. Professor George Swain was in complete agreement with the engineers who had testified before him. He told Alpert the piers under the wall tipped outward because of earth pressure from behind. There was no soil in front of them to resist that pressure.

The questioning once again became acrimonious when O'Connell began his cross-examination. He asked Swain about his visit to the collapse site, and added, "Did you go there on behalf of (defendant) Nathan Ginsberg?"

"Yes."

"Did you testify before the grand jury?"

"Yes."

"Did you disclose that you were acting for Ginsberg?"

"They didn't ask me."

"When did you become a government expert?"

"I don't remember when I learned that I was to be called."

"Are you now trying to shield Mr. Ginsberg from any responsibility in this case?"

"I am not trying to do anything of the sort."

"Did you go there (Pickwick Club collapse site) with the rest of the experts?"

"I don't know what you mean."

"Perhaps I ought not to have called them experts. I withdraw the term. I mean Mr. Bowman, Mr. DeWolfe, and Mr.–what's the other man's name–oh yes, Emerson."

"No."

"Were you there the same day the jury was, the day I took some concrete in my hands and crumbled it?"

"Now, now, now," Alpert said, "I thought the court has ruled very firmly on that."

"Counsel will make no further reference to this subject," Lummus replied.

It was almost four o'clock when the defense ended their cross-examination. George Alpert then made the long-awaited announcement, "The government rests its case, Your Honor." He no sooner returned to his seat than Attorney Francis Murray stood up and told Judge Lummus that Edward Roemer wanted to rest, and wished to enter a motion for a directed verdict of acquittal. Lummus told the jurors to leave the courtroom. He then asked each defense attorney if his client wished to rest his case without offering any defense. The only attorneys who declined were the men who represented Hendrick and Perkins. Lummus called the jury back into the room and told them:

"Several defendants have rested their cases and asked for a ruling that they cannot be found guilty based on the evidence the Commonwealth has presented, and that verdicts of not guilty be directed. I want to explain to you what a directed verdict is, because I am about to direct a verdict of not guilty in those cases where the defendants rested."

Chapter Fourteen

Lummus went on to explain to the jurors that when the Commonwealth presents evidence that could reasonably bring about a guilty verdict, the court must allow the case to go before the jury, but when that evidence is insufficient to bring about a guilty verdict, it is the duty of the court to direct a verdict of acquittal.

The court then began what the *Boston Globe* termed a "monotonous process". The clerk read the name of the first defendant who had rested his case, and the crime with which he was charged, and asked, "Have you reached a verdict?"

"We have," the jury foreman replied.

"What say you, Mr. Foreman? Is the defendant guilty or not guilty of manslaughter as charged in the indictment?"

"Not guilty."

The clerk and the jury foreman went through the same routine nine more times. After the foreman returned the last verdict, Lummus told the ten men they were free to leave. Each one rose and walked out of the courtroom, leaving only Hendrick and Perkins seated on the long settee.

Lummus spoke to the jury once again and said the actions he had just taken were to have no effect on the two remaining defendants. The two men indicated they wished to put up a defense, and the court had formed no opinion as to whether or not the Commonwealth's evidence was sufficient to warrant a guilty verdict. "You are not to draw any inference in regard to these cases," he said. Before he adjourned the proceedings for the weekend, he said the trial would resume at nine thirty Monday morning, a half hour earlier than usual, and he told the attorneys they could expect the sessions to last later in the afternoon.

The trial went into its fourth week on Monday, August 10. As

Lummus had promised, it began at nine thirty, and ran until six o'clock. The defense spent the entire day refuting the prosecution's claim that lateral pressure and lack of bracing had caused the piers to tilt, and allowed the party wall to crumble and fall.

Boston contractor William Askin was the leadoff witness. He told the court his firm had built several large brick buildings in cities such as Boston, Montreal, and San Francisco. He said he never heard of bracing concrete piers. James Powers, another local builder, followed Askin to the stand. He too said it was never customary to brace the underpinnings. James Bryne, a construction contractor, said the collapse was due to poor composition of the concrete. Shoring or bracing the piers would not have done any good. "My opinion is that the failure of the concrete in pier two caused the collapse," he stated.

Building Commissioner John Mahoney told the court pier two had cracked into pieces, and he was able to crumble some of it in his hand. During cross-examination, he stated that piers three, four, and five had also fractured, but he told Alpert, "On the other piers there was a sharp, clear fracture. Pier two was shattered." When he stepped down, Attorney O'Connell produced a corrugated box that contained several fragments of concrete that he took from the piers. Judge Lummus overruled Alpert's objection and allowed O'Connell to show the pieces to the jurors and let them see that one piece was comprised of nothing but sand and cement. Newspaper reporters never disclosed the reason for Alpert's objection, nor did they mention that Charles Leary, the general manager of the Charles Gow Company, had testified a few days earlier that his firm poured a strong concrete mixture into the tops of the forms, just under the foundation. It contained only sand and cement, and had no gravel or stone.

Chapter Fourteen

Daniel Gallagher then called Louis Ferrara of Pultz & Company to the stand. Ferrara testified that workers from the Charles Gow Company dug holes for the piers without any artificial light, and he said they often poured the concrete down into the darkness. He also told the court he suspected they were sometimes rather careless when they measured the concrete ingredients.

Joseph O'Connell had a few questions when Gallagher finished. For some reason, he repeatedly called Ferrara "Luigi". In answer to one question, Ferrara said he swung a pickaxe at one piece of concrete to see if it was rotten.

"Was it?" O'Connell asked.

"Yes. Any dub could see that."

Lummus told the clerk to strike the last part of the answer from the record.

Gallagher's main witness that day was Lawrence Perkins. The forty-one-year-old Watertown man testified in his own defense, and handled himself very well on the stand. He told Gallagher he had no idea there was any deviation between the plans and the actual piers. As far as he could see, Gow's men poured the concrete in a competent manner. He saw no reason to shore up the wall or install bracing. Alpert waited until after lunch to begin his cross-examination. He asked Perkins if he told the grand jurors that the contract between his company and Tomasello called for the Pultz Company to shore up the excavation walls. Perkins said he did.

"But your firm didn't shore up the wall adjacent to the Pickwick Club Building?"

"We weren't supposed to. The contract only called for shoring up the street side of the excavation. No one ever mentioned shoring up the side that faced the Pickwick Club building."

Alpert then read the section of the building ordinance that required shoring up an excavation wall if there was any danger of collapse.

"Are you familiar with this?"

"Yes, but it only applies to the walls of the excavation, not to the building next door. Besides, there was no danger of the excavation collapsing."

Alpert went on at length about the possibility that the support piers might tip forward, but every time he asked a technical question, Perkins replied, "I don't know. I'm not an engineer."

A chemist from the Watertown Arsenal led off the proceedings on Tuesday. Edwin MacNutt showed the jurors a chunk of concrete that engineers had sent to his lab for analysis. He said there was no bonding whatsoever between the stone and the cement. He told Judge Lummus he had no trouble breaking off the sample piece with an ordinary hammer. As for pier two, he said its composition was primarily sand and cement, and it contained very little gravel.

Retired Major General George Washington Goethals was the star witness that day. Goethals began by stating his credentials. He graduated from West Point in 1880, and then returned to his alma mater a few years later as an engineering instructor. The Army placed him in charge of construction of the Muscle Shoals Canal on the Tennessee River in 1891. In February 1907, President Theodore Roosevelt appointed him chief engineer of the Panama Canal project. He held that position for the seven years it took to complete the forty-mile-long canal. Goethals was the picture of relaxation on the witness stand. He spent very little time in the chair. When he wasn't pacing back and forth in front of it, pointing his index finger to emphasize some particular point, he often sat on the top rail of the witness box, and leaned back on the judge's bench for support while he rested his feet on the bottom rail.

He had nothing but criticism for the concrete mixture in the support piers, and he described pier two as, "the rottenest piece of concrete I ever saw." He went on the say, "There were pockets of gravel in the mixture. The cement was of poor quality, and there wasn't enough of it. When I saw the character of the concrete in pier number two, I judged that it had not been able to support its load, which I figured at 100,000 pounds. It crushed, and threw its load on the other six piers. They, in turn, were unable to support the increased load, which may not have been evenly distributed. The wall above fell and overturned, breaking off the other piers. In my opinion, the collapse was caused by the failure of pier two to carry the load placed upon it. Bracing or shoring would not have prevented the collapse."

During Alpert's entire cross-examination, Goethals never wavered from his opinion that failure of the concrete had caused the collapse. Alpert asked him if the weight of the heavy wall crashing down on top of it might have caused the concrete in pier two to pulverize. "I have seen tons of rock and clay fall down on concrete piers," Goethals replied. "They crack, they break, but they don't pulverize as this one did."

When Goethals stepped down from the witness stand, Joseph O'Connell called James Hendrick to testify in his own defense. Hendrick told O'Connell he was born in County Wexford in Ireland, and his first job in Boston was with the local transit system, the Metropolitan Street Railway. He eventually became a general foreman, and then took the civil service exam and went to work for the city as a building inspector.

He said he inspected the Beach Street building the previous fall when someone sought a permit to put in a flight of stairs, and then once again a few months later when someone wanted to get another permit to install an elevator. He told O'Connell that on both occasions, he thought it was a good building. He went back to check the building two weeks after the fire, and recommended taking down an interior wall, and enclosing the stairs. He inspected the building two more times—on June 30 and then again on July 2. Both visits were to check on the fire repairs. He said the work seemed to be going on according to regulations, and he was satisfied. He thought the wall looked very substantial, and he saw nothing during either visit that indicated there was any danger that it would fall. He told O'Connell he didn't see any cracks in the wall, and there was no need to shore up the underpinnings. He added that he had never seen anyone do that.

When it came time to cross-examine, Alpert had more questions about the support piers.

"Did you examine the piers?"

"Yes."

"Why?"

"To see that they were all right."

"Did you look at pier two?"

"Yes."

"Did you see any evidence of an improper mix?"

"No, it didn't show on the surface."

It was almost three-thirty when Hendrick stepped down, and his attorney told Judge Lummus he wished to rest. Daniel Gallagher stood up and told Lummus he too wished to rest. Lummus then adjourned the trial for the day, and said he would hear closing arguments the next morning.

The prosecution normally goes first when it comes time to make closing arguments. Because the burden of proof rests with the

Boston Building Department inspection report issued in conjunction with a permit request to repair damage caused by the April, 1925 fire in the Pickwick Club building. The remarks are in in James Hendrick's handwriting.

prosecution, it gets a chance to make one final rebuttal after the defense attorneys have made their closing arguments. For reasons that he never disclosed, George Alpert exercised his right to forgo making a closing argument, and instead chose to combine it with his rebuttal and speak last.

Joseph O'Connell was the first of the two defense attorneys to address the jury. Daniel Gallagher made his presentation afterward. George Alpert waited until after lunch to present his closing arguments. Each man summarized the key issues and, not surprisingly, ridiculed the opposition.

O'Connell began by telling the jurors that the grand jury took up the case only two days after the collapse, well before any adequate investigation had even begun. He went on to mock Alpert's expert witnesses, especially Guy Emerson, but he saved his most caustic comments for the Charles Gow Company. They started out with uncertainty, he said, and then went forward with no regard for the basic principles of engineering.

Gallagher likened the collapse of the Beach Street building to the total collapse of the government's case, and he too mocked the prosecution's expert witnesses, particularly Professor George Swain. "They did not come bearing gifts like the wise men of old," he said. "They were working for a per diem. One was wiser than the other two; he got paid by both sides. Now there's a wise man for you."

Alpert was the last man to speak. He began by deriding the defense expert who, as he put it, "referred to the theories and principles of engineering as 'bunk'." During cross-examination the day before, he had asked defense witness James Bryne if he was familiar with the angles of repose of different types of granular materials. The term refers to the steepest angle at which a sloping surface of loose material is stable. Some of the material will begin to slide back down if the angle increases. "I don't fill my head with all that bunk," Bryne replied. The prosecutor also poked fun at General Goethals, and told the jurors:

"The General didn't take into account how long the piers had stood there, and being from West Point, and being in the Army, I didn't think there was much point in trying to change his mind."

Alpert couldn't resist the temptation to take one final shot at his nemesis, Joseph O'Connell. "Experts have told us that compressive strength of concrete can only be determined by laboratory test and yet, during the trial, we have heard from a new expert who thinks it can be determined by throwing it on the floor, or crumbling it in his hands."

It was almost three o'clock when Alpert sat down, and Judge Lummus began his charge to the jurors. He said the public oftentimes demands vengeance after a catastrophe, but the court had no duty to seek such vengeance. The trial was not an inquest, nor was it an inquiry to determine the cause of the collapse. The jury's duty was limited to the actions of the two defendants. The jurors were merely to decide if anything that either of them did amounted to criminal negligence. Lummus went on to tell the jurors that death could result from accident through no one's fault. In that case, there would be no liability under law. It could result from negligence, either ordinary or gross, in which case the person responsible would be liable to civil action for damages. It could result from wanton or reckless conduct that would render the responsible person liable under both criminal and civil law. Lastly, it could be deliberate, either with or without premeditation. The legal term for deliberately taking a life under those circumstances is murder. He ended by defining the term "reasonable doubt", and then sent the jurors out to deliberate.

They reached a verdict less than forty minutes later. The two defendants, James Hendrick and Lawrence Perkins, were not guilty. Lummus congratulated the jurors on their verdict and added: "I am now free to say that if I had been a member of the jury, I would have joined in your verdict. There never was sufficient evidence that these defendants had been willfully, recklessly, or wantonly negligent."

Tom O'Brien did not take kindly to losing, and he had just suffered his third setback. The first loss came on July 16 when the grand jury refused his request to indict an additional six men. Then Judge Lummus dismissed the criminal charges against ten of the twelve defendants with the comment that the prosecution had not presented any evidence that could bring about a guilty verdict. Now, the jury had not only acquitted the remaining two, but the judge once again faulted the prosecution for not producing sufficient evidence. All that work, and not one single conviction. O'Brien was not a happy man. With little fanfare, he impaneled another grand jury and began to take yet another look into the Pickwick Club collapse. On August 25, that jury returned manslaughter indictments against five more men, this time in connection with the death of Edith Jordan:

Lyton Hart, vice president of the Charles R. Gow Company.

Charles A. Leary, general superintendent of the Charles R. Gow Company.

Nicholas Corrangelo, a foreman with the Charles R. Gow Company.

Martin M. Kane, a concrete inspector for the City of Boston.

Thomas E. Booth, an employee of Haven & Hopkins.

The five men came to the courthouse over the course of the

next few days. Each one pled not guilty and posted bail. The bail for four of the defendants was $2,500 but, for some reason, Corrangelo's bail was $3,500.

The latest round of indictments didn't garner anywhere near the press coverage that the original ones received. O'Brien appeared to be in no hurry to bring the men before a jury. The defendants were still awaiting trial four months later when a superior court judge approved Martin Kane's petition to remove Warren Patten as his defense counselor. Kane claimed that Mayor Curley had retained Patten without his consent.

O'Brien began to have second thoughts about the matter early in 1926, and he finally decided against bringing the defendants to trial. His office then quietly dropped all of the charges. That ended the criminal prosecutions. No one stood convicted of any wrongdoing. No one paid a fine, or spent even one day in prison. No one ever received as much as a slap on the wrist for anything they did—or failed to do. What's more, no one in a position of authority appeared to have any interest in finding out why the old building fell without warning. Neither the city nor the state ever conducted an investigation, or held a public hearing to look into the cause of the collapse. All the heated rhetoric about flushing out every guilty party, and handing down a quick and just punishment had been for naught. There was still hope for some justice, however. While the criminal cases were over, the civil cases had just begun.

*   *   *

On September 16, 1925, barely ten weeks after the collapse, Helen Flanagan's attorney walked into the Middlesex County Superior Courthouse in Cambridge and filed damage suits against two of the business firms that were working on the garage next door to the Pickwick Club. Mrs. Flanagan claimed the managers of the two firms had failed to take reasonable precautions to safeguard the Pickwick Club building. She believed their negligence was responsible for the building's collapse, and the loss her husband's life. She sought $15,000 in damages from each defendant. They were the first of what eventually grew to 164 separate civil suits filed against ten defendants. The plaintiffs sought more than $6.1 million in aggregated damages for deaths, injuries, and loss of personal property. That's the equivalent of about $85 million in today's dollars.

Unlike the rush to trial after the first round of criminal indictments, the civil suits plodded along at a snail's pace. Attorneys were still filing motions and counter motions and petitions for dismissal almost four years after the building collapsed. Some cynics may have even sarcastically suggested the litigation could drone on forever, like the infamous Jarndyce v. Jarndyce of Charles Dickens's *Bleak House.*

On March 23, 1929, more than three-and-a-half years after the first suit was filed, Suffolk County Superior Court Chief Justice Walter Perley Hall made an announcement that some of the plaintiffs had almost given up hope of ever hearing. The civil actions were finally coming to trial. Hall said the Suffolk County Superior Court had scheduled a joint trial of all 164 suits on April 1. They constituted the largest number of cases the court ever heard in a joint trial.

That trial never took place. Only minutes before it was due to start, the attorneys for the defendants and the plaintiffs told the court they had come to a monetary agreement. One condition stipulated that all parties refrain from disclosing the amount of the settlement. Almost thirty years later, on May 27, 1957, the *Boston Globe* revealed that after deductions for lawyers' fees, the

Chapter Fourteen

plaintiffs shared a total payout of only $40,000. It was just over one half of one percent of the amount they sought.

Beach Street today

The Pickwick Club occupied the space where the rightmost two sections of the three-story building (with large, double-height windows) now stand. The old shoppers' garage next door is still there but, after several renovations, it bears little resemblance to the way it looked when it opened in 1926.

Photo by the author

| FIFTEEN |

The incompetents and the crooks that sometimes creep into officialdom, and the greedy and the grafters that plague the world of honest business, are gambling upon what they hope is the short memory of the Boston public.

> *Boston American*
> July 9, 1925

L ocal newspapers continued to provide almost daily coverage of the Pickwick Club disaster right through the final day of the criminal trial, but their editors must have sensed that readers were beginning to lose interest after the trial judge acquitted ten of the original twelve defendants. Only a handful of spectators were in the courtroom when the jury freed the remaining two. Apparently, no one was terribly surprised or upset that the trial ended with no convictions. If they were, they

247

didn't care enough to express their outrage in a letter to the editor. The second round of indictments two weeks later made the papers, but by that time, the Pickwick Club crash was old news. Most newspapers ran the story on an inside page. When the district attorney's office quietly dropped the criminal charges some months later, editors didn't think it was newsworthy enough to mention.

Boston-based Grey Gull Records briefly rekindled memories of the catastrophe the following year when they released a 78-rpm record entitled "The Pickwick Club Tragedy". Popular vocalist Bob Thomas sang the tearjerker lyrics to a lively foxtrot tempo.

The families of the forty-four victims who lost their lives in the Pickwick Club collapse never forgot that terrible night, nor did the lucky ones who were fortunate enough to escape. Sadly, that didn't hold true for most Bostonians. Their recollection of the disaster, and the impassioned vows to seek out every guilty party and bring them to justice, began to fade soon afterward, just as the editorialist at the *Boston American* had feared. People had heard too many empty promises in the past. They had simply grown used to them.

Seventeen years later, on a chilly Saturday evening in November 1942, nearly a thousand patrons had crammed their way inside a popular nightclub in Boston's Bay Village neighborhood. It was called the *Cocoanut Grove*. Around ten o'clock that night, a young busboy in the jam-packed, smoke-filled basement lounge saw a customer in the far corner reach up and put his hand inside an artificial palm tree behind his table. As the young man watched, the customer loosened a tiny, seven-and-a-half-watt bulb. It was casting just enough light into the dimly lit room to

Chapter Fifteen

make the man's date feel conspicuous, and she kept pushing him away every time he tried to snuggle up to her. The busboy mentioned it to a bartender who told him to go over and tighten the bulb. Although he wasn't happy, the customer begrudgingly slid sideways on the zebra-striped settee so the young man could step up and reach inside the artificial tree. The busboy felt around, but he couldn't locate the bulb. He stepped down, took a book of matches from a nearby table, struck one, and once again stepped up on the settee. The flickering light from the match did the trick. He spotted the bulb and tightened it back into its socket.

For one brief instant, the tip of that match apparently came a bit too close to the edge of an artificial palm frond. A few moments later, a small, barely noticeable ring of flames broke out. Some people nearby instinctively began to make their way toward the exit, but many remained seated, amused by the bartender's frantic attempt to beat out the fire with a towel. That delay cost them their lives. The small blaze suddenly exploded across the sky-blue satin fabric that hung from the false ceiling, sending panic-stricken patrons pushing and clawing their way toward the door. Half of them didn't make it. Four hundred and ninety-two people perished in the worst nightclub fire America had ever seen.

The city's police department, building department, and licensing board wasted little time in absolving themselves of any blame. On December 1, 1942, just three days after the fire, the *Boston Daily Record's* headline proclaimed, "Three Boards Deny Responsibility". It was almost identical to those that ran seventeen years earlier, in the days following the Pickwick Club collapse.

DEATHTRAP

The Boston Fire Commissioner's subsequent investigation uncovered an all-too-familiar pattern of greed and corruption:

- Close to a thousand patrons were inside the building when the fire broke out. That was more than twice its licensed capacity.

- Two emergency escape doors were unusable. One was locked and bolted shut to prevent deadbeats from skipping out without paying, the other was hidden from view by racks of storage shelving.

- A fire department inspector had checked the club only nine days before the fire, but he failed to spot any safety violations. His report stated that he found no flammable decorations.

- A man who didn't have an electrician's license had performed all of the electrical work for a recent major renovation.

- The owner assured one contractor there was no need to bother getting a permit. "The mayor and I fit in," he said. "They owe me plenty down there at City Hall."

- The club had never applied for nor received a food service permit.

- The city granted the club a liquor license, and then periodically renewed it, even though the required inspections had never taken place.

- Bartenders routinely stamped the bar tabs of top city officials "complimentary".

- The sixteen-year-old busboy was too young to work in an establishment that sold alcohol.

250

Chapter Fifteen

• Demolition workers uncovered 4,000 cases of unscathed liquor in the ruined basement after the fire; none of the bottles bore the required Federal tax stamp.

All told, the political process was pretty much the same in 1942 as it had been in 1925. Insiders knew that only chumps played by the rules. If a person was lucky enough to know the right people, then the rules didn't apply. In Boston, some things never change.

DEATHTRAP

| EPILOGUE |

T he last of the dump trucks that the city had hired to haul away the rubble from the Pickwick Club collapse site had barely finished its task when the Rosenthal family sat down with the estate executor and began to make plans for a new building. The estate was still in probate, and the executor had legal control over all of its assets. On October 6, 1925, ninety-four days after the collapse, he applied for a permit to construct a five-story brick building at 6-10 Beach Street. It would be almost identical in size to the original building, and would house retail stores and small garment-manufacturing companies. The city gave its approval a month later. Construction took nearly a year, and the new building opened for business on October 16, 1926.

The Rosenthal estate once again leased the entire building to the David A. Shulte Co. who then hired Whitcomb and Co. to handle the sub-leasing. One of the first tenants to move into the new building was a popular cafeteria that occupied the entire ground floor for several years.

By 1935, the building was housing more than just retail stores and garment manufacturers. The police raided the building in February and found a large, well-equipped, illegal gambling den on the fifth floor. Deputy Superintendent James McDevitt told reporters it could easily accommodate 200 patrons.

A Dorchester man fell to his death four years later when he attempted to jump from the roof of the building to the parking garage next door. Twenty-one-year-old Theodore Radzik was trying to escape from the police after they spotted him breaking into the ground floor cafeteria. Special officer Timothy Wallace narrowly escaped the same fate when he tripped and crashed through a glass skylight while chasing Radzik. Wallace was able to save himself from falling sixty feet into the basement by catching hold of the edge with one hand and pulling himself to safety.

Like hundreds of similar commercial properties in downtown Boston, there was virtually nothing about the exterior of the five-story, nondescript building that would cause a person passing by to take any particular note of it. That briefly changed in 1956 when a three-alarm fire tore through the building's upper floors and heavily damaged four small garment manufacturers.

Nineteen-seventy-four was not a good year for the building, or its neighbors. That was the year the Massachusetts Supreme Judicial Court ruled that the state's strict obscenity laws were unconstitutional. The Boston Redevelopment Authority, alarmed at the prospect of vice spreading unchecked throughout the city, decided to create a 5.5-acre adult entertainment section along lower Washington Street where the sin industry could operate without hinderance. Patrons quickly named the rezoned area *The Combat Zone*. The five-story building at 6 Beach Street sat at its very heart.

A city inspection that year found several safety violations with the building's elevator. The inspector made a follow-up visit several months later only to find that the owner had failed to take any steps to correct the problem.

Another fire swept through the building in 1975. The city pulled the occupancy permit and ordered the building boarded up after loose bricks and shards of glass continued to tumble down onto the sidewalk.

The building changed hands a few times over the years as owners found themselves facing the same problem that confronted Hyman Bloomberg back in 1924—it was getting harder and harder to attract quality tenants, especially since the building right next door housed one of the city's most notorious strip clubs, and a theater just around the corner showed nothing but X-rated films round the clock. Most owners had to settle for tenants like convenience stores, adult book stores, and pornographic peep shows. In 1995, the current owner apparently decided to call it quits and throw in the towel. He applied for a permit to demolish the building. The city's Landmark Commission hoped someone might be able to save the old structure, and they were able to block demolition for ninety days. When the waiting period expired without anyone coming forward with plans to save or rehabilitate the old building, the Boston Redevelopment Authority gave the o.k. to tear it down. For some reason, the owner then changed his mind. In the summer of 1998, the city granted a permit to do some electrical work for a new Asian restaurant that planned to open on the second floor. The last permit for the property that I was able to find in the city archives was issued on July 28, 2004. The city gave the go ahead to haul away the leftover demolition debris, and clear the site.

Today, a parking garage for the 660 Washington Street luxury apartment complex occupies the space where the old Pickwick Club building once stood. The original shoppers' garage next door is still there, but after several major additions and renovations, it bears little resemblance to the way it looked when it opened back in 1926.

Twenty-five story luxury apartment buildings now sit alongside late nineteenth-century commercial buildings on Washington Street, while several of the nearby side streets remain virtually unchanged, and look much the way they did back in 1925. The neighborhood is still known as *Chinatown*, but the increasing number of Vietnamese, Cambodian, and Thai restaurants and grocery stores reflects a gradual cultural shift as more and more newcomers are arriving from other Asian nations.

Some of the locations associated with the club collapse have seen surprisingly little, if any, change. The red brick, bow-front townhouse on Beals Street in Brookline looks almost exactly like it did when Mae Lawson lived there. So does the apartment building on Worcester Square where Pauline DeLucca lived. The exterior of the five-story, brown brick building at 728 Commonwealth Avenue hasn't changed a bit from the way it looked the night Dora Stern walked down the front stairs to start her ill-fated trip to the Pickwick Club. Today, the building serves as a dormitory for Boston University.

Audubon Road, where Club Treasurer Timothy Barry and victims Mabel Dixon and Joseph Phaneuf lived, is now called Park Drive. Most sections have changed very little from the way they appeared in 1925, with one notable exception—Dixon and Phaneuf's three-story, red brick apartment building at number 461 no longer stands. It was demolished in 2002 following a six-alarm fire that gutted the building. The new replacement does manage to blend in quite well with its older neighbors.

The six-family house where Benjamin Alexander and his family lived still stands. So does Patrolman Paul Halleran's old home in Dorchester, the three-decker on Mission Hill where John Murphy lived, and Edith Jordan's former duplex in Somerville. Fayerweather Street, where Loretta Keegan and her family lived, has become one of the most sought-after neighborhoods in Cambridge. Their old house is still there but, like many of its neighbors, it has been subdivided into condominiums. In Milton, one of Boston's tonier suburbs, multi-million dollar homes in the town's exclusive Indian Springs neighborhood are scattered over the lush meadows where Stewart Henderson's dairy cows once grazed.

Not surprisingly, many of the homes and buildings that had some connection to the Pickwick Club collapse no longer exist. An overgrown vacant lot in Roxbury marks the spot where Billy and Jimmy Glennon's house once stood. The three-story Back Bay apartment house where vocalist and entertainer Johnny Duffy lived is gone. So is every other building on the street, and even the street itself. A 100-foot-wide by 690-foot-long reflecting pool at the Christian Science Center complex now occupies the site.

Of all the buildings that are gone, none ended their days on a more dramatic note than did the old, two-family house where Nora Sullivan once lived. Nora was the Roxbury widow who woke up in the early morning hours, surprised to find that her two daughters hadn't returned home as planned. She decided to wait up for them, unable to shake off a growing premonition that something dreadful had happened.

As the years went by, the close-knit neighborhood where Nora and her daughters lived began a slow but steady downhill slide, and by the dawn of the 1980s it had become something of an urban wasteland, dotted with boarded-up houses, abandoned cars, and rubbish-strewn, vacant lots. *The Boston Globe* called it "one of the most blighted places in the country." Nora's former home, like many of its neighbors, hadn't been lived in for years.

The streets of the old neighborhood were all but deserted when a dark sedan showed up a little after midnight one chilly evening back in 1982. The temperature had plunged to the mid-twenties, all but guaranteeing that few, if any, of the handful of people who still lived in the area would be venturing outdoors. Overhead, a heavy cloud cover blocked any traces of moonlight, making the poorly lit streets look even gloomier. The two men inside the car had come there for one reason—they intended to set fire to a building that night. It didn't really matter which one, as long as it was abandoned, and there was no chance of being spotted by a passerby. After driving up and down several streets, they finally settled on Nora Sullivan's former two-family, wooden home at 4 Blanchard Street.

The driver killed the headlights as the car slowly approached the derelict building. When it pulled up in front, a twenty-one-year-old dispatcher with a suburban police department stepped from the passenger side carrying a brown paper lunch bag. Tucked inside were a zip-lok plastic bag filled with lantern fluid, several sheets of tissue paper, and a book of matches. The young man glanced quickly to either side, and then headed toward the front stairs. He had no trouble forcing the old, badly weathered front door, and he stepped into the pitch-black vestibule where

Epilogue

Nora had heard the devastating news of her daughters' sudden deaths many years earlier. He lit a cigarette, spread some of the matches apart, carefully tucked the glowing cigarette between them, and then set the matchbook on top of the tissue paper. He placed the paper bag on the floor, next to a damaged section of the old plaster wall where some of the wooden lath was exposed. Satisfied that everything looked right, he hurried back to the car.

"Let's get the hell out of here," he said to the driver, "that place gives me the creeps."

"The whole area gives me the creeps," his companion replied as he steered the car away from the curb.

The interior of Nora's old home was a raging inferno by the time the first fire engine arrived. The flames had burst through the roof, and were shooting twenty feet into the air. The heat was so intense a utility pole out by the street had burst into flames.

That blaze was the first of a string of deliberately set fires that saw the young police dispatcher and his friends burn so many buildings that news reporters began calling Boston "the arson capital of the country." By the time investigators caught up with them two years later, they had torched 264 buildings in and around Boston, along with setting fires in countless dumpsters and trash piles. Their motive? They hoped the fires would force city officials to reopen the fire stations that had recently closed due to budget cuts, and rehire the firefighters who lost their jobs after the closures.

DEATHTRAP

CAST OF CHARACTERS

George Alpert continued to work as a prosecutor in the district attorney's office for two years after the Pickwick Club trial, and then resigned to open a law practice with his brother. He was a longtime fundraiser for Jewish charities, and he served as vice president of the United Jewish Appeal for several years. Alpert played a major role in founding Brandeis University, and was the chair of the University's Board of Trustees from the school's opening in 1946 until 1954. He continued to sit on the Board until his death. In 1956, he was named president of the New York, New Haven and Hartford Railroad, and held that position for the next five years. Alpert succumbed to pneumonia at his home in suburban Cohasset in September 1988. He was ninety years old.

Timothy Barry faded from the limelight after his acquittal in the criminal trial. His billiard parlor on Tremont Street was one of the thousands of businesses that failed during the Great

Depression. Barry then moved back to South Boston and found work as a supervisor with the school department. He later worked for the US Customs Service. He died in Boston at age sixty-nine in June 1960.

Frank Callahan was still working as a Boston Police Department patrolman on Saturday, February 17, 1945, almost twenty years after the collapse of the Pickwick Club. He was walking his beat on Warrenton Street late that afternoon when the sound of pounding footsteps caught his attention. A young man wearing eyeglasses was racing through a parking lot across the street, heading right toward him.

"Hey, what are you running for?" Callahan shouted.

"Here's a couple for you," the man replied, and rapidly fired two shots.

Both bullets struck the veteran police officer, sending him reeling backward into a snowbank. One of them tore through his right lung. The bespectacled young man kept running up Warrenton Street. Patrolman Francis Connerney heard the shots and turned around just in time to see Callahan fall. Connerney chased the gunman as far as Shawmut Avenue, and then opened fire when the fleeing man attempted to commandeer an Army truck. One of the bullets struck and critically injured the assailant—later identified as twenty-four-year-old Patrick Devlin of Waltham, the married father of two young children. He died at Boston City Hospital early the next morning. Devlin used his Navy-issued service revolver in the senseless shooting spree that began with a botched holdup attempt at a pawnshop on nearby Washington Street. When the elderly owners, Mr. and Mrs. David Pearlstein of Allston, refused to open the cash register, Devlin opened fire, killing them instantly.

Cast of Characters

Doctors at Boston City Hospital gave Callahan fifteen pints of blood in a vain attempt to save his life. He remained in critical condition for three days before he finally succumbed. His wife and daughter were at his bedside when he died. The veteran officer had been a member of the Boston Police Department for twenty-six years, and had celebrated his fifty-third birthday only one day before the shooting. An honor guard of sixty uniformed police officers escorted his funeral procession from Saint Columbkille Church in Brighton to Holy Cross Cemetery in Malden. Francis Connerney later learned that he and Devlin's father had been classmates at Roslindale High School.

James Michael Curley had been Boston's mayor for seven years when the Pickwick Club collapsed, and had one more year to go in his second four-year term. After a brief hiatus, Curley captured the mayor's office once again in the fall of 1929, and went on to win the race for governor in 1935. His political career began to falter soon afterward. In 1936, he lost his bid for a seat in the US Senate. He ran for mayor of Boston once again the following year, but came in second. In 1938, he failed to regain the governor's office, and he made another try for mayor in 1941, but lost out to the incumbent. His fortunes took a turn for the better a year later. He won a seat in the US House of Representatives in November 1942, and was reelected two years later. He vacated his seat in Congress the following year to make another run for mayor. He won that contest by a landslide, and was half way through his four-year term when a federal jury convicted him of mail fraud. He served five months in the federal prison at Danbury, Connecticut before President Truman yielded to pressure from the Massachusetts congressional delegation and commuted his sentence. Curley made three more attempts to capture the mayor's office, but lost all three bids. He died at his home in Boston on November 12, 1958 at age eighty-three. The 1956 best-selling novel *The Last Hurrah* closely parallels Curley's life and political career.

Frank Decker married a girl from Jamaica Plain two years after his narrow escape from the Pickwick Club, and eventually settled in Jamaica Plain's exclusive Moss Hill neighborhood. He was the New England regional manager of a national retail consulting firm for many years. He died in Boston in June 1970 at age seventy-six.

Arthur Dreyfus was fifty-nine when the Pickwick Club collapsed, and lived in semi-retirement on his farm on Moose Hill Street in suburban Sharon. He still owned the Hotel Dreyfus in Providence, but he had relinquished much of the operating responsibility to his son Harry. A few years later, he moved to Cranston, Rhode Island where he died in 1938 at the age of seventy-two. Dreyfus left two sons, Harry and Edmund. Harry managed the hotel in Providence; Edmund owned a restaurant in nearby North Attleboro, Massachusetts. The Hotel Dreyfus remained a fixture in downtown Providence until 1975 when Johnson and Wales University purchased the building for use as a dormitory.

Harry Dreyfus became the sole owner of the Hotel Dreyfus in Providence following his father's death in 1938. He retired seven years later, placed control of the hotel in the hands of its long-time general manager, and moved to Florida. The *Miami News* included his custom-built, single-family home in a 1956 article about local properties that had elaborate, outdoor Christmas lighting displays. Dreyfus died in Miami in September 1978 at the age of eighty-seven.

Thomas Elston was in the newspapers once again in March 1928 when the leaders of Congregation Beth El in Fall River sued his firm for damages, claiming its employees were responsible for the conflagration that destroyed their temple. Elston's company was demolishing a textile mill next door when it accidently caught fire. His daughter suffered critical injuries the following year when she fell against the side of a passenger train as it pulled into a station. Officials faulted her for standing too close to the tracks. Elston died at his home in West Roxbury in October 1930 after a brief illness. He was sixty-four years old.

Louis Epple still headed the Boston Licensing Board when an inferno tore through the Cocoanut Grove nightclub in November 1942, claiming 492 lives. He came under fire when investigators learned that his department had routinely issued and then renewed liquor licenses for the ill-fated club without making the required investigations or holding public hearings. Epple retired from the board a year later after serving as its secretary for thirty-seven years. He died in Bay Pines, Florida in January, 1954 at the age of seventy-six.

Governor Alvan Fuller beat Boston mayor James Michael Curley in the closely contested 1924 gubernatorial race. He was successful in his bid for reelection in 1926 and, once again, he refused to accept any compensation. The controversial Sacco and Vanzetti murder trial took place during Fuller's second term in office, and their conviction brought widespread appeals to the governor, asking him to commute the death sentences of the two

Italian anarchists. He responded by appointing a three-member panel to determine if there was any evidence of impartiality during the trials. The panel members spent two weeks reviewing the transcripts, and concluded the trial had been fair and unbiased. Fuller then refused to delay the executions or grant clemency. Soon afterward, postal authorities discovered a bomb inside a package addressed to the governor. Fuller never ran for public office again, and devoted his energies to looking after his successful Boston automobile dealership. He suffered a fatal heart attack in April 1958 while watching a film in a Boston theater. He was eighty years old. His youngest son Peter owned the thoroughbred racehorse *Dancer's Image* when it won the Kentucky Derby in 1968.

Billy Glennon and his orchestra continued to play at local dance halls, and were frequent headliners at Roxbury's Hibernian Hall. That's where he met his wife Barbara. They lived with his widowed mother at the family home on Marcella Street while he commuted to his daytime job as an engineer at the General Electric aircraft engine plant in Lynn. Billy was only four days short of his forty-second birthday when he unexpectedly died of pneumonia on December 15, 1942. He left his wife and four young children. The oldest was six, the youngest just nine months old.

Theodore Glynn was a longtime friend and political ally of Boston mayor James Michael Curley. He was working as a food salesman when Curley tapped him to be the city's fire commissioner in August 1922. Glynn tossed his hat into the ring early on in the 1925 mayoral race and, with the backing of Mayor Curley, he seemed to be a sure winner. Any thoughts of an easy victory were dampened a few days later when legendary Boston ward boss Martin Lomansney threw his support behind former mayor John "Honey" Fitzgerald, the grandfather of President John F. Kennedy. That led to a free-for-all during which no fewer than twenty people—one of them Pickwick Club prosecutor Thomas O'Brien—announced their intent to run for the vacant office. Although several of those candidates eventually dropped out, voters still had ten names to choose from when they cast their ballots that November. Charles Innes coasted to an easy victory, becoming the first Republican mayor of Boston in twenty years. Glynn relinquished the fire commissioner's post in January 1926, but remained active in Boston politics. In August 1935, Curley appointed him Clerk of the Roxbury District Court. Glynn died in Boston at age sixty-nine in February 1950.

Herbert Goodwin had been the commanding officer of Station Four for fourteen years when the ill-fated club collapsed. At the time of his promotion, he was the youngest captain on the force. Goodwin stayed at Station Four for five more years, and then transferred to Jamaica Plain. He retired in November 1932 after a forty-year career with the Boston Police Department, and moved to St. Petersburg, Florida. He died at this home there in January 1935 at age sixty-eight.

Harry Haven was showing unmistakable signs of major depression as the winter of 1927-28 set in. Sometime during the early morning hours of February 6, 1928, almost two and a half years after Judge Lummus acquitted him of four counts of manslaughter, Haven quietly descended his cellar stairs and walked into the basement laundry. The stately old house in Winchester was originally illuminated by gas; when a contractor wired it for electricity some years later, he left the old gas fixtures in place. Haven slipped a rubber tube over the tip of one of those fixtures, gently turned the old valve handle, and then took a deep breath that filled his lungs with illuminating gas. Sarah Haven discovered her husband's body a few hours later. It wasn't the first time the fifty-six-year-old architect tried to take his own life. Only nine days earlier, his son found him sitting behind the wheel of his car inside his closed garage with the car's engine running. Fortunately, a police officer was able to revive him. Haven left his wife and three sons; the youngest was sixteen.

Martin Kane had worked as a foreman with the City of Boston Bridge and Ferry Department for a number of years before he took a concrete inspector's job with the city's building department. He passed away at his East Boston home in April 1928, a little more than two years after the District Attorney's office decided against bringing him to trial on a manslaughter charge. The former resident of Co. Wexford, Ireland was seventy-three, and had been a widower for more than twenty years. He was buried alongside his wife Annie at Holy Cross Cemetery in Malden.

Dr. Timothy Leary had been the Medical Examiner for the Southern District of Suffolk County for seventeen years when the Pickwick Club collapsed. Governor Curtis Guild named him to the position in July 1908, and Leary went on to serve in that capacity for the next forty-two years. His office gained national attention when hundreds of badly burned bodies arrived at the Southern Mortuary following the disastrous Cocoanut Grove nightclub fire in 1942. In addition to working as a medical examiner, Leary also served as dean emeritus of the Tufts Medical

School. He stepped down from his medical examiner's post in 1950, and died at his home in Jamaica Plain four years later. He was eighty-four years old.

Henry Lummus continued to sit on the Massachusetts Superior Court for another seven years after the Pickwick Club trial. In July 1932, Governor Joseph B. Ely appointed him Associate Justice of the Massachusetts Supreme Judicial Court. In 1937, Lummus gave a series of lectures to law students at Northwestern University in Chicago. The following year, the Foundation Press incorporated those lectures into a book, *The Trial Judge*. To this day, every newly appointed trial judge in Massachusetts receives a copy. Lummus also gained some acclaim as a discerning antiques collector, and a connoisseur of fine wines. He retired from the bench in October 1955, and died at his home in Swampscott in August 1960 at the age of eighty-three.

Rev. Lawrence Morrisroe made news once again in March 1941 when newspapers labeled him a "hero priest" after he dashed inside the still-smoldering Strand Theater in Brockton to administer the last rites to thirteen fire fighters who perished when a large part of the roof unexpectedly collapsed during what was thought to be a routine fire. The East Boston native was the pastor of Saint William Church in Dorchester at the time of his death in December 1961. He had been a priest for forty-two of his seventy years.

Thomas O'Brien became the Suffolk County District Attorney at the culmination of an unusual chain of events—Governor Channing Cox appointed him to the office in 1922 to fill a vacancy that the state's highest court created when they removed his predecessor from office after uncovering numerous instances of extortion, graft and corruption. O'Brien was a 1911 graduate of Harvard Law School, and had formerly served as the Massachusetts Deputy Director of Prisons. In November 1925, four months after the Pickwick Club collapse, he made an unsuccessful run for mayor of Boston. In 1936, O'Brien tossed his hat into the ring again—twice! He was the Union Party's candidate for two races—a seat in the US Senate from Massachusetts, and the US Vice President. O'Brien fared poorly in both contests. He and William Lemke, the party's nominee for president, received less than two percent of the nationwide votes cast. The short-lived political party was formed by supporters of Fr. Charles Coughlin, the politically conservative and anti-Semitic "radio priest" in 1936. It collapsed on the heels of its disappointing showing in that year's November elections. O'Brien was a lifelong resident of Brighton, and died in November 1951 at the age of sixty-four.

Joseph O'Connell was fifty-two years old when he repeatedly clashed with the prosecutor and the trial judge while representing defendant James Hendrick in the Pickwick Club trial. One of O'Connell's claims to fame was being a founder and member of the first football team at Boston College. In addition to practicing law, he also served as vice president of the Board of Trustees at Suffolk Law School. He made an unsuccessful run for the US Senate in 1930, and failed in his bid to win election as Mayor of Boston three years later. O'Connell died in Boston on December 10, 1942, three days after celebrating his seventieth birthday.

Cast of Characters

Daniel Sennott was only six months into his new job as the city's fire chief when the Pickwick Club collapsed, but he had been a Boston firefighter for forty-three years. People who knew him considered him a consummate professional. An incident that occurred shortly after he was named chief shows how far he carried that professionalism. The Saint Croix Club arranged a banquet in his honor at Boston's Copley Plaza Hotel in January 1925 at which Fire Commissioner Glynn was the principal speaker. When Glynn finished his talk, several firemen dressed in comic firefighter uniforms ran helter-skelter through the ballroom in a Keystone Kops-fashion. One carried a toy axe while another pulled a toy fire engine on a rope. Sennott made no attempt to hide his displeasure, and he told the men to get back into uniform and return to their stations. He retired in May 1930 after forty-eight years of service, but continued to take an active role with the Massachusetts Fire Chiefs Club, and was a featured speaker at several of their meetings. Sennott died in January 1947 at the age of eighty-seven. An honor guard of one hundred uniformed fire fighters accompanied his funeral procession.

Felix Toupin made a run for the governor's office a few months after the Rhode Island stink bomb incident, but he lost decisively when Republicans easily captured all of the major statewide offices. Toupin later served three terms as the Democratic mayor of Woonsocket, Rhode Island. He repeatedly clashed with the Board of Aldermen, and in 1935 he got into a widely-publicized fistfight with one of its members. He lost his bid for reelection the following year, but recaptured the mayor's office a few years later when he ran as a Republican. Toupin died at his home in Woonsocket in October 1965 at the age of seventy-nine. At the time of his death, he owned extensive real estate holdings in

Rhode Island and Massachusetts.

Herbert Wilson had been the Boston Building Commissioner for four years when Massachusetts Governor Channing Cox tapped him to be the city's police commissioner in September 1922. Today the mayor fills that post. Even though Wilson had no background or training in law enforcement, he made a determined effort to streamline police operations, and he backed several pieces of legislation that would help that goal. He instituted numerous reforms, and he ordered several department-wide shakeups to combat what he thought was a general breakdown in morale and efficiency. He also fought unsuccessfully to close several loopholes in the civil service procedures that some politicians exploited to pressure officials into promoting unqualified individuals.

His career as police commissioner came to an abrupt and unhappy end in the spring of 1930 when he became embroiled in the Oliver Garrett scandal. Garrett was twenty-five years old and a recently discharged Navy veteran when he joined the Boston Police Department in 1919. It marked the beginning of what turned out to be a meteoric rise. Within a few years, he had become head of the vice squad where he gained fame by personally leading several Prohibition raids. It wasn't long before rumors began to circulate that he was on the take. A secret investigation into Garrett's finances uncovered at least a dozen bank accounts, most of them in his wife's name, along with several pieces of property, three expensive cars, a horse racing stable, and a large dairy farm in suburban Hingham. In ten years, his net worth had grown from only a few dollars to more than $300,000. It was a big jump for a man who earned only forty dollars a week. Investigators didn't buy his explanation that his wife came from a wealthy family. His superiors demoted him to patrolman, and assigned him to night duty at Station Three. Garrett immediately took a one-month vacation. He was still on vacation when he applied for a disability pension. He claimed he was involved in an automobile accident while on duty two years earlier that left him seriously injured with a fractured skull. He said an x-ray taken at the time confirmed the injury. Wilson was skeptical, especially in light of the timing, but Garrett produced a doctor's letter that said the injury had left him "irresponsible". Wilson approved the pension application.

Some people at the state house thought Garrett had gotten off too easily, and they urged the Attorney General to look into the matter. Garrett's doctor soon admitted that he amended his original report after he learned of Wilson's doubts, and added the notation about Garrett being irresponsible. Investigators located several of his fellow officers who heard Garrett say he would never return to street duty, and would try to use the accident as a way out.

He reportedly traveled to Washington, DC and sought employment as a federal prohibition agent only a week before he submitted his pension application. When doctors at Massachusetts General Hospital told investigators there was no evidence that Garrett had suffered a fractured skull as he claimed, the Attorney General's office summoned Wilson to a state house hearing to defend his decision to grant the disability pension. On May 3, 1930, Governor Frank Allen demanded that Wilson resign his position for awarding a fraudulent pension. When Wilson declined to step down, Allen signed an executive order removing him from office. The ouster left Wilson bitterly disappointed, and he blamed local politicians for making him a scapegoat. A newspaper columnist happened to meet him by chance several months later, and said he was still extremely angry about the treatment he received.

Herbert Wilson died at his home in Brighton in May 1934 after a lengthy illness. He was sixty-four, and left an estate valued at $304,000—nearly $5.5 million in today's dollars.

A Suffolk County grand jury had indicted his nemesis, Oliver Garrett, on 152 counts of conspiracy and extortion four years earlier. Garrett and his wife fled from Massachusetts a few days before his trial was to begin, but he turned himself in five months later. After his first two trials ended with hung juries, he entered a guilty plea at the start of his third trial in May 1931 and served a two-year prison sentence. He worked as a nightclub emcee for a few months after his release, but then left that job and opened an auto repair shop. Garrett passed away in Yacolt, Washington in 1979 at the age of eighty-four.

Appendices

DEATHTRAP

| ONE |

The Victims of the Pickwick Club Disaster

Benjamin Alexander, 42, 1635 Dorchester Avenue,
    Dorchester
Ella Calley, 33, 96 Peterborough Street, Boston
Burt Chapman, 32, 175 Callender Street, Dorchester
Michael Cheffalo, 34, 33 Prince Street, Boston
William Cochrane, 20, 63 Upham Street, Malden
Ralph Congdon, 43, 44 North Bennet Street, Boston
Charles DeCostis, 28, 47 Pembroke Street, Boston
Pauline DeLucca, 35, 41 Worcester Square, Boston
Mabel Dixon, 34, 461 Audubon Road, Boston
Francis Driscoll, 43, 7 Copeland Street, Roxbury
John Duffy, 30, 44 Falmouth Street, Boston

DEATHTRAP

Edward Flanagan, 29, 68 Avon Street, Malden

Clara Frederick, 41, 209 Park Street, West Roxbury

Patrick Glavin, 32, 711 Washington Street, Dorchester

James Glennon, 32, 86 Marcella Street, Roxbury

Arthur Graham, 27, 18 Kingsboro Park, Jamaica Plain

William Grossman, 31, 27 Allen Street, Boston

Paul Halleran, 33, 17 Inwood Street, Dorchester

Stuart Henderson, 36, 730 Canton Avenue, Milton

Edith Jordan, 28, 35 Boston Street, Somerville

Loretta Keegan, 36, 161 Fayerweather Street, Cambridge

Mary Lawson, 29, 40 Beals Street, Brookline

Gellato Lombardi, 33, 16 Fleet Street, Boston

Wayne Marr, 30, 433 Centre Street, Dallas, Texas

Mary McEachern, 22, 4 Blanchard Street, Roxbury

Lillian McIsaac, 21, 4 Blanchard Street, Roxbury

John McLaughlin, 19, 60 Castle Street, Boston

Francis McLean, 20, 51 Norwood Street, Malden

Thomas McManus, 23, 206 West Broadway, South Boston

Mary Moore, 29, 1847 Columbus Avenue, Roxbury

Max Mulmat, 33, 24 Homestead Street, Roxbury

John Murphy, 23, 146 Hillside Street, Roxbury

Margaret Murphy, 29, 127 Warren Street, Roxbury

James Murray, 28, 20 Chase Street, Dorchester

William Murray, 35, 8 Hamilton Road, Somerville

Bartholomew O'Donnell, 25, 11 Saint Charles Street, Boston

Carl Paulson, 24, 15 Greenville Street, Roxbury

Joseph Phaneuf, 46, 461 Audubon Road, Boston

John Scales, 22, 2 Spring Terrace, Roxbury

Appendix One

Dora Stern, 22, 565 Jerome Street, Brooklyn, New York

Frank Tillo, 28, 56 Clinton Street, Chelsea

Frank Vara, 25, 58 Billerica Street, Boston

Charles Whalen, 27, 206 West Broadway, South Boston

Esther Wilson, 26, 74 Bragdon Street, Roxbury

DEATHTRAP

| TWO |

Officers and Incorporators of the Pickwick Club

The original incorporators of the Commercial Men's Club, Inc. (March 20, 1924):

Keron Clemens, 147 Old Plymouth Road, Sagamore
Francis Nevins, 248 Nevada Street, Newton
Joshua Paine, 2 Commercial Street, Provincetown
Max Pilder, 726 Washington Street, Brookline
Edward Powers, 153 Warren Avenue, Boston
Louis Rosenfield, 879 Beacon Street, Boston
James Troy, 4 Mayhew Street, Dorchester

The original officers:

President, Edward Powers, 153 Warren Avenue, Boston
Treasurer, Francis Nevins, 248 Nevada Street, Newton
Clerk, Keron Clemens, 147 Old Plymouth Road, Sagamore

In December, 1924, the Commercial Men's Club, Inc. filed a request with the Massachusetts Department of Corporations and Taxation to change the name of the organization to the Pickwick Club, Inc. The Department of Corporations and Taxation returned the application for needed corrections. The Commercial Men's Club failed to resubmit their application, so the Commonwealth of Massachusetts never officially chartered a "Pickwick Club, Inc.".

On February 2, 1925, the Pickwick Club, Inc. filed a revised slate of officers:

President, John Roth, 226 West Newton Street, Boston
Treasurer, Timothy Barry, 85 Audubon Road, Boston
Clerk, Charles Gluck, Hotel Avery, 589 Washington Street, Boston

On February 24, 1925, the Pickwick Club, Inc. filed another revised slate of officers:

President, Daniel Barry, 41 Woodward Street, South Boston
Treasurer, Timothy Barry, 85 Audubon Road, Boston

Appendix Two

Clerk, Frank Ross, 24 Homestead Street, Roxbury (*)

(*) Frank Ross was a fictitious name. The clerk's real name was Max Mulmat, a convicted bootlegger. He lived at the Homestead Street address.

DEATHTRAP

| THREE |

Suffolk County grand jurors who heard testimony in the Pickwick Club collapse

Seymour M. Abraham, supervisor, 127 P Street, South Boston

Albert M. Austin, banker, 85 Ocean Street, Revere

Joseph F. Brennan, clerk, 33 Hillside Street, Roxbury

William A. Cruise, motorman, 604 Saratoga Street, East Boston

Jeremiah deYone, carpenter, 62 Lonsdale Street, Dorchester

James Dolan, shoe worker, 10 Creighton Street, Roxbury

John F. Dolan, plasterer, 29 Mount Ida Road, Dorchester

Arthur T. Downey, clerk, 362 Arborway, Forest Hills **

Michael J. Doyle, clerk, 37 Parker Hill Avenue, Roxbury

Mortimer F. Fitzgerald, compositor, 69 Sedgwick Street, Jamaica Plain

Daniel Kelly, clerk, 822 Parker Street, Roxbury

Patrick E. Little, manager, 7 Jackson Street, Charlestown

Henry M. Martin, chauffeur, 135 Franklin Street, Roxbury

Patrick H. McGrath, salesman, 30 Leamington Road, Brighton

John McNeice, factory worker, 580 Freeport Street, Dorchester

Carl L. Mittell, vice president, 6 Newsome Park, Roxbury

Richard J. Neville, salesman, 159 Bradstreet Avenue, Revere

Philip F. O'Brien, machinist, 7 Mark Street, Roxbury

Dennis F. O'Connor, foreman, 217 M Street, South Boston

Matthew T. Patterson, machinist, 25 Trenton Street, Charlestown

Lawrence S. Peck, accountant, 1745 Dorchester Avenue, Dorchester

John V. Riley, laborer, 686 East 8th Street, South Boston

George T. Tannam, bookkeeper, 15 Magnolia Street, Roxbury

** Arthur Downey served as the jury foreman

Suffolk County Superior Court petit jurors who tried the twelve Pickwick Club defendants

John S. Brawley, salesman, 83 Colgate Avenue, Roxbury

Dennis J. Enright, grounds superintendent, 93 North Harvard Street, Allston **

Robert W. Evans, clerk, 670 Bennington Street, East Boston

Michael Harrigan, laborer, 224 West 4th Street, South Boston

James J. Harrity, machinist, 140 Marcella Street, Roxbury

David F. Leahy, clerk, 90 I Street, South Boston

Joseph F. Magee, printer, 5 Chauncy Place, Boston

James L. McMahan, manufacturer, 2 Thane Street, Dorchester

Albert J. McNamara, florist, 18 Mallon Street, Dorchester

J. Edward Mullins, salesman, 46 Glenwood Street, Jamaica Plain

Walter F. Murphy, clerk, 25 Alpine Street, Roxbury

John H. Naylor, carpenter, 51 Brooks Avenue, Boston

** Dennis Enright served as the jury foreman. His address, 93 North Harvard Street in Allston, is the site of the historic Harvard Stadium. Mr. Enright was the superintendent of groundskeeping at the stadium from its opening in 1903 until his retirement in 1939, and the only person who ever lived inside the stadium. His small frame house was located just inside Gate One.

DEATHTRAP

| FOUR |

Partial list of the witnesses who
testified before the Suffolk County
Grand Jury

Captain Ainsley C. Armstrong, Boston Police Department
Timothy Barry, Pickwick Club treasurer
Hyman Bloomberg, lessee of 6-12 Beach Street
Patrolman Frank B. Callahan, Boston Police Department
George E. Callahan, Pickwick Club doorman
Nat Clark, co-owner of the Greenwich Village Café
Frederick W. Cook, Massachusetts Secretary of State
Patrick Curran, piano player, Pickwick Club orchestra
Patrolman Robert J. Dalton, Boston Police Department
Earl Davis, Pickwick Club busboy

E.W. Davis, employee of Parke Davis Pharmaceutical
Company

Frank Decker, Pickwick Club patron

Inspector James A. Dennessy, Boston Police Department

District Chief Charles Donahue, Boston Fire Department

Louis Epple, Secretary of the Boston Licensing
Commission

Nathan Fritz, president, Fritz Construction Company

George Funk, architect

Augustine J. Gill, Boston Police Department stenographer

William Glennon, Pickwick Club orchestra conductor

John Glynn, co-owner of the Greenwich Village Café

Theodore Glynn, Boston Fire Commissioner

Captain Herbert W. Goodwin, Boston Police Department

Charles A. Gow, president, Charles A. Gow, Inc.

Sergeant William Hartigan, Boston Police Department

Harry M. Haven, partner, Haven and Hopkins, architects

James J. Hendrick, district inspector, Boston Building
Commission

Harris "Mike" Hirshberg, Pickwick Club waiter

M.E. Hopkins, partner, Haven and Hopkins, architects

Martin Kane, concrete inspector, City of Boston

Charles R. Leary, general superintendent, Charles R. Gow
Company

Dr. Timothy Leary, Suffolk County Medical Examiner

Henry F. Long, Massachusetts Commissioner of
Corporations and Taxation

John H. Mahoney, Boston Building Commissioner

Patrolman Neal McDevitt. Boston Police Department

Mildred McGilvary, Pickwick Club patron

Malcolm McIntosh, Boston Fire Department

Appendix Four

Matthew H. McIntosh, night watchman, Pultz, Inc.

Arthur McNeil, Pickwick Club patron

Sergeant John F. Montague, Boston Police Department

Patrolman Frank Mullen, Boston Police Department

Patrolman Sylvester Murphy, Boston Police Department

Lawrence J. Perkins, foreman, Pultz, Inc.

John L. Pultz, president, Pultz, Inc. , contractors

William J. Reed, foreman, A.G. Tomasello & Son, Inc.

District Chief Victor H. Richter, Boston Fire Department

Rocco Scarparto, Pickwick Club doorman

Chief Daniel F. Sennott, Boston Fire Department

Deputy Chief Edward J. Shallow, Boston Fire Department

John J. Sullivan, a building wrecker who helped with the
   demolition

John M. Tobin, a superintendent at Pultz, Inc.

Joseph A. Tomasello, president, A.G. Tomasello & Son,
   Inc. excavation contractor

William F. Turner, handwriting expert

Hugh Urquhart, construction engineer

Michael Ward, co-owner of the Greenwich Village Café

DEATHTRAP

| FIVE |

House Bill 91

The Massachusetts House Committee on Social Welfare held a public hearing on the proposed legislation on February 19, 1925. Section 4 would have given Boston mayor James Michael Curley the very controls he claimed to have sought. Assistant Corporation Counsel H. Murray Pakulski attended the hearing as the mayor's representative, and told committee members the legislation wasn't needed, as there were already enough statutes on the books to adequately control private clubs and dance halls. After hearing Pakulski's comments, the committee issued a negative report that effectively killed the bill, and it never came up for a vote on the House floor. The bill read as follows:

DEATHTRAP

An Act to provide for Licensing and Regulating Semi-Public Dances and Dance Halls.

Be it enacted by the Senate and House of Representatives in General Court Assembled and by the authority of same as follows:

Section 1 ---- Any building wherein dancing is permitted, suffered or tolerated, and in which or connected with which by an interior communication, food or drink is sold to be consumed on the premises, or in which after free admission, money or any valuable consideration is received for remaining thereon for any purpose whatever, shall be deemed a semi-public dance hall, and dances therein semi-public dances.

Section 2 ---- Whoever manages, promotes, or holds a semi-public dance without first having obtained a license so to do from the proper authorities shall be punished by a fine of not more than one hundred dollars or six months in the House of Correction, or by both such fine and imprisonment.

Section 3 ---- The license shall be expressed to be subject to the following conditions and to be subject to revocation upon the breach of any thereof:

First ---- That the dance shall be conducted and that the persons in and about the dance hall shall be required to conduct themselves with propriety and decorum.

Second ---- That there shall be no drinking of intoxicating liquor on the premises nor any person admitted or suffered to remain thereon who is under the influence of intoxicating liquor, or who has intoxicating liquor in his possession.

Third ---- That no muscle dancing or Apache dancing shall be tolerated on the premises.

Section 4 ---- The Licensing Board of the City of Boston, or the officer or board at the head of the police in cities, and the board of selectmen in towns, may grant a license to conduct semi-public dance halls to such person or persons as are of good character and repute, under such terms and conditions as they deem reasonable, and they may revoke the same at their pleasure.

Section 5 ---- Whoever in a public or semi-public dance hall shall engage in a muscle dance, an Apache dance, or any other indecent dance shall be punished by a fine of not more than one hundred dollars or three months in the House of Correction.

Section 6 ---- Whoever shall enter a public or semi-public dance while under the influence of intoxicating liquor, or remain thereon having the same in his possession, shall be punished by a fine of not less or more than one hundred dollars or three months in the House of Correction.

DEATHTRAP

| SIX |

Selected statements made by advocates of House Bill 91 at a public hearing conducted by the Massachusetts House Committee on Social Welfare on February 19, 1925

The historic Park Street Church in Boston traces its origins to 1804. The present structure was built in 1810, and from its opening until 1856, it was the tallest building in the United States. Rev. Arcturus Zodiac Conrad, DD, the pastor of that church, had some decidedly heated words about "midnight clubs", as organizations like the Pickwick Club were often called, when he spoke at the hearing:

"These places are responsible for young girls being led astray by the hundreds because of the facilities for destruction that are being offered them. It is impossible to choose words describing the conditions that actually exist. The situation is unspeakable. The resorts are run by shameless men who fatten on the ruined characters and the destroyed bodies and souls of our young people.

"It is a nefarious, infamous, hell-filling business and should be stopped, not with a feather duster, but with a decidedly big club. That is the only way of meeting such a situation."

J. Frank Chase, Secretary of the Watch and Ward Society, was equally vociferous. From its founding in 1878, members of the Watch and Ward Society served as self-appointed arbiters of public morality. Their censorship activities popularized the phrase "Banned in Boston". The organization's influence began to fade after journalist H.L. Menken successfully sued them in 1926 for restraint of trade after they tried to block the sale of his American Mercury magazine. Chase told the committee members:

"It is difficult to describe the conditions in these places because what goes on there is almost unbelievable. In the midnight club the principal activity carried on is the indulgence in hootchie-kootchie dancing and the drinking of liquor. In the dances the woman participant is so attired as to attract the man. She is accoutered with a view to tempting him. She is allowed to park her intimate personal apparel before going on the dance floor.

"These midnight clubs open at midnight and close at six o'clock in the morning. They do a large business in the sale of liquor. If this liquor is not taken to the club on the hip of the person who indulges, he can get it on the premises from a waiting bootlegger. It is Scotch from Chelsea (Massachusetts) that is being served, and it brings in twelve dollars a quart. These clubs and roadhouses are run by men who, before prohibition, were the owners of cafes. They are in the business for money and are making it plentifully. Scores of these places are springing up. They are a menace to the communities of our Commonwealth and I believe it is time for the lawmakers to do something to check the evil."

Clarence R. Preston of the Florence Crittenton League also spoke in favor of the proposed bill. His organization fancied itself a rescue mission for wayward girls, and it provided a home for unwed mothers. Preston told the committee members that many of the girls who sought help from the mission attributed their downfall to attending parties at midnight clubs and roadhouses.

DEATHTRAP

| SEVEN |

"The Pickwick Club Tragedy"
(Grey Gull Records, 1926)

'Twas the night before the glorious Fourth,
   in staid old Boston town,
When the building known as the Pickwick Club,
   came rumbling, tumbling down.
The place was filled with people,
   a carefree lot were they,
Full of the joys of nightclub life,
   singing and dancing away.

Then all of a sudden, the walls gave way,
   the floor slid out into space;
The lights went out, and moans and groans,
   were heard all over the place.

DEATHTRAP

In a buried heap of ruins,
    the helpless victims lay;
Rescuers worked with might and main,
    digging and searching away.

When the work was done, the terrible news,
    was broadcast far and wide,
And the records show, in the final count,
    that forty-four had died.
Those unsuspecting people,
    a carefree lot were they,
Never a thought of future harm,
    singing and dancing away.

'Twas the hand of God, a great many said,
    who from His throne on high,
Tore the building down as a punishment,
    and caused these folks to die;
That future sons and daughters,
    might learn a lesson there,
And cast off the chains of reckless life,
    and travel along on the square.

But this was the eve of the jolly Fourth,
    when men go looking for fun,
And lots of things can be excused,
    by nearly everyone.
In the golden realms of heaven,
    where angels hold full sway,
All of the folks, they're happy now,
    singing and dancing away.

DEATHTRAP

| ACKNOWLEDGEMENTS |

Several people made significant contributions to this book, and I want to express my sincere thanks for their help. My wife Rose Marie was a constant source of encouragement and support. Attorney John McAdams always had a ready answer for my questions on criminal law. Brian Harkins, the reference librarian at The Social Law Library in Boston, provided valuable help in my search for details of the criminal and civil cases. Jennifer Fauxsmith, the reference supervisor at the Massachusetts Archives, Ellen Wendruff, the local history librarian at the Robbins Library in Arlington, Alyssa Pacy, the archivist at the Cambridge Public Library, and Henry Scannell of the Boston Public Library's Microtext Department went out of their way to help. Sadly, I wasn't able to get the name of the Salem Library's reference librarian, but I am extremely grateful for her help in unraveling the mystery surrounding the mistaken identity of victim Thomas McManus.

Thanks also go out to three very special people. Barbara Warner provided personal, unpublished information about her father, orchestra leader Billy Glennon. Tim Heffernan shared his memories of his grandfather, John Heffernan, who suffered severe injuries in the collapse. Elizabeth Krance, the granddaughter of Lieutenant Benjamin Alexander, gave me an update about his family, and told me of some of the many tributes he received.

Finally, I would be remiss if I did not single out one person for special thanks. I wouldn't be writing a book about the Pickwick Club collapse today if my father hadn't told me the story many years ago. Dad certainly had firsthand knowledge of the disaster—he was one of the holiday celebrants who were inside the club that night. He had the good fortune to leave only a short time before the building fell, but it wasn't soon enough to keep the Boston Sunday newspapers from including his name in their reports of the missing and feared dead. His friend Johnny Duffy wasn't that lucky. Firefighters found his body almost forty-eight hours later, buried under fifteen feet of rubble. I wish that I had asked my father a lot more questions about what happened, but it's too late now. Dad died many years ago, but I feel extremely privileged to have learned about the collapse from someone who was in the club that fateful night.

DEATHTRAP

INDEX

Index

Index

DEATHTRAP

ABOUT THE AUTHOR

John Keefe is a Massachusetts native whose Boston roots go back nearly 200 years. He graduated from Boston College, served with the U.S. Army Corps of Engineers, and then embarked on a successful, four-decade career in the high tech industry. Retirement gave him the opportunity to pursue his long-standing passion for historical research. His first book, *Carroty Nell: the Last Victim of Jack the Ripper*, was published in 2010. Keefe and his wife live in a northwest suburb just outside of Boston.

DEATHTRAP

www.ingramcontent.com/pod-product-compliance
Lightning Source LLC
Chambersburg PA
CBHW020433130626
46549CB00001B/124